Ecclesiology in the Trenches

CHURCH OF SWEDEN

Research Series

§

Göran Gunner, editor
Vulnerability, Churches, and HIV (2009)

Kajsa Ahlstrand and Göran Gunner, editors
Non-Muslims in Muslim Majority Societies (2009)

Jonas Ideström, editor
For the Sake of the World (2010)

Göran Gunner and Kjell-Åke Nordquist
An Unlikely Dilemma (2011)

Anne-Louise Eriksson, Göran Gunner, and Niclas Blåder, editors
Exploring a Heritage (2012)

Kjell-Åke Nordquist, editor
Gods and Arms (2012)

Harald Hegstad
The Real Church (2013)

Carl-Henric Grenholm and Göran Gunner, editors
Justification in a Post-Christian Society (2014)

Carl-Henric Grenholm and Göran Gunner, editors
Lutheran Identity and Political Theology (2014)

Ecclesiology in the Trenches
Theory and Method under Construction

Edited by
SUNE FAHLGREN
AND JONAS IDESTRÖM

Foreword by
GERARD MANNION

☙PICKWICK *Publications* · Eugene, Oregon

ECCLESIOLOGY IN THE TRENCHES
Theory and Method under Construction

Church of Sweden Research Series 10

Copyright © 2015 Trossamfundet Svenska Kyrkan (Church of Sweden). All rights reserved. Except for brief quotations in critical publications or reviews, no part of this book may be reproduced in any manner without prior written permission form the publisher. Write: Permissions, Wipf and Stock Publishers, 199 W. 8th Ave., Suite 3, Eugene, OR 97 401

Pickwick Publications
An Imprint of Wipf and Stock Publishers
199 W. 8th Ave., Suite 3
Eugene, OR 97 401

www.wipfandstock.com

ISBN 13: 978-1-4982-0864-2

Cataloguing-in-Publication data:

Ecclesiology in the trenches : theory and method under construction / edited by Sune Fahlgren and Jonas Ideström.

xiv + 242 p. ; 23 cm. —Includes bibliographical references.

Church of Sweden Research Series 10

ISBN 13: 978-1-4982-0864-2

1. Church. 2. Practical Ecclesiology. 3. Theology—Methodology. I. Title. II. Series.

BV598 E25 2015

Manufactured in the U.S.A.

New Revised Standard Version Bible, copyright 1989, Division of Christian Education of the National Council of the Churches of Christ in the United States of America. Used by permission. All rights reserved.

Contents

Foreword: The Point of Ecclesiology— Gerard Mannion | ix

1. Ecclesiology Under Construction: A Report from a Working-Site —*Sven-Erik Brodd* | 1

PART ONE: *Systematic Ecclesiology under Construction* | 29

2. Ecclesiology as Juxtaposition of Social Theory, Hermeneutics, and Theology: Learnings from a Dissertation on Afrikaner Theology —*Hans Engdahl* | 31
3. Systematic Ecclesiology as Primary Ecclesiology—*Michael Hjälm* | 49
4. To Compare or Not to Compare, That is the Question: Some Thoughts on Comparative Method in Ecclesiology—*Tiit Pädam* | 63
5. Reflections on Understanding Ecclesiology—*Harald Hegstad* | 75

PART TWO: *Empirical Ecclesiology under Construction* | 85

6. Studying Fundamental Ecclesial Practices—*Sune Fahlgren* | 87
7. The Active and Concrete Church: Operative Ecclesiologies in the Visitation of the Sick in the Middle Ages and Reformation —*Stina Fallberg Sundmark* | 106
8. Implicit Ecclesiology and Local Church Identity: Dealing with Dilemmas of Empirical Ecclesiology—*Jonas Ideström* | 121
9. Reflections on Particularity and Unity—*Clare Watkins* | 139

PART THREE: *Embedded Ecclesiology under Construction* | 155

10. Ecclesiology in Liturgical Texts: In Search of a Method —*Karin Oljelund* | 157
11. Church Floor Plans as Ecclesiological Texts—*Gunnar Weman* | 173
12. (De)gendering Ecclesiology: Reflections on the Church as a Gendered Body—*Ninna Edgardh* | 193
13. Reflections on The Church at Worship and the "Lieutenant Nun" —*Teresa Berger* | 208

Bibliography | 221

Illustrations

Figure 1. Rev. Lewi Pethrus (1884–1974). | 89

Figure 2. Sanctury in Filadelfia Church, 1931. | 90

Figure 3. The stage area in Filadelfia Church | 91

Figure 4. Ecclesiology based on a communication theory. Each "body" is also interrelated to others in time and space. | 104

Figure 5. A procession with priest, assistants and attending parishioners on their way from the church to the sick. Part of altarscreen, Basilica di S. Lorenzo Maggiore, Milano, fifteenth century. | 113

Figure 6. The priest gives communion to the sick. Woodcut from *Ars moriendi* printed by Konrad Kachelofen, Leizig 1493. | 117

Figure 7. The priest anoints the feet of the sick. Woodcut from *L'art de bien vivre et de bien mourir*, Paris 1492. | 118

Figure 8. A theoretical model of implicit ecclesiology, part 1. | 133

Figure 9. A theoretical model of implicit ecclesiology, part 2. | 135

Figure 10. The Church of Västra Ryd at the end of the nineteenth century and throughout the twentiethcentury. | 180

Figure 11. The Church of Västra Vingåer in the early nineteenth Century and at the beginning of the twentieth century. | 182

Figure 12. The church of Västra Ryd after the renovation from 2004–2010. | 185

Figure 13. The church of Västra Vingåker after the renovation of 2011–2012. | 188

Foreword

The Point of Ecclesiology

GERARD MANNION

What is ecclesiology, who does ecclesiology, and why do they do it? These are the challenging questions that contributors to this collection have set themselves to tackle. In order to do so, the editors have brought together a range of perspectives from scholars of differing background—ecclesial and global location. These scholars explore approaches to the study of the church from differing ecclesial and methodological starting points; they uncover ecclesiological work going on in surprising places; and they engage practical, moral, and organizational issues where ecclesiology can offer genuinely transformative resources. The essays look at foundational and methodological question; historically, contextually, and denominationally divergent approaches; and they explore the realities of "embedded ecclesiology" in terms of the practical and ethical challenges in areas such as church ordering, liturgy, gender and worship. They seek to demonstrate the encompassing and integrative nature of what is called ecclesiology as well as to offer significant food for thought toward the future of the discipline.

One only has to look at the interest in the global media generated by recent developments in not only in so many churches—from the evangelical movement's growth across multiple continents, the rapidly changing face of official Roman Catholicism under Pope Francis or the Anglican Communion's internal divisions, to the forthcoming pan-orthodox synod—but also in global Christianity in general to see that ecclesiological questions are of great interest to the wide human family. So a collection that seeks to explore the wider parameters of this theological "science" in an interdisciplinary fashion is both timely and most welcome.

ECCLESIOLOGY IN FASHION

In recent years, ecclesiology has become one of the fastest growing areas of enquiry in theological and religious studies. Simply witness the rapid growth in the number of monographs, articles, collections, journals, networks, conferences, and symposia that take ecclesiology in one or more of its many forms as their focus. Or again look at how many courses and classes in universities and church-related institutions of training and education have come to the fore in these times. Often studies will say that ecclesiology as a discipline in its own right really only emerged in a distinctive fashion in the twentieth century, with important nineteenth century developments foreshadowing this. But, while the term "ecclesiology" itself emerges in use only in the nineteenth century (and in English primarily to describe the study of church architecture and interior design), with more frequent use of the term in its present-day usage only developing throughout the following century, in fact there have been many different ways of exploring the church and its story, its aspirations, its trials and tribulations, its failings and achievements, as well as differing interpretations of key teachings about the church and its life, organization, structures, ministries, offices, and so on throughout the history of the church. What is true is that the twentieth century gave more structure and methodological order and organization to the differing ways of studying and exploring the church and its life. This served to accentuate the rich diversity of ways and means of carrying out what we today call ecclesiology and, therefore, of actually being church, itself.

Stretching back to the New Testament itself, there have obviously been reasoned-informed enquiries exploring the church from theological, historical, and philosophical standpoints, as well as from other, often more context-informed and practical-focused standpoints. Biblical scholars have long charted the ecclesiological themes and priorities, for example, of the epistles of Paul, and we can say that so much of what Paul wrote to the young churches of the day was driven by practical, social, and ethical concerns (as well as political issues having an impact in some instances). The increasing influence of the church in the Empire and the multiple contributions from the early church fathers and, indeed, mothers, would often be concerned with ecclesiological issues and priorities as well. The growth of monasticism and eventual rules of community, and the emergence of important new styles of communities and schools in places such as ancient Ireland fostered much further reflections that today we must clearly deem ecclesiological in orientation. Again, much of this would often be driven by issues pertaining to the lives of actual communities, everyday issues, and social concerns, as much as by historical reflections and theological and philosophical approaches.

In the second millennium, with the advent of what came to be the new-style schools that were the European universities, the scholastic era also gave birth eventually to weighty treatises on the church, not least of all in response to the challenges coming forth "from below," from movements for reform of varying kinds. The emergence of canon law as a discipline and fluctuating models and priorities of and for papal authority led to further reflections, historical, theological, philosophical and practical on and for the church. The emergent renaissance and humanist scholarship took such reflections into new methodological waters altogether as did the era of European reformations, itself permeated by ecclesiological reflections focused upon the "macro-" and more local levels of ecclesial existence alike as so many existing church communities found themselves facing new ways of organizing and living out their faith, just as multiple new churches were also being born. From the post-reformation period to the growth of modern missionary ventures and on to the Enlightenment, ways of exploring, charting, and indeed shaping the church and its story have increased in their diversity.

So, yes, the nineteenth and twentieth centuries in particular did witness the emergence of solid foundations for approaches to ecclesiology from the standpoint of systematic theology, and that remains the branch of theology today under which ecclesiology is most commonly bracketed (others might say "dogmatic," "fundamental," or "foundational" theology). But the last century also saw theology interact with other disciplines, some of these new disciplines, others disciplines developing in new and innovative ways—so history and historical consciousness; new schools of philosophy such as existentialism; and the various social sciences and hybrid methodological approaches such as hermeneutics, critical theory, and organizational studies also left their mark upon theology. So, too, did they upon ecclesiology. Newly emergent ways of doing theology such as political theology; the theology of hope; liberation theology and its multiple forms in differing contexts and for differing communities including black theology, feminist, womanist, and *mujerista* theology; as well as further interdisciplinary approaches such as ecotheology and animal theology—each of these also left their mark upon ecclesiology. Indeed, for example, contributions appeared that self-termed their approach as "political ecclesiology," "liberation ecclesiology," "feminist ecclesiology," "black ecclesiology," "ecclesiological cybernetics," as well as a host of other innovative and fruitful ways and means of doing ecclesiology.

In the light of such developments, by the time we reach our own twenty-first century there emerge ecclesiological methods and sub-disciplines which take into consideration so many of those other schools, methods, and pathways for understanding the church better and helping the church and churches to live out their lives better too. In particular, what has been termed historical ecclesiology and then the umbrella approach that is called comparative ecclesiology (which compares one or more distinctive ways of understanding the church) have been developed in multiple ways in recent years. Here, in the work of Roger Haight, for example, distinctions have been made between more doctrinal approaches toward doing ecclesiology "from above" and more historically, socially and contextually attentive approaches to doing ecclesiology "from below."

During this same period there emerged—in many ways as a result of several of the developments noted above, and on occasion in parallel with them—ways of doing ecclesiology shaped and motivated by the core methods, areas of focus, and concern for practical and pastoral approaches to theology. Likewise the emergence of missiology. Many of the people working at the ecclesial "coalface," so to speak, saw to apply the fruits of many of the above developments in ecclesiology and so to offer further methodological tools still for speaking to the real-life communities that call themselves church in today's richly diverse world (who face real-life issues and challenges on a daily basis). So congregational studies, to take but one example, has also contributed much. Liturgical studies has seen considerable overlap with ecclesiology in this period too, alongside aspects of sacramental theology.

There have also been distinctive approaches to ecclesiology within and across particular denominations which have also led to multiple studies in recent times. Then there is the fact that global, multi-lateral, and bi-lateral representative bodies across and within differing Christian traditions have increasingly turned their attentions toward ecclesiological themes and foci in recent decades, for example the several ecclesiological commissions and reports that have emanated from the World Council of Churches. So "ecumenical ecclesiology" has emerged as a sub-discipline in its own right, the challenges of which should be of the utmost importance for any and every ecclesiology.

Further developments of relevance here have included the approach to the history, story, and challenges for and aspirations of the church from the standpoint of particular global regions and different ethnic and national communities. The method of "world christianities," therefore, has also brought so much to the ecclesiological table and tool-box for us and our successors. There have also been some innovative approaches to applying aspects of ecclesiology to a comparative theological study of religion and community in differing faiths.

I would say that so many of these ways of doing ecclesiology, especially in recent times, and throughout much of the twentieth century but also at so many other points of church history, are shaped and motivated by a further underlying concern—the ethical. Moral theology, Christian Ethics, and approaches to ethics and socio-political challenges in general have also left their deep mark upon eccesiology throughout the story of the church and especially since the later decades of the twentieth century and early twenty-first century. In fact, I would suggest that ecclesiology can never be separated from moral concerns because the church itself is a moral community, and the shaping and story of any community *per se* will have multiple moral dimensions. Perhaps this moral timbre to the science of ecclesiology is what so many of the most innovative and promising approaches to the study of the church share in common. It is certainly something that many of the essays in this collection you hold in your hands have in common. Bridging ecclesiology and ethics in a consistent fashion is *the* challenge for the church in our times. Even ecumenism is, ultimately, as much a moral challenge (and thus an obligation) as it is a theological and sacramental calling. Perhaps this is what some of the contributors have in mind in seeking to portray ecclesiology as a practical discipline first and foremost.

A CONSTRUCTIVE APPROACH

This collection seeks to cross the disciplinary boundaries of approaches to ecclesiology in a constructive and especially innovative fashion. They demonstrate how so much of the work of ecclesiology must by necessity be a continuous undertaking, carried out as though on a construction site or, as they term it, "in the trenches." Of course the latter phrase can also have darker connotations—reminiscent of the so destructively futile tactic of warfare that encapsulates for many the First World War, that terrible blight upon collective humanity's history, the centenary of which was observed. It was a time when Christians were sadly and especially divided and the wounds that war left among the Christian family took very long to heal, with a number still lingering. So ecclesiology also needs to be especially mindful never to forget the divisions that exist among the church of churches nor to "paper over the cracks" (to continue the construction site metaphor) by ignoring their reality. The rich ecumenical range of authors who have contributed to this volume will help ensure this collection might serve the cause of ecumenical ecumenism well, with its very starting point of ecclesiology as being "an ecumenical endeavor."

These essays also help to bridge disciplinary divides and ecclesiological "preferences," such as the doctrinal or systematic approach with the empirical or practical approach, and to encourage readers to see the differing approaches to ecclesiology from a complementary and thus (again) "constructive" standpoint. They see ecclesiology, in the word of Sven-Erik Brodd, as "an integrative force."

The title of this collection evokes many personal memories for me in a number of ways. Both before and during my university education, I spent a great deal of time down in trenches of various form on actual construction sites. Being from an Irish family in the UK, my Father and so many of my relatives worked in the many different areas of construction. There was great camaraderie and humor on those sites and many great characters were encountered and friends made, as well as many valuable lessons and skills learned. But being down a trench for much of the day can be messy, tough, unpleasant, and laborious work. Often the hard work goes unnoticed, not least of all by those who long into the future will benefit from the laying of, say, the pipes that carry their water to their home, their waste away, or prevent the storm waters from flooding their streets. But the work that goes on in trenches is *vital*. Long after the trench is closed the benefits of such work will go on, sometimes for centuries as we know from historical and archaeological studies into the feats of groundworkers from long ago. This collection helps demonstrate that those who toil in the ecclesiological trenches do not do so in vain.

Above all else, the collection will help readers to explore further and find some answers to the question that the contributors set out with—why do ecclesiology and why do *we* do ecclesiology in the ways in which we do so? Ecclesiology has a bright and prosperous future. This collection of essays embodies so much of the creativity and promise alike that have helped make this branch of the theological sciences the vibrant and exciting field in which many of us are privileged to work.

1

Ecclesiology Under Construction

A Report from a Working-Site

SVEN-ERIK BRODD

EDITORS' INTRODUCTION

In this introductory chapter Sven-Erik Brodd discusses some of the central themes that are considered in the trajectory of this volume, such as ecclesiology as an empirical discipline, ecclesiology as a theological discipline in a secular university, different definitions and scholarly approaches to ecclesiology, and questions of normativity and divine revelation as an inevitable condition in and for ecclesiological studies.

Brodd's chapter gives the reader a sense of the context in which the authors in this volume have conducted their research. As Brodd underlines, such contexts are important life worlds for scholarly work. Theories and methods are not created and used in isolation.

In the trenches, where the actual work of reading, writing, interpreting, and analyzing is done, there are many factors that are part of the necessary preconditions for research. Brodd points to some of these factors and integrates them in an overall argument for Ecclesiology as a theological discipline with great potentials for studying the church as a theologically defined empirical phenomenon.

Sven-Erik Brodd (born 1949), professor in Ecclesiology at Uppsala University since 1993. Between 2004 and 2006, Brodd was also a

> member of the Faculty of Education at Uppsala University. He was the Dean of the Faculty of Theology between 2001 and 2009 and thereafter Deputy vice-rector for the six faculties in the domain of humanities and social sciences at Uppsala University. Brodd received his doctoral degree at Uppsala University in 1982, and his dissertation was on *Evangelical Catholicity*, its content and function.
>
> From 1982–1985, Sven-Erik Brodd was employed as a researcher at the Swedish Government Research Councils. Between 1985–1990 he was director of the Church of Sweden's International Research Department and served as an advisor in international affairs to the Lutheran World Federation and the World Council of Churches in Geneva.
>
> Brodd has been a visiting professor at General Theological Seminary, New York and at Chichester University, England. He has published several books and a large number of articles and papers in Swedish and international periodicals and books.
>
> Brodd has participated in different international research projects, and he initiated the first international theological project—financed by the Swedish International Development Cooperation Agency (Sida) and realized by four African Universities (2005–2008)—on the response of the Churches to HIV and Aids.

Scholarly work takes place in a context, based on tradition and aiming at future shared insights. Thus, with any given exceptions, studying ecclesiology is not an enterprise undertaken by isolated individuals but by persons influenced, inspired, and encouraged, opposed, and disputed by the environment in which they work.

In the introductory part of doctoral theses there are usually "acknowledgements" of various sorts indicating this. There are references to dissertation directors or supervisors reading "endless drafts of the text," and to colleagues to whom the author is indebted for their advice and support. Sometimes there is a sort of brief theological autobiography that locates the author in a specific ecclesial tradition. But I have not found any deliberations about the milieu, the theological "ecosystem," so to speak, in which the scholarly work has been brought about. To get any answers to that, one has to wait until yet another scholar undertakes research on a person or a movement establishing the "background" of persons, ideas, or events.

Theologians know too little about each other's circumstances or real working conditions. Sometimes, when meeting at conferences or visiting each other's universities and institutions, we become fairly aware of what is going on, and we recognize similarities and differences and thus learn from each other. But normally language barriers, confessional boundaries, and other hindrances make this sort of exchange on working conditions impossible. At the same time it is important to underline that there is an exchange of ideas between researchers, perhaps even on a personal level, which initiates life-long friendship.

The purpose of this book is not to present a full-blown treatment of ecclesiology, its theories and methods, but rather to contribute to the understanding of how we, at the outskirts of Europe, in a secular university, in Uppsala, Sweden, are working with ecclesiology. For us this work is not finished—it is "under construction." It is done in a "working-site," (or to use the eponymous American expression of this book, it is done "in the trenches") and it is probably the case that the process of construction is as important as the edifice itself.

Ecclesiology as a scholarly discipline is very young, even compared, for example, with social sciences. It is internationally visible and diverse and is producing new working styles and contents. Our experience, based on different international evaluations of the research done at the university and in the faculty of theology, is that colleagues undertaking the evaluation have their own understanding of ecclesiology as a norm for their stance. We simply have difficulty explaining what we are doing. This is still another reason for this book.

What we have been doing in Uppsala is embracing various types of ecclesiological research, mostly developed out of theoretical curiosity and practical needs for understanding. We have borrowed ideas from where we have found them and developed them into theories and methods that we have found to be productive. So, one of the expectations reading this must not be to find any very precise set of coherent concepts and a subtly defined scholarly subject. It is more of a short survey of how we have tried, during the last twenty years, to handle ecclesiology as an unavoidable and fundamental element in the Christian faith, and an attempt to offer some hints of its future.

THE TERM ECCLESIOLOGY

When the German theologian Dietrich Bonhoeffer visited Uppsala in 1933, he wanted to give a lecture about "concrete ecclesiology" (konkrete Ekklesiologie), but his Swedish hosts had no idea what that cryptic title would imply. Bonhoeffer was persuaded to give a lecture about the visible and invisible church, at the time a common Lutheran problem.[1] The term ecclesiology was, for those theologians with good connections with the Church of England, first associated with the study of church buildings. In the Swedish language the term ecclesiology was introduced during the 1970s and remained rather obscure until it was pushed for and actually gradually accepted, not least because of the wrestling with ecclesiology and ecclesiological themes in an ordinary research seminar (*Kyrkovetenskap*) in the Faculty of Theology at Uppsala University.

Let me stay briefly with the term ecclesiology. From conversations with Nordic and international colleagues I have understood it to be a common experience that sometimes the concept has been either confusing because of its roots in dogmatics and thus *eo ipse* is seen as confessional and normative or, in parts of the Nordic world, something alien. This has also been the experience in the Uppsala ecclesiology seminar. As late as 2001 it was concluded in a doctoral thesis that "ecclesiology certainly is an alien word in the Swedish language, really only used in a limited academic and theological context."[2]

In a 2008 Uppsala thesis the author, an English scholar in the field of Orthodox ecclesiology, has to relate both to the background of the term in the Anglican tradition, i.e. the study of church buildings and style, and also to the fact that "the category 'ecclesiology' as such" is both a novelty and sometimes questioned in Orthodoxy."[3] This reflects, of course, an awareness that ecclesiology as seen from outside is somewhat strange. Seen from within it is a challenging and dynamic field of studying the church.

Ecclesiology from the Uppsala perspective is very much an unfinished project and will hopefully remain so. It is, as expressed in these introductory remarks, something under construction.

A Meta-Reflection in an International Context

Looking around the academic world it becomes rather clear that in many places there is an ongoing struggle with how to handle ecclesiology. Sometimes it is located in the context of an academic discipline, integrated into dogmatics, practical theology, ecumenics, church history, canon law, etc., and is just becoming evident through individual scholarly works. Sometimes, as in the Faculty of Theology in Uppsala, ecclesiology is established as a discipline in its own right. The fundamental difference between the two models is that one makes ecclesiology one component among many,

---

1. Ryman, *Brobyggarkyrka*, 37–38.
2. Edgardh, *Feminism och liturgi*, 16.
3. Hall, *"Pancosmic" Church*, 22–23.

while the other establishes ecclesiology as a comprehensive and integrating perspective. Liturgy and ecclesiology, for instance, become parallel tracks in the field of theological studies in the first case; in the second case, liturgy is integrated into ecclesiology.

This dynamic but rather fragmented situation has inspired different researchers to discussions, from a more theoretical perspective, of how to understand ecclesiology in the framework of other disciplines while establishing and preserving its own characteristics.[4] There is also a development starting in these discussions on theory, namely the developing ideas of specific methods in ecclesiology.[5] One of the tasks of the research seminar is certainly to test the limits of what is possible in an academic milieu. That demands a dialogical and open setting.

There seems, however, to be a lacuna in our knowledge about the actual meta-processes going on when the idea of conceptualizing ecclesiology is confronted with concrete research or with actual university politics. This is a type of ongoing reflection about the scholarly work as such: what are we doing and why are we doing that in ecclesiology? It is a reflection on what ecclesiology is emanating from concrete academic work. In Uppsala this is done in the research seminar.

RESEARCH SEMINAR: AN INTRODUCTION

In a foreword to a book presenting some results of an externally funded research project (*The Meaning of Christian Liturgy*) situated in the framework of the research seminar, the North American liturgist Gordon Lathrop describes the seminar as "one of the most interesting long-term graduate level theological projects found in current European and American university life: the ecclesiology (*Kyrkovetenskap*) seminar at Uppsala university in Sweden."[6] These kind remarks suggest it might be helpful to briefly explain what a research seminar is in the Swedish university milieu.

In all disciplines or departments there are research seminars—what earlier was referred to as "higher seminars." Members of the seminar in *Kyrkovetenskap* (Ecclesiology) are doctoral students, research master's students (the master's degree was introduced in Uppsala University in 2007),

---

4. Ormerod, "The Structure;" Ibid., "A Dialectic Engagement;" Ibid., "Ecclesiology and the Social Sciences;" Sterkens, "Challenges for the Modern Church;" Watkins, "Organizing the People of God;" Ibid et al., "Practical Ecclesiology;" Haight, "Historical Ecclesiology;" Ibid., "Systematic Ecclesiology."

5. Bretherton, "Coming to Judgment;" Barruffo, *Sui problemi del metodo in ecclesiologia*; Dianich, *Ecclesiologia*.

6. Lathrop, "Foreword," viii.

postdoctoral researchers, and senior scholars. In 1997, when Gordon Lathrop was a member of the seminar, it counted among its members six different denominational belongings and managed at least to read eight different modern languages. That has, of course, shifted over the years.

The research seminar meets once a week. It works with texts presented by its members, discusses theory (including disciplinary theoretical problems), methodological challenges, and communicates information, for example, about individual members' participation in networks, experiences from visiting other institutions, and travels abroad.

The responsibility of the individual members of the seminar, not least the doctoral students, is important. Tutoring is not instructions but deliberations out of which the student has to make decisions. When the student presents a text or an idea in the research seminar, the goal is to give positive critique in such a way that the member of the seminar can find it useful. We have tried in this case to break a long tradition in Sweden that focused on rather negative criticism.

But the research seminar is also a forum for professors and doctors in the discipline, as well as invited guests, to get their work scrutinized and to discuss theoretical and methodological problems.

In the seminar we also invite guests, who give presentations. Sometimes they also are called to scrutinize parts of doctoral works.[7] That means that we get new impressions and contacts, and this participation in the work of international well-known scholars contributes to the development of the discipline as well as the individual scholars.

The preceding serves an introduction that demands some reflection about the history of ecclesiology. The chapter, thus, proceeds in two parts. The first part (pp. 7–11) comprises the necessary reflection about the history of eccelsiology. The second part (pp. 12–28) focuses on the various meanings of ecclesiology and can be read separately without the historical background of part I.

---

7. For instance, over the years Gail Ramshaw (USA), Gordon Lathrop (USA), Miroslav Volf (USA), Kari Veiteberg (Norway), Nicolas Healy (USA), Stanley Hauerwas (USA), John de Gruchy (South Africa), Ola Tjørhom (Norway), Teresa Berger (USA), Graham Ward (UK), and Paul Avis (UK), have visited the seminar.

I.

The History of Ecclesiology at Uppsala University

In order to make the core of this presentation understandable, I have to give some historical background, partly because the development in Sweden sometimes differs from the development internationally, and partly because the reasoning needs a context.

The dominating church in Sweden has been and is the national Church of Sweden, and up to the 1960s that affected the Faculty of Theology, both in form and in content. The Faculty of Theology (as, for example, in Germany, the basic academic institution at a university) was in various ways confessional. The professors were almost without exception priests in the Church of Sweden, the faculty sent representatives to the General Synod of the Church of Sweden, and the professors were represented in the diocesan chapter of the Archdiocese of Uppsala.

ACADEMIC STUDY OF THE CHURCH IN RECENT HISTORY

Already during the first decades of the twentieth century the issue of the Church was present in the Church of Sweden and in academic theology. In 1912 Gustaf Aulén (1879–1977), then a docent in Uppsala, later an internationally well-known theologian, wrote a thesis about the concept of the Church.[8] Other famous Uppsala theologians who worked on the question of the nature of the Church, were Nathan Söderblom (1866–1951)[9] and Einar Billing (1871–1939).[10] The result of their work was conceived as the Folk Church idea. Already during the nineteenth century the Church had been in focus both in the revivalist movement, in the emerging Free Churches, and among the high church Lutherans. The Free church theologians, however, were left out of the Faculties of Theology in Uppsala and Lund.

The last noteworthy example of the confessional academic studies of the Church was the so-called "new view on the Church," which emerged at the end of the 1930s and had an international impact during the 1940s and the 1950s.[11] It was a cooperation between New Testament scholars and systematic theologians in Lund and Uppsala. To most of them, the Church

---

8. Aulén, *Till belysning*.

9. Brodd, *Evangelisk katolicitet*, 101–34.

10. Wrede, *Kyrkosynen*.

11. Usually one single book is singled out to represent this movements, translated into English and German, namely *En bok om kyrkan*, *This is the Church*, *Ein Buch von der Kirche*.

was instituted by Christ, was sacramental in character, and was actually an ongoing incarnation of the Lord.[12]

During this period, the academic study of the Church remained confessional and dogmatic. The references and authorities that theologians used mirrored that orientation. Simultaneously, the confessional position (based on e.g. Martin Luther, the Church Fathers, the Scriptures, or whatever authorities used) formed the foundations of their conceptual constructions and coherent understandings of the Church. The studies were deductive and historical in character, and historical texts were used argumentatively—and every now and then polemically. The distance to practical theology and praxis at large was apparent. During the 1970s everything changed.

ECCLESIOLOGY IN THE CONTEXT OF A FACULTY OF THEOLOGY

Since the 1970s, theology departments in many universities around the world have been reorganized, and the various disciplines have been submitted to changes in structure, content, and theory. The study of the Church in the Faculty of Theology at Uppsala University is no exception to that.[13]

When, as a newly ordained priest in 1974, I was accepted into doctoral studies in Practical Theology, the immediate forerunner to what became the discipline of ecclesiology, it was mainly a historical discipline. The focus had been largely on the Swedish reformation and history of liturgy, sacramental theology, canon law, and other themes of a practical theological character. But it also included topics of research related to the social sciences of religion. That made the discipline the sum of its parts, and it lacked an overall focus. In spite of that, of my fellow doctoral students one became professor in Church history in Gothenburg, another in Sociology of Religion in Uppsala, another professor in Pedagogics of Religion in Lund, and still another one, Oloph Bexell, in Ecclesiology and later Church History in Uppsala.

What happened in the university at large and in the Faculty of Theology in Uppsala during the 1970s was a theoretically grounded reshuffling of the structures. New disciplines, such as Sociology of Religion and Philosophy of Religion, were added, and the old disciplines, such as Dogmatics, became Studies in Faiths and Ideologies (nowadays once again changed to Systematic Theology). The basis for this was a transformation from a more or less confessional theology to religious studies.

Practical theology changed its name and became Studies in Churches and Denominations. Sociology and other elements of social sciences were

---

12. See for example Brodd, "The Church as Sacrament."
13. Andrén, "Kyrkovetenskap."

moved, and dogmatics, as far as it related to the study of the Church in a more narrow sense, was integrated into the reordered discipline. These changes demanded a theoretical anchoring.

Swedish university theology had, since the nineteenth century, been what the Lundensian theologian Gustaf Wingren called a German province.[14] To the extent that there had been a theoretical discussion about the character of practical theology it had been stamped by that. Whatever the position taken, practical theology was always a *theologia applicata*, an applied theology, mostly historical in nature. This dimension gave practical theology a sort of legitimacy also from the perspective of religious studies. There had been systematic theological elements in the studies presented in the discipline, but they had always been subordinate to the historical perspective and not clarified as such.

Practical Ecclesiology?

What had already taken place in Uppsala, before the new university structures were implemented in 1973, was that the discipline had become the sum of its sub-disciplines. In the 1989 Faculty program, however, it was said that the research field is "practical ecclesiology."[15] When the University asked the government to give permission to advertise the professorial chair in 1991, the Faculty deliberated on "practical ecclesiology" and interpreted it as "the study of the Christian Church (in its different traditions and denominations) precisely as Church and with specific attention paid to its concrete expressions."[16] The letter to the government also quotes the Faculty program of 1982, in which it says: "The research [in the discipline] regards ecclesiology as viewed through history and at present in Christian churches and denominations and as it takes shape in various forms in harmony, tensions and conflicts." In the 1982 Faculty program, as well as in the advertisement for the chair ten years later, it was said that the development of the discipline had led to the integration of the earlier sub-disciplines and the introduction of a disciplinary integrity. The task was, "in the framework of ecclesiology, to keep together and research various ecclesial manifestations, in order to clarify the reciprocity, interaction—and content—in theological structures within the life of the Christian Church."

---

14. Wingren, "Deutscher Einfluss."

15. Fakultetsprogram, *UHÄ-rapport 1986:24*, 14; *Teologisk forskning. Fakultetsprogram 1989*, 13–14.

16. The universities in Sweden are state universities. Up to the end of the twentieth century, the universities had to ask the government for approbation of each professorial chair, and the government—and at one time, the King—appointed the professor proposed by the university.

The question is, however, how it was possible for the Faculty of Theology to reach these conclusions. This took place when the faculty was transformed from being a place which was rather "Lutheran" in character to a place for religious studies, and when Åke Andrén (1917–2007), the holder of the professorial chair since 1954, retired in 1983.[17] In 1974, I introduced Karl Rahner's view on practical ecclesiology as one possibility of pursuing practical theology,[18] and Andrén used that one year later in a presentation of the discipline.[19] It was, however, developed by another professor in the field, Alf Härdelin (1927–2014), but then in the framework of spirituality, which he at the time presented as a possible conception of the reshaped discipline.[20]

When the renamed discipline (Studies in Churches and Denominations) no longer had to formally consider its confessional heritage, new theoretical possibilities were opened. In search of a disciplinary identity, the faculty found Karl Rahner's presentation of practical theology to be helpful. His distinction between dogmatic ecclesiology (*Essentialekklesiologie*) and practical ecclesiology (*Existentialekklesiologie*) offered a possibility to give the discipline both a framework and a center.[21] This was, as mentioned, mirrored in the research programs of the faculty during the 1980s and when the profile of the chair was decided at the beginning of the 1990s, ecclesiology was the center of the discipline. The content remained, however, undefined. This became a challenge for the whole research seminar, and the development of ecclesiology in Uppsala can be traced not only in articles, in journals, and in books but also in doctoral theses presented during the years.

In 1995 the name was changed again, now to *Kyrkovetenskap*, and given the English translation Ecclesiology.[22] The question is: How is it possible to change a discipline that is characterized by its different sorts of research using a concept that is not unambiguous?

THE DEVELOPMENT OF A DISCIPLINARY IDENTITY

The chair of ecclesiology was very much in accordance with the Swedish university tradition that was stamped by the idea of the strong discipline.

---

17. Brodd, "Åke Andrén."
18. Brodd, "Vad är praktisk teologi?"
19. Andrén, "Kyrko- och samfundsvetenskap."
20. Härdelin, "Spiritualitet—ny deldisciplin."
21. Andrén, "Practical Theology."
22. Brodd, "Kyrkovetenskap." See also the Norwegian theologian Olav Skjevesland, who reflects on ecclesiology in Uppsala as Practical Theology. See Skjevesland, *Invitasjon*.

The professor *ordinarius*, who was at that time appointed by the Swedish government, was expected to mould the discipline in a more or less autocratic way. When I took office in 1994, this had begun to change so what was called collegiality could include not only professors but also other categories of teachers and researchers, even if, I dare to say in retrospect, it took a long time. In reality the development of ecclesiology in Uppsala has been very much built up by those who have worked with their master- and doctoral theses in the research seminar.

In 1994 the research seminar contained almost 40 doctoral students, most of them inactive. I met all of them for conversations and many chose to conclude their doctoral studies. Some wanted, however, to finish their work and did so. This means that at the end of the 1990s there were doctoral students accepted in Practical theology, in Studies in Churches and Denominations and in Ecclesiology. During (at least) the first ten years of my professorship, many of the doctoral students were presumably confronted with ideas of the identity of the discipline that were foreign to their own doctoral work, while at the same time new doctoral students were accepted under the new theoretical understanding of the discipline. This, of course, created tensions.

Another problem has been the theoretical tension between those who actually wanted to keep the traditional practical theological character of the discipline—i.e. making ecclesiology the traditional doctrinal element in a wider conception of the discipline—and those who wanted to develop theories making ecclesiology the all embracing theme. This means that discussions about theory have accompanied the research seminar through the years and still do, even though the change from a more general practical theology to ecclesiology as the kernel and frame is now well established. In this development the professor heading the discipline has, of course, a crucial role. This change would, however, never have been possible to achieve without the participation of colleagues, including doctoral students. And I also think that there has been a sort of mutual influence of ideas involving all parties during this historical process.

In the next part, I will elaborate on the term ecclesiology and present different theories and methods in the research seminar—and discuss what holds it all it together.

II.

Several Meanings of Ecclesiology Under Construction

After this historical review (Part I), we are back to the term ecclesiology: Is it possible to make ecclesiology a center and focus of a whole discipline without a firm conceptualization? The word ecclesiology has, in any case, three meanings: it is the object of the study, it is the way of studying something, and it is the result of the study.

At the beginning, still under the influence of Rahner's distinction, we actually separated ecclesiology (doctrine) and ecclesial life (practice). We did that for some years, and this approach is also used theoretically in some scholarly works in other Nordic countries, but we have since abandoned this. There were several reasons for that, for example that this difference favors an idealistic view of ecclesiology that it in one way or the other supports a theory of doctrine that is not only distinct from practice but separated and sometimes makes practice doctrinally irrelevant. It creates, to allude to the German Lutheran theologian Edmund Schlink, a sort of ecclesiological docetism that is difficult to handle in ecclesiological research.[23]

Another question was about the possible connotations of ecclesiology. Who is the owner of the concept? Is it possible to cross the borders of the Church and identify and analyze ecclesiologies outside the Church? The first modest step we took was in a thesis about the understanding of the Church in the Swedish Social Democratic Party. The author had to defend the idea that political texts could be studied ecclesiologically because it was said by his opponents that only a church could have an ecclesiology.[24] So the question remained of how intimately the term ecclesiology should be attached to doctrine.

THE MAIN CHALLENGE: KEEPING DOCTRINE AND PRACTICE TOGETHER

We have continuously been asked what we mean by Church; what is the object we study? Originally we answered that question rather pragmatically. The researcher decided how to define what is Church from his or her understanding of the object studied. In texts claiming a normative understanding of Church this position of the researcher had to take into consideration the three strata in ecclesiology that we had established: ecclesiology as an

---

23. Schlink, "Das wandernde Gottesvolk," 687.
24. Ahlbäck, *Socialdemokratisk kyrkosyn*.

analytical tool, ecclesiology as an object of study, and ecclesiology as a result of a scholarly investigation.

In short, that means both that the object is identified as an ecclesiological phenomenon or object (not, for example, as exclusively sociological or historical) by means of research theories, and that the result then is ecclesiological in character, answering the adequate ecclesiological questions.

That, however, did not entirely solve the problem of the use of the concept of Church in our theories and methods. So there has been a development in our understanding. We can still talk about *the* Church (definite), which implies given normative and exclusive traits, and we can also handle that theoretically. But we can also talk about church in an undefined way which according to given criteria can be studied also in texts and practices that do not claim to deal with or represent church in any traditional meaning. So we can analyze a novel or research results in political science, for example.[25]

In the beginning we were very reluctant to study any other materials than written texts, partly because of the focus on given doctrinal presuppositions. Doctrine was the sole object in ecclesiology. There was also a historical argument for this, which took into account both the practical theological heritage of the discipline and a wish to avoid it once again becoming the sum of loosely added elements. Later on, other competences were integrated in the seminar giving new perspectives on the importance of social sciences; not least the possibilities ethnography offered ecclesiology. That opened the door for cooperation with other disciplines.

The last example of components of the theoretical framework in ecclesiology is the different perspectives offered by studying implicit ecclesiology, operative ecclesiology, meta-ecclesiology, or fundamental ecclesial practices. One of the challenges to ecclesiological research is to combine deductive and inductive studies. The churches can be studied not just from what they teach but also from the way they practice. It is important to bear in mind that different mindsets in the life of the believers in a particular church disturb the deductive processes grounded in magisterial documents and the ideas offered by individual theologians.

In practice there are hidden ecclesiologies that are operative and contribute to the understanding of the churches.[26] These operative ecclesiologies are often presented as meta-ecclesiologies; the church is described *as* something, for example *as* a school or *as* communicative fellowship. When

---

25. Brodd and Weman, *Kyrka i olika meningar*.

26. Brodd, "Upptäckter av dolda uppfattningar;" "Kirche als Kultursystem?"; "The Hidden Agenda;" "L'agenda nascosta."

latent ecclesiologies are revealed, they may be related to—or give rise to—a constructive ecclesiology of some sort, which is based, for example, on implicit communication theories.[27] Hence ecclesiology has the possibility of proposing conceptualizations that will be different from other theoretical fields and disciplines and thereby make evident what was earlier unknown.

On the other hand doctrinal, textual ecclesiology continues to be important. This research is often based on history but is not necessarily historical in character, which complicates the work. Examples would be ecumenical texts or doctrinal texts from different periods.[28] During the period when we stressed the study of texts, we distinguished between ecclesiology and ecclesiality, holding that the first was dogmatic and the second the expression of ecclesial life.[29] Later on this distinction came to be applied differently, and ecclesiality became an interpretative tool in ecclesiology.

Thus, the main challenge is to keep together various kinds of ecclesiological research in a productive way. From time to time that gives rise to discussions in the research seminar about what is common for the work undertaken, and those conversations remain important. The goal is to realize that the different projects held together by the seminar are together perspectives of one reality where practice and doctrine are held together. What we agree on is that ecclesiology is a theological discipline.

ECCLESIOLOGY AMONG OTHER DISCIPLINES

We are quite often asked how ecclesiology relates to other disciplines, both in the Faculty of Theology and in the university at large. There are several underlying connotations in that question, not unique at all in a university where natural sciences and social sciences, disciplines are continuously redressed or abandoned in favor of others.

One question that has followed the seminar during the years is whether the idea of ecclesiology is integrative enough, that is, what is the factor that is shaping the integrity of the discipline. In ecclesiology it has been the construction of ecclesiology as a discipline that has kept the discipline as such going, not in a theoretical vacuum but in praxis by answering to certain needs in actual ongoing research. It means that the usefulness and adequacy of theories for specific research has been decisive. The references to—and developments of—ecclesiological theories and methods in doctoral theses

---

27. Brodd, "Papal Ministry;" "Kyrkan som kommunikativ gemenskap;" "Electronic Church."

28. Brodd, "The Trinitarian."

29. Brodd, "Ecklesiologi och ecklesialitet." See also the comments to this made by the Danish theologian Hans Raun Iversen, "Ekklesiologi og ekklesialitet."

written in the discipline hints at the fact that there is an integrative force in place in the ecclesiology worked with in Uppsala. I think that we have found a way to make ecclesiology a discipline capable of integrating, for example, liturgy,[30] ecumenics,[31] canon law,[32] Mariology,[33] and religious life.[34]

But there is also a need for interdisciplinary work in ecclesiology, because of the complexity of the object studied, namely ecclesiology. I will soon return to that. One example: as already mentioned there is a tradition of a church historical character in the discipline. Here, two comments might be necessary. On the one hand, history, including church history, has been stamped by positivism, both internationally as well as in Sweden. That gives little or no room for theological interpretations of history, even if post-positivist theories give some openings for that. On the other hand, the Church is incarnational, and theologically the history of the Church is labeled tradition, which is, in one way or another, constitutive of the Church. Therefore the history of the Church ought to be an integral part of ecclesiology.

I can offer another example of the specific character of ecclesiology, this time in relation to political science. If ecclesiology is threefold (with an object, means, and result), that means that it differs from disciplines like political science, which can study the ecclesiology of, for example, a political thinker using theories inherent in political sciences, without presenting ecclesiology as a result of the study. The difference is that ecclesiology might use the same method as the political scientist, but the ecclesiologist has to combine it with theologically-based theories to understand the texts and/or practices ecclesiologically. As there is a difference between "study of theology," as an object and theological studies, theology has to be integrated into ecclesiological theory, which affects the result.[35]

Another challenge from our critics has to do with what, in a simplistic way, is called inductive and deductive studies. Here we have made a conclusive decision related to the use of social sciences according to theories and methods offered by them to establish texts that can be analyzed ecclesiologically. We can use these texts in combination with written texts and thereby establish a common text for all materials possible to read. The purpose is, of course, to attain knowledge otherwise not accessible.

---

30. Oljelund, *Kristi kropp och Guds folk*. A more extensive presentation in English is Oljelund, "Method in Liturgical." See also Hjälm, *Liberation of the Ecclesia*; Brodd, "Kyrkosyn och gudstjänst;" Brodd, "Liturgy Crossing Frontiers."

31. Pädam, "Toward a Common Understanding;" "The Diaconate after the Signing."

32. Heith-Stade, *Marriage as the Arena of Salvation*.

33. Adolfsson, "Mother of Jesus, Mother of Me."

34. Brodd, "A Female Face of the Church."

35. Brodd, "Kyrkosyn och kyrkohistoria."

As mentioned, ecclesiology as a research discipline developed from a study of the doctrines of the Church or studies of groups' and persons' understandings of the Church to include also ecclesial practices.[36] The next step was to include ecclesiological analyses of political standpoints, music, and other cultural phenomena, where it is possible to elucidate implicit or explicit ecclesiological patterns in cases where until now these phenomena have been studied as "religious." We think that the Church or church without the definite article is no religion. To attribute the concept of religion to church makes it either too narrow or too broad, i.e. important aspects of the Church are lost or decisive elements in the description of religion—which are irrelevant for ecclesiology—are added. The introduction of the concept of Christianity in the modern sense makes that obvious. In nineteenth century history of religion, Christianity, by means of abstraction, became a religion possible to compare with other religions.

In talking about the theoretical basis of ecclesiology and its relation to other disciplines, it seems necessary to say something about the relation between the parts and the totality of ecclesiology. Of course, even if every single study undertaken in ecclesiology in Uppsala were to recall the theoretical foundation and the relation to other disciplines, that would still not be a complete description of the individual research done. This seems self-evident, but experiences make it necessary to say it. The individual scholarly work is undertaken in a specific scholarly culture, affected by the theoretical and methodological debate, integrating influences from the work in the seminar but at the same time not restricted to that. Creative new inputs in the research seminar are of the utmost importance, and I think it would be disastrous if, from the methodological and theoretical point of view, all the research followed the same pattern, in a monolithic and imitative way.

Ecclesiology as a research discipline is not something fixed and given; it remains under construction. The object, the Church, in any given meaning, is something *sui generis*. It is a unique, ideal, and empirical community, which is a presupposition for the practice and understanding (historically and theologically) of all Christian faith in history and in contemporaneity. The content of this *sui generis* is ecclesiology, and the discipline of ecclesiology is the study of that.

At the same time—and now I am returning to the idea that we study ecclesiology—we do not only research the Church, but also church, and lastly ecclesiology. Once more, what is the relation between the three? It is not so simple that we can reduce the problem and say that the study objects of the Church and church just are included in the overarching concept of

---

36. For more on the discussion on practice, see Bexell, "Om kyrkans praxis."

ecclesiology, even if that is true. The use of church, without the definitive article, implies that we can study phenomena like a performance of Bach's St. John Passion to understand what ecclesiology might be found in that event, what elements of being church is present, and how to understand the totality of the event (music, texts, the gathering of people, their behaviors, etc.) ecclesiologically. Then we still can say that we study church in some sense. But when analyzing what ecclesiology emerges from studies of, for example, dominating financial flows, management, or personell administration in a specific Church, we are talking about studying an *implicit* ecclesiology. We are researching a cluster of non-theological factors, which we cannot define as the Church or church. So, in the end, when we talk about the object, it may be the Church, church, ecclesiology, or a combination. But it the object may be diversified like that, the study taken on is always ecclesiology.

Ecclesiology as an Integrative Force

Several times I have mentioned the importance of integrating various elements in the study of ecclesiology, not as the sum of them but allowing ecclesiologically motivated questions to structure studies of liturgy, art, ministry, Trinitarian models, or whatever. This does not imply that these or other themes or objects cannot be studied otherwise, but the ecclesiological perspective puts them in a specific perspective that might be surprisingly new. The questions and the themes become integrated in a wider entity of which they are parts, namely ecclesiology. I am not only referring here to the redundancy of sub-disciplines in favor of a disciplinary integrity but also to the theory that ecclesiological perspectives on a subject, say diaconal work, which can bring about new insights into the nature of both *diakonia* and the Church. This is self-evident, and a reminder is therefore necessary.

My experience of this actually started when I was the director of the Church of Sweden International Study Department and had to deal with the rather limited question of whether or not the deacon was a part of the threefold ministry. There were two dominating ideas in earlier discussions and also in earlier research: that it was possible to deduce the diaconate from the concept of *diakonia* (in the German Protestant meaning of *Diakonie*) and that the ministry of deacons was formed by its tasks. Impressed by John Collins's research[37] and later on inspired by the researchers in the Anglo-Nordic Diaconate Research Project (ANDREP)[38] I brought together formerly isolated elements from tradition, canon law, pastoral practices,

---

37. Collins, *Diakonia*.

38. For a summarizing and assessing presentation of the project, see Hall, "Research on the diaconate."

etc., into the framework of ecclesiology and from the perspective of ecclesiology, it became possible to describe a diaconate that "is important not simply functionally, nor in itself, but ecclesiologically for understanding what the nature of the Church is."[39]

One should also say that to a part of this ecclesiological enquiry was added a sort of necessary historical deconstruction of ideas.[40] The result, anyhow, was that ecclesiology proved productive in working out problems that otherwise had been handled in rather fragmented ways.

ECCLESIOLOGY IN A SECULAR UNIVERSITY

Sometimes I am asked to account for the theoretical basis of ecclesiology as a discipline at a secular university. My answer departs from Saul's dramatic meeting with Christ on the road to Damascus, later recalled in St. Paul's letter to the Galatians, "I was violently persecuting the church of God and was trying to destroy it" (Gal 1:13). Three times in Acts (9:4; 22:7; 26:14) what Christ said is remembered: "Saul, Saul, why do you persecute me?" The identification between the small churches and Christ is made evident. This identification is given already in the teaching of Christ before the resurrection, e.g. in John 15:1–15: "I am the true vine and you are the branches." This is developed by St. Paul in the analogy of the Body of Christ. At the same time the analogy between Christ and church is always paradoxically contradicted by the sinfulness and failures of the Church, the People of God *in via*, always on its way to perfection, always the object of Christ's grace. In the framework of academic theology, this is not an object of faith but a fundamental part in a theory.

Firstly, it gives possibilities of acknowledging the character of the object of research, for example its claims to be of a theandric nature. A foundation in any theory in ecclesiology is that all aspects of the researched phenomenon are taken seriously, to avoid unnecessary deficit. It is also a part of the necessary *benevolentia* of the researcher. If the Church is theandric, it opens up for the study of all aspects of human life in the Church from the perspective of ecclesiology.

Secondly, the Christological basis for ecclesiological research is in principle Trinitarian, which gives the opportunity of widening ecclesiological study and ecclesiologically investigating a broad spectrum of themes, not least from the perspective of implicit ecclesiology, motivated by the simple argument that where Christ is, there is also the Church.

---

39. Rowell, "Editorial preface," 256, Brodd, *Diakonatet*; "A Diaconate Emerging from Ecclesiology."

40. Brodd, "Diaconia through Church History."

Thirdly, there is a possibility of discovering, defining, and ecclesiologically researching various phenomena that normally are not identified as church. This is also theologically motivated by the insights from the New Testament and tradition. Neither "vine" (John 15:4) nor "ship" is automatically associated with a social body like the Church or church (indefinitely), so why not study church as a financial system[41] or as music?[42] In any case, given the presence of the Church in unexpected circumstances, it should be one task of ecclesiology to reveal this, identifying elements of church or ecclesiological elements wherever they are traceable.

Making the identity and difference between Christ and church the basis of an ecclesiological theory underlines that, fundamentally, ecclesiology is theology.

One question that could be raised is if it is possible to have a theoretical framework, which can so easily be interpreted in faith categories. The problem is, however, that we need hermeneutical tools, not so much when we study traditional ecclesiologies or traditional ecclesiological phenomena as when we cross that border.[43] One example is research of management and administration in a church. The idea is that we actually can explore various ecclesiologies by doing that, even if they differ from a church's doctrinal teaching about itself. To make that study more than a business study, to make it ecclesiological, there must be hermeneutical tools available. These tools consequently function on such an abstract level that they allow the acknowledgement of biblical concepts like Body of Christ or traditional concepts like ship being no more "ecclesiological" than concepts borrowed from economics, when a church or an ecclesiology is described in economic/financial terms.[44]

The necessity of a fundamental theory becomes obvious when texts and practices are researched using the basic question of whether they are ecclesiological or not. Then there ought to be some idea of what is looked for. If a novelist is writing about a war during the sixteenth century reformation period, and the researcher wants to analyze the ecclesiology in the story, which might be essential but not accessible for a scholar of literature, then she uses all the ideas the author might have in her understanding of

---

41. Brodd, "Stewardship and Ecclesiology." This article is a contribution to the ecclesiological reflections in the Lutheran World Federation. Also, for a critical discussion of my article (the German edition), see Zeuch, "A comunhão na confissão;" Brodd, "Stewardship Ecclesiology: The Church as sacrament."

42. Brodd, "Ecclesiology and Church Music."

43. Brodd, "Ecclesiological Research and Natural and Human Sciences;" "Ecclesiology."

44. Brodd, "Church, Organisation;" Nordlund, *Isomorfismer i kyrklig organisation*.

church and all the author's knowledge about sixteenth century ecclesiology. Still she needs a fundamental theory in order to avoid a methodology based on accidental elements, a theory offering additional and new insights compared to studies in the department of literature. The understanding of the HIV and AIDS pandemic differs depending on whether it is analyzed from the perspective of medicine or ecclesiology.[45]

In sum, to study ecclesiology in a secular university is not faith-based, but it must be theoretically grounded. The fundamental tools offered for this are presented by a given divine revelation, and I cannot actually see any alternative to that.[46] It is, however, non-confessional, multi-confessional, or ecumenical. The alternative would be an atheistic approach, which is alien to ecclesiology and therefore a hindrance for an adequate understanding of the object studied. When several traditions are present in the research seminar, no position is self-evident and that positively influences the creativity but also acts as a reminder of the need for clarifications. Visiting confessional theological faculties abroad it is rather easy to identify the confessional culture that to a great extent influences the choice of research problem and of subject and theory.

In the research seminar we have discussed this position and asked whether it creates a sort of dichotomy between belief and scholarly theory. I think this is complex, but if we talk about the given divine revelation, which is a necessary element in understanding the Church and why the Church acts as it does, the theory does not exclude the researcher's personal belief in divine revelation but gives a non-believer access to equal possibilities for ecclesiological research. This also means that the more "empirical" the research is, the more important the theological analysis. Theology presupposes the divine revelation and cannot be an additional extra in ecclesiology; it must be integrated into the scholarly work itself. The question is how this affects the research process and how it can be controlled by the researcher in her work.

Evaluations by International Panels

International panels evaluated the discipline of Ecclesiology in 2007 and in 2011.[47] It was well received with good ratings but the international panels

---

45. Brodd, "Theological Focus."

46. Brodd, "Die Zukunft der Theologie;" "Theology/religious studies." Erik Eynikel criticizes me for making an old-fashioned division between religious studies and theology, but that has to do with my postulation of a divine revelation. Eynikel, "Western European Theological Challenges."

47. The entire Uppsala University, with all its faculties, research disciplines, and research centers was evaluated in 2007 and 2011. The international panels assessed the

showed some uncertainty about the identity of the discipline. In 2007 the panel writes that "the discipline needs to develop its identity in the cross field of Systematic Theology and Church History."[48] In 2011 the panels wrote: "Ecclesiology as an independent unit, separated from Systematic Theology (especially Dogmatics), Church History or Practical Theology; it is peculiar in the field of theology. Formed in 1995, it understands itself to cover areas of classical dogmatics, practical theology and church history."

The panels acknowledged 2011 that the identity of the discipline had developed since the last evaluation, that it "steadily produces a good number of doctoral theses," that it is involved in international networks and symposia, and "that a considerable amount of titles is published in international anthologies and periodicals." Still, the panel wrote, the discipline's "identity separated from its natural partner disciplines seems problematic."[49]

It could be said that, apart from the political errand of the panel during the last evaluation when their remit was to establish larger units out of the disciplines, there is confusion about what ecclesiology is as a discipline. We are doing well, but we have not managed to explain the inner coherence of the discipline.

Church History and Ecclesiology

The panel's discussion about Ecclesiology and Church history requires some comment. It has, of course, been very much discussed in the international context, and important ecclesiological research has been historical in character, to mention only Yves Congar as an example. The historical dimension in ecclesiology is important because tradition is a decisive element in being Church, and, at least after the Incarnation, the Church is a subject in history. Nevertheless, there is a difference between the two disciplines, mainly because of how the object is studied.

It is important here to mention the impact professor Oloph Bexell has had in the discipline. I was Dean of the Faculty of Theology from 2000 to 2008 and thereafter Deputy Vice-Rector for the scholarly domain of six faculties in humanities and social sciences from 2008 to 2014. Bexell took major responsibility for the discipline from 2000, when he was appointed Professor of Ecclesiology, until 2006, when he became Professor of Church History. Before that he was my colleague and associate professor since 1993. Two of the authors in this book, Stina Fallberg Sundmark and Gunnar

---

quality of research. *Quality and Renewal 2007, Quality and Renewal 2011*.
    48. *Quality and Renewal 2007*, 242.
    49. *Quality and Renewal 2011*, 253.

Weman, are among those who wrote their doctoral theses under the supervision of Professor Bexell.

In his inaugural lecture to the University in 2005, Bexell presented his understanding of the discipline.[50] He repeatedly emphasized that it is historical in nature but also a theological discipline studying concrete practices:

> Ecclesiology thus balances the historical- and praxis-orientated and the ecclesiological-theoretical issues. [. . .] Ecclesiology [*Kyrkovetenskap*], is then a historical discipline that analyzes theologically the churches own reflections on their peculiar nature, as this is concretely manifested by practices in history and contemporaneity. The discipline is kept together by the sum of its fundamental ecclesiological questions at issue.[51]

The ongoing debate in Uppsala was about the domination of research dealing with twentieth century phenomena. Another problem we discussed was whether we should keep the distinct profiles of "sub-disciplines." Bexell defended the "sum," while I wanted a total integration in a comprehensive ecclesiological conception of the discipline. And lastly, we discussed the relation between systematic theology and ecclesiology. Oloph Bexell reminded us that there was a real threat that dogmatics would dominate the historical studies of ecclesial practices.[52] These contributions remain important elements in the ongoing discernment of ecclesiology.

EXAMPLES OF ECCLESIOLOGY IN DOCTORAL THESES

In 1994 we had a "box," the discipline, but the content was neither decided on beforehand nor concealed by a presupposed tradition; instead, it grew by means of ongoing work in the research seminar. What is unique in this case is that ecclesiology was developed very much by the doctoral students and later also by the students writing their master theses. Therefore, it seems appropriate to introduce some examples of the work done in the seminar by presenting a few of the 30 doctoral theses completed since 1995—which in various ways mirror the development and content of ecclesiology—and see how they can contribute to the understanding of the identity of this "peculiar" discipline. Or, to put it differently: if the small community of

---

50. Bexell, "Kyrkan som forskningsobjekt."

51. Ibid., 103.

52. The debate during a seminar arranged by The Royal Academy of Letters, History, and Antiquities from the twelveth to fourteenth of November 1998 is very well recorded in Heberlein, "Var står vi."

researchers that is called the research seminar is a working-site, could one say something about the concrete work going on?

Giving a brief introduction to the theses below, I obviously refer to the completed doctoral work. That implies that the given year for the defence of the work is preceded by a process lasting at least four years, stamped by labour individually and in the research seminar, and contributing to the development of our self-understanding.

When Kjell Blückert presented his doctoral thesis *The Church as Nation: A Study in Ecclesiology and Nationhood* in 2000,[53] he initiated a series of doctoral theses offering new and original approaches to the study of the Church, well-anchored in international ecclesiological academia. He thereby also reflected the intense work with theoretical questions going on in the research seminar. In his extensive theoretical discourse, Blückert introduces the concept of "meta ecclesiology" when studying the ideas of church and nation in the developing modern Swedish nation-state. What he was struggling with is the problem of identifying ecclesiologies, which are not explicitly dealt with in texts but become obvious in analyses of political discourse or action, for instance, and can be conceptualized as theories; in this case the church can be identified *as* nation.

On the meta level it is possible to "reconstruct" an ecclesiology by means of analyzing three "levels": the visions of the Church, the Church in praxis, and the dynamic and mutual influences between the empirical church and its context of culture and society. "The first level is a study of ideas, the second is a study of how these historical ideas materialize in institution and spiritual life and how they are thought to be materialized. The third level is a pure study of history: a study of the context of the text."[54] In the framework of historiography Blückert analyses "implicit ideals of the church and certain philosophical implications" in a reconstructed history.[55]

In 1995 Ninna Edgardh introduced feminist studies to the research seminar, resulting in her doctoral thesis *Feminism and Liturgy—An Ecclesiological Study* (2001). This was in a way a turning point and a start for a process of change in the self-understanding and certainly the character of the seminar. From a more or less practical theological discipline dominated by historical perspectives, it moved on its way to include new perspectives.[56] I had been in office one year, and most of the participants in the seminar

---

53. Blückert, *Church as Nation*.
54. Ibid., 96.
55. Ibid., 313.
56. Edgardh, *Feminism och liturgi*.

were thus more established than we. Ninna Edgardh actually worked with both feminist theory and made feminist liturgies the object of her research. The problem was, however, that the research seminar fundamentally lacked competence in feminist theology and even more so in feminist ecclesiology. About the latter it should be said that Ninna Edgardh had to follow the very few theologians working on feminist ecclesiology at the time. Further, a part of the process was to educate the research seminar. This is, of course, a normal procedure, and part of the idea of the research seminar is to broaden the scholarly scope, but in this case the point of departure was from nothing

The question to this is, of course, if it was responsible to accept Ninna Edgardh as a doctoral student under these circumstances and if she made a sound judgment when applying for the post. The answer is obviously positive since she is now professor in the discipline.

The subtitle of her dissertation *Feminism and Liturgy—An Ecclesiological Study* reveals an ongoing debate in the research seminar as to whether ecclesiology is merely an object to study, explicit or restructured, or if it also implies distinct or even separate theories and methodologies. In her thesis Ninna Edgardh is working with three areas: liturgy, feminism, and ecclesiology. "Ecclesiology in the meaning of concrete liturgical form of Christian church is one of the areas studied," she writes. "But ecclesiology is also my overarching perspective by which I seek to keep together dogmatics and liturgical practices, feminist ambitions and Christian, and empirical and observable church and the church of faith and visions."[57] The object of the study is liturgies created for women by women unaware of the underlying or implicit ecclesiological elements or even of ecclesiologies that are possible to uncover by means of ecclesiological analysis. Edgardh also uses the operative concept of "reconstruction" for the deductive establishment of ecclesiologies she finds in the analyzed liturgies and their contexts.

In a conference in 1998 hosted by the Swedish Royal Academy of Letters, History, and Antiquities, Kjell Blückert and Ninna Edgardh, both then doctoral students, were among the speakers.[58] Edgardh spoke about "Ecclesiology as Gender Studies."[59] She noticed a gender-blindness in ecclesiology in general and certainly in her own discipline. She argued that feminist analyses make ecclesiologically relevant practices and texts visible and that this s a precondition for access and understanding of vast fields in understanding what is church. She also underlined the importance of understanding the empirical data from a theological perspective. Blückert,

---

57. Ibid., 17.
58. *Kyrkovetenskap som forskningsdisciplin*.
59. Edgardh, "Kyrkovetenskap som kvinnoforskning."

in his contribution, "The Church as—Studying Ecclesiology from Different Horizons," discussed my position that it is acceptable in the study of ecclesiologies to postulate a divine revelation, not grounded in a personal faith but as a scholarly position, as an expression of the researcher's *benevolentia* in his relation to the object of research.[60] Very much of the conference was centered on this idea.

Mikael Mogren's doctoral thesis, presented in 2003, was called *The Romantic Church: Conceptions of the Ideal Church on Earth by the New School [of Swedish Romanticism] up to 1817*.[61] Mogren stated from the beginning that ecclesiology refers to conscious or unconscious conceptions of church, the latter, of course, being established through analysis of ideas and practices. He also established that an ecclesiology is not necessarily a coherent system of ideas but can even consist of contradictory parts. Without using the term meta-ecclesiology, Mogren constructed the concept of "romantic church" (cf. the title of the dissertation), which should be distinguished from the "ideal church" that belongs to the ideal world and the "empirical church" which is the concrete Church of Sweden at the time.

The "romantic church" is made up of perceptions of the "ideal church" when it coincides with the "empirical church" and the material and the phenomena included in that church. The texts written by the romantic authors are very diverse and often written in such a way that they consciously hide the theological content. The "romantic church" became operative when it was shown that the two worlds in Swedish romanticism, the ideal world and the empirical world, were not totally separated but that there were possibilities of transcendence in the empirical church as well as in the embodiment of the ideal church. This made it possible for Mogren to introduce Sacramentality as a hermeneutical key, and the formulation of that hermeneutical key was generated from the romantic text used. Mikael Mogren used the hermeneutical key to lock up three areas for analysis of three perceptions: of religion, of gender, and of art. The result was that Mogren was able to "reconstruct" the "romantic church" by identifying philosophical, cultural, or other elements that that could be translated into theological language.

Sune Fahlgren, in his doctoral thesis in 2006, introduced the concept of preachership as an ecclesiological category: *Preachership and Church: Six Case Studies of an Ecclesial Fundamental Practice within the Free Church Traditions in Sweden*.[62] Preachership is a construction used in order to iden-

---

60. Blückert, "Kyrkan som."

61. Mogren, *Den romantiska kyrkan*.

62. Fahlgren, *Predikantskap och församling*. See also Fahlgren, "Preacher and Preachership."

tify a personal function, task, and identity without becoming involved in traditional questions about ordination and ordained ministry. Preachership is a structuring factor in being Christian in communion, in being church. It is established in the social interplay between preacher and listener, the room they share, the message, the situation, and other factors. Even when people listen to a radio broadcast of a sermon, or when people during the 1960s listened to sermons on cassette tapes, a virtual community was created, fulfilling the role of church in some sense and establishing characteristics of being church.

The basis for Fahlgren's research is the theory of operative ecclesiology, namely that the praxis of a Christian community, when analyzed, can disclose one or several hidden ecclesiologies. The underlying hypothesis in his work was proven, namely that different kinds of preachership unveiled various kinds of ecclesiologies, different ways of being church. Therefore preachership is described as an "ecclesial fundamental practice" defined by inductive analysis of the preaching event—preacher, sermon, listener, reception, and situation. The object of the research makes it obvious that the common ecclesiological model in this case can be designed "communicative community."

In her 2008 thesis, *"Pancosmic Church"—"Specific Românesc." Ecclesiological Themes in Nichifor Crainic's Writings between 1922 and 1944*,[63] Christine Hall analyzed the ecclesiology of a controversial but nevertheless prominent Romanian Orthodox figure in the field of culture and politics, a man who was also an Orthodox theologian. Hall identified Crainic's "life experience" as composed of personal experiences, cultural ideas, and Orthodox spirituality founded in mystical and ascetical theology. Like Mogren earlier, she brought together a diverse material and handled it by means of a cluster of ecclesiological concepts from which she created her hermeneutical tools. Hall also made use of the dialectics between Crainic's idea of the "pancosmic" Church and the empirical church, in relation to *"specificul Românesc,"* a concept of the Romanian "particularity" carried by ideas of an ethnically grounded Romanian identity. Hall's thesis was historical in character but was not church history in a traditional way. Her analysis showed that it is possible to bring into view political and cultural history as an object of ecclesiological analysis.

The "ecclesiological approach" in Jonas Ideström's 2009 thesis, *Local Church Identity—A Study of Implicit Ecclesiology with the Example of The*

---

63. Hall, *"Pancosmic Church."* Hall has, in her continuous research, developed her understanding of the intimate relation between spirituality and ecclesiology. See for example Hall, "Spiritual tradition and ecclesiology."

Church of Sweden in Flemingsberg,⁶⁴ is presented as "theologically reflective and abductive." In this case, abduction offers the possibility of concurrence with disclosed empirical data and theory, which offers the possibility to develop the theory from the perspective of data. The object for Ideström's study is manifestations of a concrete church, a "social body," a study undertaken through means presented by social theory. At the same time, the church as a social body is also the Body of Christ and therefore the theological analysis is necessary. This social body, defined by being the body of Christ, is not a static phenomenon but always in via, moving and developing. The central concept is "implicit ecclesiology," which is used by Ideström "to summarize the understanding of the relationship between ecclesiology and ecclesiality," and the concept is also to designate "un-understanding of being church, which is visualized when a theoretical perspective is used when studying various forms of expressions taken on by that church."⁶⁵

I have chosen these doctoral theses to illustrate some of the differences, the diffusion of sometimes new ideas, and the continuity characterizing the research seminar in ecclesiology. These theses also hint at the possibility of studying different kinds of practices and utilizing analytical tools and instruments that are not traditional in theology.

CONCLUDING REMARKS: ECCLESIOLOGY AS AN ECUMENICAL ENDEAVOR

Let me return to the initial reference to Bonhoeffer and the lack of understanding of what ecclesiology is and my mentioning of the idea of making ecclesiology the center and frame of an academic discipline. When describing the scholarly milieu, it becomes obvious, I think, that ecclesiology as the object of the study, the way of studying something, and the result of the study is complex and multiplex and must remain so, because that creates the dynamics of the work and offers new challenges. There is, however, a unity in that diversity requiring reconciliation. This reconciliation takes place when different theoretical and methodological positions reciprocally communicate in such a way that they become mutually fruitful.

Observing ongoing doctoral work in the seminar in 2014, what, for example, do work about catholicity and ethnicity in South Africa, Bonhoeffer's ecclesiology, an identification of ecclesiology in people's experiences of music in the church, or Max Thurian's ecumenical model, have in common? Observing that members of the research seminar do not constitute a monolithic but a rather diverse group of people from different ecclesial

---

64. Ideström, *Lokal kyrklig identitet*.
65. Ibid., 23–24.

traditions, what, for example, do a Roman catholic, a Congregationalist, a Baptist, a Pentecostal and an Orthodox theologian, have in common?

Observing that the members of the research seminar themselves not only profess different ecclesiologies but also have various understanding of how that functions in the academia, how can historical and deductive theories and methods be on good terms with those who are working inductively in various ways?

To me it is important that the participants in the research milieu have different ecclesial affinities. It would obviously be rather dull if every work were cast in the same mould. But this is also very demanding on all the members in the seminar, and no one knows if it is possible in the long run. In the introduction to his thesis "Ordination of Deacons in the Churches of the Porvoo Communion," Tiit Pädam elaborates on ecclesiology and ecclesiologies and concludes: "Ecclesiology is thus a mosaic, consisting of various elements which only together constitute a whole."[66]

One could say that the work in the research seminar has distinct affinities with the process in ecumenical dialogues and that we might learn from that. An ecumenical dialogue should not be negotiation but a common effort to understand the given divine revelation.[67] The aim is to understand the actual positions, explain them from their historical background, and investigate whether a dominating perception is the only possible one and if the traditional doctrinal formulations could be reformulated in such a way that conveys a common understanding for the time being. To do that, it is necessary to relate doctrine to practice. I assume that these experiences should be taken into account in ecclesiological research. A conscious but self-critical position in relation to one's own tradition contributes to a necessarily broadened and deepened understanding of the Church. It is very much a question of overcoming prejudices and thereby detecting new possibilities of understanding.

---

66. Pädam, *Ordination of Deacons*, 16.

67. Brodd, "En gemensam förståelse av den gudomliga uppenbarelsen."

PART ONE

Systematic Ecclesiology under Construction

This book can be read as various arguments in the dialectics between the empirical versus the systematic within ecclesiological studies. Therefore, the book is composed of three parts, each proposing a possible argument in a dialectic thinking through the 13 chapters. Each part also represents the use of different forms of data in ecclesiological studies.

In the first part of the book, the authors are reflecting on Ecclesiology as Systematic Theology, but through contextual analysis they also challenge traditional approaches within this discipline. Their studies are examples of how systematic ecclesiology is under construction today. The arguments presented in the three following chapters are based on traditional data within ecclesiology, such as theological and philosophical works, dogmatic and liturgical texts from churches and ecumenical documents.

Read in relation to the proposed dialectical trajectory of this book, this part represents the *thesis* of ecclesiology as essentially systematic ecclesiology. Even though each chapter reflects upon how the empirical realities of the church might be analyzed and interpreted in ecclesiology, such reflections are done within the framework of systematic ecclesiology.

Even if these authors are using the philosophical methods in systematic theology—the field in which ecclesiology has had its loci for centuries—they have written their dissertations in ecclesiology as a research field of its own. Making the church the central study object in this discipline is challenging the conventional theological approaches to "church."

The argumentation in this part of the book makes clear that when the concrete church is the study object, its context must be a part of the study. This challenges the immanent approach of conventional systematic theology. It is not enough to argue coherently and consistently. These three chapters are examples of hermeneutical theology, fundamental theology, and comparative theology, and they will meet their antithesis in Part Two where empirical data are interpreted as theological texts and brought into the analysis.

Part One can also be read in conversation with Sven-Erik Brodd's introductory chapter and his concerns for developing ecclesiology as a fundamentally theological discipline, and at the same time ecclesiology is crossing the conventional borders of systematic theology.

> Making the identity and difference between Christ and church the basis of an ecclesiological theory underlines that, fundamentally, ecclesiology is theology.
>
> One question that could be raised is if it is possible to have a theoretical framework, which can so easily be interpreted in faith categories. The problem is, however, that we need hermeneutical tools, not so much when we study traditional ecclesiologies or traditional ecclesiological phenomena as when we cross that border. One example is research of management and administration in a church. The idea is that we actually can explore various ecclesiologies by doing that, even if they differ from a church's doctrinal teaching about itself. To make that study more than a business study, to make it ecclesiological, there must be hermeneutical tools available.[1]

At the end of Part One, professor Harald Hegstad reflects on understanding ecclesiology and highlights its character of *inter-disciplinarity* and *intra-disciplinarity*. These two models in ecclesiology are richly exemplified in the following chapters.

---

1. See Brodd's chapter in this volume, 19.

2

Ecclesiology as Juxtaposition of Social Theory, Hermeneutics, and Theology

Learnings from a Dissertation on Afrikaner Theology

HANS ENGDAHL

EDITORS' INTRODUCTION

Hans-Georg Gadamer and Jürgen Habermas are two important voices within the broad field of hermeneutics. Both of them play an important role in Hans Engdahl's reading of F.J.M. Potgieter and B.J. Marais, two Afrikaner theologians in South Africa. They are both shaped by the violent politics of apartheid which, according to Engdahl, makes any innocent reading of them impossible. In the following chapter, Engdahl reflects over the research steps he took to be able to read and interpret Potgieter and Marais in a responsible way.

Ecclesiology becomes a necessary tool to read and interpret the two theologians. Engdahl argues that their texts cannot be understood in a meaningful way unless the ecclesial context is outlined. He opts for two readings: a *close reading* that mainly stays within the text itself, and a *contrast reading* that relates the text to other texts and perspectives (fundamentalism and deconstruction). Engdahl's argument raises questions on how ecclesiology, theology and social sciences are related to one another in studies of the churches' life worlds. In this respect

PART ONE: SYSTEMATIC ECCLESIOLOGY

> Engdahl's and Michael Hjälm's arguments are clearly related to one another.
>
> Engdahl points to the fact that present research on church in Africa is almost exclusively sociological and anthropological, and he argues for research approaches where ecclesiology is juxtaposed with empirical science and theology. Engdahl's research is also an example of how ecclesiology can play an important role in theological studies that are not primarily ecclesiological.
>
> **Hans Engdahl** (born 1943) is Extraordinary Professor in Theology at the University of the Western Cape, Cape Town, South Africa. His dissertation, *Theology in Conflict: Readings in Afrikaner Theology*, is an ecclesiological study of two South African theologians. Engdahl received his doctoral degree at Uppsala University in 2006, and he is also a minister in Church of Sweden. Presently he is working on a study of African theology, ancient and modern, investigating the theologies of Origen and Mbiti. Together with Anders Göranzon he has published "Ecumenical Space—Expanded for Whom" in *The Ecumenical Review*, July 2013.

MY METHODOLOGICAL TRAJECTORY

In this chapter I want to demonstrate that a juxtaposition of social theory, hermeneutics and theology could provide an edifice for ecclesiology. The contention, then, is that theology will qualify the other two by providing a truth claim.[1] Such a theory sketch has been useful for my methodological intimations in my dissertation on Afrikaner theology.[2]

To make a study of two Afrikaner theologians, F. J. M. Potgieter and B. J. Marais, both of whom were deeply marked by the apartheid system in different ways, proved to be a particular challenge.[3] Not only was it impossible to do an "innocent" reading; soon enough it became clear that I had to take

---

1. This truth claim will be discussed more in detail in this chapter under "Reading Afrikaner Theology—a Meta-Reflection/Close Reading: Building an Inter-disciplinary Edifice."

2. Engdahl, *Theology in Conflict*.

3. An authority on John Calvin and Abraham Kuyper, F. J. M. Potgieter (1907–1992) taught systematic theology at Stellenbosch for 25 years. B. J. Marais (1909–1999)had a doctorate on the early church, taught church history at Pretoria, and was also influential as student chaplain. Both held leading positions in the Dutch Reformed Church. See Engdahl, *Theology in Conflict*, 61–63.

the context of these texts into account in a literal sense. For example, just because these texts both represented the white side and that of perpetrators, it would be necessary in some way to also represent what Schillebeeckx calls "the contrast experience as a result of injustice" which is critical to such a study such experience having "peculiar epistemological value."[4]

What I could be certain about was that these texts had been written during a time and in an environment that were highly charged by oppressive apartheid in both society and church. I should hasten to add that this oppressive atmosphere was there whether or not one expressed support of apartheid. The authorship of the founder of the Black Consciousness Movement, Steve Biko, is a case in point. He admitted readily that all in such a system would be complicit one way or another.[5]

I opted for two readings of the texts, one a close reading, the other a contrast reading. The first could be compared with so-called immanent reading[6] in the sense that little effort would be made to compare the texts with other, similar texts. The text itself would stand out as the primary object. On the other hand I quickly opted to go well beyond ordinary immanent reading and invited commentary from the side of social as well as interpretive reality. There was also a need to establish, from a theological point of view, what kind of social reality the church is. It was my firm conviction from the outset that it would not be possible to understand the texts meaningfully unless their ecclesial context was outlined. What fascinated me was that here I was finding myself in an interpretive and interpreted space that was formulated with philosophical (social theory and hermeneutics) and theological tools.

Stirred up by the prevalence of the daunting contrast experience of extreme suffering due to oppression,[7] I also had to opt for a contrast-reading that would either stereotype the notion of church (fundamentalism) or work in the direction of anti-ecclesial dispersal (deconstruction).[8]

While my dissertation was not about ecclesiology, per se, but about whether it would be possible to understand theological texts highly charged by apartheid, this chapter is an attempt to highlight the ecclesiological

---

4. Engdahl, *Theology in Conflict*, 6. See also Schreiter, *Edward Schillebeeckx*, 54.

5. Biko, *I Write*, 29–31, 74; Engdahl, "Theology as Politics," 16–17; Engdahl, *Theology in Conflict*, 11.

6. Engdahl, *Theology in Conflict*, 11.

7. I use the term meaning either contrast as comparability or as contrariety, here with the latter meaning, Engdahl, *Theology in Conflict*, 21. See also Schreiter, *Edward Schillebeeckx*, 56.

8. Engdahl, *Theology in Conflict*, 26.

construction that took place as a methodological concern in the very attempt to understand such texts.

MY SOURCES IN METHOD CONSTRUCTION

There is no innocent, objective reading of theological texts. Many factors, hidden or obvious, influence such reading. The chapter wants to demonstrate the need for establishing certain foreunderstandings when analyzing texts. The study of Potgieter's and Marai's texts has triggered far-reaching reflections regarding social theory, hermeneutics, deconstruction, theology and not least ecclesiology.

The section on close reading deals with various fore-understandings relating to social theories and hermeneutics. Gunnar Myrdal has become known for his emphasis on valuations and beliefs in his research (influenced in this by Axel Hägerström). However, residues of positivism can be detected in his writing, for example in his way of accepting facts as given, regardless if they are facts in terms of humans or material goods.[9] Here Jürgen Habermas comes to the rescue. What is of importance here is his secular understanding of the social life-world of the 1980s. In a lasting way he problematizes not only the difficulty in identifying one's foreknowledge in doing research but also the subject matter (facts to Myrdal), that is already an interpreted, interpretive reality and the social theory that becomes, at best, "a second-order construct."[10] Habermas develops a theory (that can be used as a research method) that involves both empirical social science and interpretive science. His interest is contemporary society and the social dynamic between people. His conviction at this time is that one could expect cooperation between humans in a dialogical function that would lead to harmony.[11]

Under close reading one needs to include the hermeneutics of Hans-Georg Gadamer, who is arguably very different from Habermas. For example, unlike Habermas he has a historical perspective in dealing with texts. In his hermeneutic circle, notions of prejudice, tradition, the fusion of horizons and effective-historical consciousness all have bearing on what is close reading.[12] It is, for example, possible to argue with Gadamer that unless the Biblical Scriptures are interpreted on a regular basis in the church's liturgy,

---

9. "If theory is thus *a priori*, it is, on the other hand, a first principle of science that the facts are sovereign," Myrdal, *Value in Social Theory*, 233.

10. Engdahl, *Theology in Conflict*, 15; Habermas, *On the Logic of Social Sciences*, 107.

11. See footnote 47.

12. Gadamer, *Truth and Method*.

these texts will either lose importance or even no longer be understood. The church remains a vehicle for constant reinterpretation.

However, the point to emphasize between Habermas and Gadamer concerns how *interpretandum* should be used. Gadamer goes as far as saying that the interpreter has the right to apply (Application, Anwendung) what s/he has understood. But Habermas goes further and claims that what is interpreted has to be shared in a social environment. One could say that he wants to break one-sidedness and make a shift from text to context, from text to texts, from one author to a colloquium of co-writers, from a message or a kerygma to a discourse or a community. It goes without saying that Habermas here creates an environment that is somehow conducive to ecclesiology.[13] As one can see it is not about an easy, straightforward close reading, but about a rather critical look at what the context entails, be it in the social respect or in terms of interpretation.

Secondly there is also a contrast reading. This holds the close reading as supposition and could not be done had the initial close reading not been there. Here I make use of two tools: *contemporary fundamentalism*[14] and *deconstruction*.[15] In the next section I will show how they have been applied.

Thirdly, one cannot just use these secular sources in order to build an ecclesial environment conducive to the reading of the texts at hand. There is indeed a *sui generis* stance that plays a part, probably the most important one. The church is a social reality as well as an interpretive, interpreted fellowship. What has to be recognized is that theology also, and not least of all, has to account for its own social realities. Theology is not only a reflection on belief systems but also on how these systems are lived. Again, this insight does not in any sense delegitimize searching for the wider context, be it economic, social, or political. The problem is that theology all too often has seemed to make do with borrowing from others, while it represents something which itself is full of social meaning. It is as simple as it is ingenious and yet often disregarded— and here we quote John Milbank: "[T]here can only be a distinguishable Christian social theory because there is also a distinguishable Christian mode of action, a definite practice." Christian theology

---

13. Habermas: "Processes of reaching understanding are aimed at a consensus that depends on the intersubjective recognition of validity claims; and these claims can be reciprocally raised and fundamentally criticized by participants in communication." Habermas, *Theory, Volume One,* 136.

14. A useful resource in this instance is Marty and Appelby, *The Fundamentalism Project.*

15. I make use of Jacques Derrida's deconstruction of the anthropologist Claude Lévi-Strauss.

as social theory is inextricably tied to that practice that is the church. One can therefore also talk about this theory as ecclesiology. Milbank, again:

> The theory, therefore, is first and foremost an *ecclesiology*, and only an account of other human societies to the extent that the Church defines itself, in its practice, as in continuity and discontinuity with these societies. As the Church is *already*, necessarily, by virtue of its institution, a "reading" of other human societies, it becomes possible to consider ecclesiology as also a "sociology."[16]

Radical Orthodoxy pursues the argument saying that things are in fact are even worse. Signs are on the wall telling us that we must move beyond the secular. There is no permanent realm of secular existence: "the logic of secularism is imploding."[17] In addition the secular may even be the result of bad theology.[18]

For my methodological purposes I do not draw such far-reaching conclusions—yet. The contention in this chapter, then, is that a dialogue between the two strands of research, one taking secular models into account and the other building what is already there in the church is of greatest importance. This is in fact the gist of the argument in this chapter: how ecclesiology could function as an intermediary between empirical science and theology. There are at least two pitfalls here. First, if theology is too keen to learn from other sciences these will inevitably define theology. Here radical orthodoxy has an argument that cannot be overlooked. However, working from *sui generis* in an exclusive way leads to an isolationism that is not very helpful to theology. The church as community is unique also in the sense that it always everywhere is concerned with the whole of the world.

---

16. Engdahl, *Theology in Conflict*, 28; Milbank, *Theology and Social Theory*, 380.

17. "For several centuries now, secularism has been defining and constructing the world...[Y]et in its early manifestations secular modernity exhibited anxiety concerning its own lack of ultimate ground... And today the logic of secularism is imploding... it proclaims its own lack of values and lack of meaning... it promotes a materialism which is soulless, aggressive, nonchalant and nihilistic." See Milbank, *Radical Orthodoxy*, 1.

18. "It is, ironically, certain particular modes of theology which first invent and encourage 'secularization' and then, because of their unbelievability, invite an agnostic and atheist scepticism which eventually engenders nihilism as a kind of truncated theological via moderna." See Milbank, *Beyond Secular Order*, 3.

READING AFRIKANER TEXTS WITH SPECIFIED ECCLESIOLOGICAL GLASSES

Two Ecclesial Gateways

First I need to provide the two ecclesial gateways that helped me to get into the study of Potgieter and Marais. Potgieter is deeply influenced by the great Dutch scholar and politician Abraham Kuyper who held the Stone Lectures in Princeton in 1901 about neo-Calvinism as a *life system* rooted in Calvinist beliefs.[19] It was thus a "root and plant system"[20] that had to be differentiated from for example the Enlightenment and Modernism on the one hand and Roman Catholicism on the other. Potgieter makes real efforts to dress the apartheid system in Kuyperian clothes. Apart from life system he also adopted the notion of *sphere sovereignty*, which was for Kuyper a support of independent life spheres like those of family, education, church or any other activity in civil society that the state should protect but not disturb.[21] To Potgieter these concepts became useful in support of existing apartheid structures in church and society. Here I argue that life system is a good description of what was church to Potgieter. The whole life system of neo-Calvinism, which had free reign in South Africa at the time, was in effect his ecclesiology of which the actual life of the church as denomination (Dutch Reformed) was just a minor part.[22]

Marais's gateway is the ecumenical church. While at the time Marais defended the upholding of apartheid for purely practical reasons (in order to avoid chaos), his theology was completely dismissive of any type of segregation or separation. Despite being an Afrikaner among Afrikaners his whole life and accordingly also a faithful member of the Dutch Reformed Church, his theology was ecumenical, greatly inspired of what took place in the World Council of Churches during its first two general assemblies (Amsterdam 1948 and Evanston 1954).[23] Here, the gap in relation to Potgieter starts widening. With these gateways a close reading is undertaken.

---

19. This is the expression that Kuyper, who had been advised by American scholars, adopted— instead of "world view"—to denote Calvinism as a movement.

20. Expression used in these lectures also denoting Calvinism.

21. Bratt, *Abraham Kuyper*, 461–90.

22. Engdahl, *Theology in Conflict*, 65–75.

23. Decisive is his doctoral thesis on communitarian Christian living (1 Pet 2:17) in the early church: Marais, "Die Christelike broderskapsleer: sy agtergrond en toepassing in die vroeë kerk."

Reading Potgieter and Marais through these Gateways

Potgieter could be typified in four ways.[24] He works from the assumption of Biblical revelation taking the form of a plurality of truths.[25] He also claims, supported by Kuyper, that there are *"principia, axioma*, a prioris and these are directly derived from *phanerosis*, revelation."[26] There is also an intimate relationship between theology and philosophy: "[T]heology has the task of drawing principles from Scripture and revelation, which is theology's object of study, also for use in philosophy."[27]

Finally he claims that the church is pluriform. One should here also recall his usage of the term re-creation ("herskepping" in Afrikaans). It seems that the term has lost its salvific radicalism in favor of being conducive to existing creation: renewed creation along already existing principles, like that of pluriformity.[28]

To Marais the notion of the Kingdom of God is paramount. But the coming of the kingdom is dependent of what he calls the radical and the conservative principle, a principle "derived from the workings of the early church," but also used by scholars like Ernst Troeltsch and Emil Brunner.[29] His dissertation on Christian brotherhood (communitarian living) in the early church helped him to take seriously the social dimension of the church as a concrete social and moral reality.[30] Finding that the early church actually did not talk about race in a South African sense of the 1940s, he stressed its antitheses like "universalism, cosmopolitanism, the church becoming the world or the church transforming the world (Origen)."[31] In a strange way the early church had all the answers that Marais could possibly ask for in regards to his own contemporary society, yet on one point he refrained from being influenced by the early church:

> The (early) church was maybe a free zone devoid of race divisions or racial thinking, but there was something else, namely the social scourge of slavery. All through his life Marais fails to

---

24. Equally decisive is the doctoral thesis: Potgieter, *Die verhouding tussen die teologie en die filosofie by Calvyn.*
25. Engdahl, *Theology in Conflict*, 289.
26. Ibid., 290.
27. Ibid., 290.
28. Ibid., 291.
29. Ibid., 292. See also Troeltsch, *The Social Teaching*; Brunner, *Justice*.
30. Engdahl, *Theology in Conflict*, 293.
31. Ibid., 293.

apply the early church's dealing with slavery to the South African church's dealing with apartheid. We do not know why.[32]

With the interpretive tools at my disposal it immediately became obvious that the gap between Potgieter and Marais had widened drastically. There was here reason to talk about theology in conflict, which could be seen in the following areas, Potgieter first, then Marais: in terms of methodology, one deductive, the other inductive; scriptural interpretation: verbal inspiration versus gospel-centered interpretation; theological thrust: trinity versus "God was in Christ;" and social life: diversity versus unity, nationalism versus universalism, neo-Calvinist confessionalism versus ecumenism.

> [T]he question has to be asked: Apartheid, was it a blessing to the one and a sin to the other? We cannot see one quotation where Marais says that apartheid is a sin, but he comes pretty close. He could for example say that if racial separation in the church means division and remoteness between people of different groups, then it must be against the will of Christ.[33]

Potgieter was something of an apartheid ideologue, but he denounced the term segregation instead favoring the term separation, thereby thinking that he could demonstrate some kind of justice in this separation. "He strongly believes that God has ordained each population group to live separately in their own God-given spheres."[34]

Potgieter and Marais Confronted with Fundamentalism and Deconstruction

Finally something should be said about the fall-out of the contrast reading of Potgieter and Marais. I have used the notions of "contemporary fundamentalism" and "deconstruction" in order to interfere with the two theologies. Potgieter could be said to embrace this kind of fundamentalism. He has decided to stick to a select tradition in his Calvinist faith that is to be applied in his own day without reservation: the pluriformity of life, understood as strictly following racial and ethnic lines in society and church as an expressed will of God. In addition, such a fundamentalism may have religious roots but is at the same time political in a stark way, not least in the implementation of the doctrine at stake. Marais could not be said to be a fundamentalist in any sense of the word, so we can leave that.

---

32. Ibid., 293.
33. Ibid., 243.
34. Ibid., 243.

With deconstruction it becomes very interesting as both can profit from such an exercise. I have used Derrida's deconstruction of the social anthropologist Claude Lévi Strauss with the following pattern: disclosure of various "fields of force,"[35] displacement, bringing in a new theory (of language) top down, and finally dispersal.

There is ambivalence in Potgieter that could be used against him, even as he tries to defend pluriformity at all costs. He also says that the church is able to bring in renewal to such an extent that it means a revival of the status that life had before the fall to sin.[36] He is also of the opinion "that in a pre-fall situation, people would worship God together as one unity."[37] Potgieter is here talking about unity as a gift to the church! Such disclosure is enough to displace his whole apartheid theology, i.e. a first-order deconstruction. Marais thinks differently:

> [H]is masterly portrayal of the early church as a moral community, not least in dealing with slavery, has been of lasting importance to Marais. This is the hidden "grand narrative" that has impacted on his thinking and is the key to his insistence on the church as an ecumenical, largely visible reality.[38]

But this grand narrative was never allowed to have full impact on his theology and world view; above all such deconstruction of Marais would displace and even disperse his almost lifelong conviction completely: namely, that for practical purposes we still need apartheid.

READING AFRIKANER THEOLOGY: A META-REFLECTION

Here we will look at three things: the gateways prepared for the two theologians, the edifice of close reading, and then the edifice (or lack of edifice) of contrast reading.

The Two Gateways—Again

Potgieter's ecclesiological gateway is Kuyper's notion of life system. As stated this notion goes well beyond what normally is church, and yet there

---

35. Derrida's gesture is to treat Lévi-Strauss as an example or symptom of a way of thinking more pervasive and more persistent than any one individual thinker, a kind of metaphysical field of force that would enclose and shape or constrain our apprehension and conceptualisation of the world, cf., Engdahl, *Theology in Conflict*, 24, 275; Johnson, *Derrida*, 51–55; Derrida, *Of Grammatology*, 99.

36. Engdahl, *Theology in Conflict*, 258.

37. Ibid., 258.

38. Ibid., 278.

is an ecclesiological dimension that is rooted in being church. The very fact that Potgieter's Afrikaner people literally were in church, under the Word of God Sunday after Sunday is enough proof to say that their religion was something more than just Afrikaner civil religion.[39]

When speaking about life system as ecclesiology, as we do in Potgieter's case, we are taking seriously the charge that Sven-Erik Brodd is making regarding the church.[40] Life system as meta-ecclesiology is *the church as*; it is about how the church expresses itself in a particular circumstance. And yet, as we will see, the life system that Potgieter builds is not ecclesiologically faithful in the ordinary sense. Reformed notions of common grace and Scriptural principles make it possible to form a system that is in effect dislodged from the church (at least as institution).

Marais had the ecumenical church as gateway. He was writing in the 1940s, and it is fascinating, to say the least, to realize that his notion of the ecumenical church—as a moral community and formation, as well as a body with conciliar and covenantal qualities —was revisited in the 1990s in two ways. About three decades in the ecumenical movement had been spent saying what the church is not, but rather what it was called to be and do for others. In the 1990s the study process, resulting in the report *Ecclesiology and Ethics*[41] had the courage to pronounce the church as a life in *koinonia*, a life of fellowship in solidarity. At about the same time, in 1995, reflecting on the newly won liberty in democratic South Africa, the South African Council of Churches had serious talks about the church as being the ecumenical church, a church in solidarity, across confessional and racial lines, with the qualities of conciliarity as well as covenant.[42] These recent insights make Marais's writings remarkably fresh and almost prophetic.

---

39. See Moodie, *The Rise of Afrikanerdom*. Moodie talks about civil religion as fostered by the political leadership and the language movement without actually seeing the church; Engdahl, *Theology in Conflict*, 29.

40. Sven-Erik Brodd has a discussion regarding church and organization. His claim is also that all organized activity inspired by the gospel somehow or other has an ecclesial function and meaning. The church is not an organization but "the church makes use of many different tools (organizations) which all are realizations of what is Church," Brodd, "Church, Organization," 10.

41. *Costly Unity, Costly Commitment, Costly Obedience*, also called "the three costlies," are the three studies undertaken in the 1990s by the World Council of Churches, published under the title *Ecclesiology and Ethics*.

42. *Being the Church in South Africa Today*. See also de Gruchy and de Gruchy, *Church Struggle*.

Close Reading: Building an Inter-disciplinary Edifice

Secondly, much more could be said about the meta-level of methodology also as prolegomena for ecclesiology. It is evident that Myrdal grapples with the need for valuations in research. His two monumental research tasks attest to this. As an economist he soon moves into an inter-disciplinary mode and deals with the predicament of African Americans (the word Negro was used) and later on problems regarding development in Asia.[43] All his life he reflected on what are the presuppositions for research and developed thinking around what he called "valuations." One here comes close to the discussion on *Vorverständnis*. The question is whether you can declare what your presuppositions are in actual terms, in your values and your valuations. In the US he used the American Creed (Constitution) as the core value; in his *Asian Drama* he opted for equality of opportunity and political democracy as value premises.[44]

Then, it is worth noticing that Habermas has read Max Weber carefully when it comes to social theory. He echoes in a way a basic insight already visible in Weber. The latter is already suspicious of the ever presence of evaluative terms but maintained that there was a space for value-free descriptive presentation. Habermas would here disagree.[45]

What could be said for all three is that they worked in an interdisciplinary fashion and saw clearly the commonality between various sciences; in Weber's case it was obvious that he boldly embarked on work that dealt with social theories as well as interpretive ones. His classic work on capitalism and protestantism is a proof of this.[46]

These scholars belong to a meta-level discussion and play a role in terms of theory and method construction to the benefit of the study of *ecclesia*.

---

43. Myrdal, *An American Dilemma*; and his monumental work on under-development in South Asia, *Asian Drama*.

44. "In spite of its enormous complexity, the American Negro problem is in one respect relatively simple. As the discussion in the book shows, in America there is a set of rather homogeneous valuations, ready-made for the use of the social scientist, in the form of the American Creed, which is particularly explicit about the Negro problem," and "In my recent publications on the problems of under-development and development I have used as value premises the desirability of equality of opportunity and of political democracy, and I am now setting out to use these value premises for a more intensive study of the problems of development and integration in South-East Asia." Both quotes from Myrdal, *Value in Social Theory*, 260–61.

45. Habermas, *On the Logic*, 14; see also Weber, *Aufsätze zur Wissenschaftslehre*, 174–78.

46. Weber, *The Protestant Ethic*.

Again, we have to look at the edifice of close reading. It has been my contention that social theory and hermeneutics could serve as important building blocks when creating a room for close reading so that we in equal measure draw from Habermas as well as Gadamer.

There is a mutual dependency here that opens for a space that is the church. (See above under "My Sources in Method Construction," the last paragraph.)

Despite his secularist tendency, being a traditional, sociological supporter of the disenchantment of religion (but this view of his has almost vanished in the new millennium), Habermas is very useful to our purposes. His notion of a "dialogical function" makes out a social milieu without which mere interpretation on an individual basis does not go very far. But his dialogical model is also criticized as it seems to take for granted some kind of harmony. Justice rather than consensus is of lasting value:[47] "This critique could mean leverage for Gadamer's application (and contrast reading) while claiming (some) validity for Habermas' consensus dialogical function model (and close reading)."[48]

In the end, however, social theory and hermeneutics have to be qualified by theology. What we regard as essential in Radical Orthodoxy is not only a theology located in the church in general. We have here a theology with a truth claim. In order to sustain this truth claim an interpretive and interpreted milieu is needed, i.e. the church. We benefit from this location also in terms of theory. Social reality has a bearing on the church. It is a realization that our social theory is designed to have a meta-ecclesiological function. It is not a matter of curbing or changing what is in effect a social theory but of adding a certain qualification. It is a matter of affirming a social theory that is circumscribed by ecclesiological realities, qualified by theology.

To be honest, this truth claim of theology is far more radical than a mere qualification of the rest (of the sciences). Rowan Williams talks about the unity of Christian truth, which invites the existence of everything and everybody in a particular frame work:

> With (Dietrich) Ritschl I believe that "the conception of the unity of humanity, which has a theological basis, calls for the

---

47. Engdahl, *Theology in Conflict*, 19. See also Cilliers, *Complexity and Postmodernism*, 137, and Lyotard, *Postmodern Condition*, 66. Hjälm in this volume, 58. Even though Habermas is quite helpful in method construction towards an edifice of ecclesiology I am also aware of his secularist confinement. Hjälm does not seem to see this, which simply may be due to the fact that he uses Habermas in a philosophical sense, i.e. the relationship between theory and practice.

48. Engdahl, *Theology in Conflict*, 18n21.

venture of an overall view" [. . .] To belong to the community of Christian belief at all is to assume that the pattern of relation between persons and between humanity and God which is displayed as gift and possibility in the Church is open to humanity at large, and to act on that assumption in respect both of the internal structures and of the external policy of the Church. Christian belief involves exposure to what the New Testament calls "the judgment of this world," and its corporate articulation and living out claims to be a mediation of that judgment to the nations, and a mediation also of the hope that lies in and beyond the judgment. In other words, the fact of a community committed to mission, to inclusiveness, to calling human persons and society to account, is the source of the question about the unity of Christian truth.[49]

Here two things are achieved. First, by claiming that Christian faith ultimately is about the unity of all humanity and that there is a God-given purpose for all, without exception, there is a universal and catholic truth claim that is so radical that it could be called in New Testament terms, "a judgment of this world." Secondly, this truth claim is an ecclesiological statement, coming from the heart of the church. It is above all a theological statement coming out of the church's common life of "a community committed to mission, inclusiveness, to calling human persons and society to account."

Williams here neither adopts a monothematic theology (Luther, Barth), nor a theology following the *loci* method (Tillich, Weber), but opts for a third way, as just described. He is here on the same wavelength as Radical Orthodoxy, seeing the church as the fountain of (all) theology. If there is no such challenge from the Christian community to secularity the result would be one of no communication and of "irreconcilable human ends." History would have no meaning but would be completely contingent, as "the 'salvation' of the medieval peasant and of the twentieth century bourgeois would operate in mutually inaccessible frames of reference." It would be "only the blanket dismissal modernity is usually happy to pronounce."[50]

Williams is here breaking out of the ranks of recent theology, which took a plurality of truths for granted. It is noticeable that as late as 1986 Leslie Houlden can still assume quite a readership (and hearing) when he, in the editorial of *Theology*, states that due to modern scholarship, it no longer seems to make sense to talk about a coherent biblical Canon:

---

49. Williams, "Unity of Christian," 20.

50. Ibid., 21.

The heyday of the Christian Bible began with Origen, with allegory and a sense of a single divine process of creation and redemption as the twin bonds giving it unity. So it largely remained, the single verbal entity, until the distrust of allegory in medieval and Reformation times began that intrusion of historical perspectives which ultimately sapped the unity of the very Scriptures on whose authority that Reformation so firmly rested.[51]

It is logical that the Editorial was titled "Is the Bible still there?" and it stands clear that theology without ecclesiology is in trouble.

Putting the Edifice Under Pressure: Contrast Reading

Thirdly, there is the contrast reading of the texts. Generally one could say that making use of fundamentalism and deconstruction is to put the Afrikaner texts under quite some pressure. This is also the aim as these texts were written in a country under conditions of extreme conflict. The title of my dissertation also indicates a theological conflict. As part of this meta-reflection I will say a bit more about fundamentalism and deconstruction as phenomena.

A clear picture emerges; it is possible to describe a substantial part of fundamentalist anatomy. Yet, there is a major uncertainty or tension that is unresolved. On the one hand fundamentalism has claims that are universalistic and it is clearly demonstrated that there are links to other heterodox movements emanating from axial orthodox religions such as revolutionary movements. There is a claim to radically change this world here and now.

On the other hand, fundamentalism is described as enclave and perhaps even as sectarian. Frequently there is an ethnic or nationalist confinement. It is typical of fundamentalism to select a few religious fundamentals and build a system on these. One result of this selectivity is that other elements in the tradition in question will become subordinate and perhaps redundant. An easily identifiable moral code and behaviour are other cornerstones in fundamentalism. These serve as a confirmation of right and true beliefs.

At the same time the religious fundamentals selected are there for a wider and more ultimate purpose. They serve more than anything else as the basis of a political agenda. In turn, the political agenda creates an unavoidable surge for power, from the periphery to the center, from the enclave to hegemony. The setting up of a political agenda means an absolute preparedness for execution of power, which may include aggressive power,

---

51. Houlden, "Is the Bible still there?"

violence, and war. There are normally no inhibitions regarding the use of aggressive power. The religious fundamentals are such that they by principle condone violence if it serves a "rightful" purpose.[52]

Then there is this special mode of critical analysis called deconstruction. There are three things to take into account. First, deconstruction here does not at all mean destruction or demolition of the works by any other thinker, like Lévi-Strauss. It is rather an attempt to unearth symptoms and ways of thinking "more pervasive and persistent than any one individual thinker, a kind of metaphysical field of force that would enclose and shape—constrain—our apprehension and conceptualization of the world."[53] "Rather than direct refutation, therefore, deconstruction could be described as a form of critical dialogue, which uses the example of particular case histories. . .as symptoms of a more general configuration or structure."[54]

Secondly, Derrida does not merely critique the phenomenon called logocentrism. He does not simply denounce the fact that speech and writing have been seen as opposites for a long time: "Derrida questions the traditional oppositions of speech and writing [. . .] not in order simply to reverse or overturn these oppositions, but rather in order to *displace* them."[55] He comes up with his own theory and by doing that he also opens up the whole discourse into something much wider. "The second stage or moment of deconstruction would therefore be the widening of the frames of reference, the loosening of the rigid systems of oppositions, which habitually shape and constrain our understanding of the world."[56] What has to be kept in mind is the fact that the whole process of deconstruction from the beginning was intimately linked to the unfolding of a new theory of writing. "It is important to emphasize the extent to which deconstruction is embedded in the question of writing as it is explored in *Of Grammatology* and other related texts of the same period, since there is often a tendency to decontextualize deconstruction, to present it as a method of critical analysis separate from the theory of writing which is its original and essential corollary."[57]

---

52. Regarding the section on fundamentalism see for example Eisenstadt, "Frameworks;" Almond, "Politics, Ethnicity."
53. Johnson, *Derrida*, 51.
54. Ibid., 53.
55. Ibid., 53.
56. Ibid., 53.
57. Ibid., 54.

Thirdly one has to bear in mind the importance of language. In Derrida's understanding that means holding together the two, the "literary" as well as the "philosophical," the rhetorical as well as the conceptual.[58]

Christopher Johnson demonstrates that Derrida is interested in a process and a certain procedure. Derrida wants to deal with and engage in what others have composed and inscribed. But this procedure is not without structure and purpose. It is done top-down in the sense of first finding out the main features and the genre to which the literature belongs in the first place. In this top-down handling of the work there is also, we firmly maintain, a very definite plan, a theory of how the work should be done. Again, it is not overboard here to talk not only about theory of writing, but also, in a sense, a rather definite doctrine of script and trace that goes much deeper than is obvious at first sight. The very predicament of being human is somehow addressed. Despite what he says himself, Derrida is quite metaphysical.[59]

ECCLESIOLOGY REVISITED

In my dissertation I attempted two things in terms of method—a more theoretical construction of the church as an edifice and secondly, I used the empirical, contextual South African church as a gateway for my analysis.

I built a theory for close reading of what could be church using Myrdal, Habermas, Gadamer, Milbank, and Williams. I built a space or edifice in which communication could take place. I here described a study of the church in terms of social theory and as hermeneutics. I also claimed, with Milbank, that ecclesiology is sociology in its own right, not understood through secular concepts but with theological underpinnings. With the assistance of Williams it was also possible to formulate a truth claim for theology.

But the second reading of the Afrikaner texts, that is contrast reading, put this edifice to a very severe test: through contemporary fundamentalism which is about complete rigidity through a select core doctrine, and secondly, through deconstruction, which threatened to dissolve the whole edifice.

---

58. Ibid., 54.

59. In my dissertation I also relate these two phenomena to theology as both have theological inclinations. For deconstruction: "It always tends to look for the ultimate. Deconstruction might be called a prophetic, apophatic theology with a purpose, a theology by and large anti-ecclesial." For fundamentalism: "[E]asily falls into some kind of ecclesiology, [. . .] a religious ideal made concrete, [. . .] building the kingdom of God here and now, overdone in an overtly violent way." Engdahl, *Theology in Conflict*, 25–26.

I have also used the empirical, contextual church as a gateway for understanding the Afrikaner readings. These ecclesiological gateways focused on the church as life system (Potgieter) and the church as ecumenical church (Marais).

In other words, ecclesiology is a discipline among others or a science among others. I have made an attempt at sketching a theory, albeit rather multifaceted, of what could be church; this theory could be used as one pleases, and one would have to realize that ecclesiology is juxtaposed with social science, hermeneutics, philosophy, and theology (empirical science and philosophy/theology). I have used this theory of what could be church as methodological tool in my dissertation dealing with texts of two Afrikaner theologians.

My contention has been that ecclesiology is indeed juxtaposed with empirical science and theology.[60] And this juxtaposition of ecclesiology with the broader field of science should be taken seriously as opportunities for new alliances may abound; qualified by theology it is now wide open to other empirical and non-empirical sciences and engagements.

As an example of the need for such an opening, it is of quite some importance to take note of the present flourishing research on the church in Africa, which is almost exclusively sociological and anthropological. The task is to juxtapose such research with ecclesiology, which will prove to be an intermediary of such research and theology. Only when ecclesiology, qualified by theology, is brought onto the scene will these vibrant African churches be given full authenticity as churches.

---

60. In the first paragraph of this chapter I put my case somewhat differently: social theory, hermeneutics and theology in juxtaposition could provide an edifice for ecclesiology. I mean there is no conflict here. Ecclesiology is indeed a discipline in its own right owing its existence to a phenomenon called church. At the same time, as regards any other discipline, ecclesiology could indeed also be said to be constituted by other disciplines, in this instance theology, philosophy, and empirical science. That is what excites me. There is something tangible here, but this physical presence of the church (people, buildings, rituals of bath, and table) has another side that somehow is in charge of the whole thing, which is quite elusive and difficult if not impossible to grasp. See for example introduction in Dulles, *Models*.

3

Systematic Ecclesiology as Primary Ecclesiology

MICHAEL HJÄLM

> **EDITORS' INTRODUCTION**
>
> Jürgen Harbermas's emancipatory perspectives play an important part in the arguments formulated by Michael Hjälm in the following chapter. As in Engdahl's chapter we are invited into reflections concerning ecclesiology and its relations to the empirical realities of church.
>
> Hjälm's argument should be read in relation to the field of liturgical ecclesiology. He wants to question and challenge a view on liturgy that isolates it from the broader life world of the church. For the sake of his argument he makes a distinction between *primary* and *systematic* ecclesiology. The former is concerned with the human resources of the church, with a focus on patterns of meaning and change on a micro level. The latter moves the level of reflection to a macro level.
>
> In his chapter Hjälm argues for a primary ecclesiology that embraces the entire church. As the argument evolves he raises questions on how theory and practice are treated in relation to one another. He sees a tendency towards a mediation of the two, which he finds problematic. Instead he opts for a dynamic ecclesiology and a focus on how the church constantly adapts to change through ecclesial system dynamics. It is interesting to compare Hjälm's reflections on theory and practice with Sune Fahlgren's in Part Two. Fahlgren also uses the concept primary ecclesiology, although in a slightly different manner.

> With his argument, Hjälm challenges the researcher in ecclesiology to put the world of the subject in focus and thereby move beyond objectifying descriptions of the church.
>
> **Michael Hjälm** (born 1968) is Assistant Professor in Eastern Christian Studies at Uppsala University. His dissertation, *Liberation of the Ecclesia: The Unfinished Project of Liturgical Theology*, is a critical and constructive study of liturgical theology using Jürgen Harbermas' emancipatory theories.
>
> Hjälm received his doctoral degree at Uppsala University 2011 and is currently the Dean of Sankt Ignatios Theological Academy. His research areas are Eastern Christian Studies and Political Ecclesiology.

A NEW PARADIGM

The Patriarchal Encyclicals from Constantinople on Christian Unity and Ecumenism (1920, 1952) resulted in the Orthodox Church fellowship opening up to the worldwide Ecumenical Movement.[1] The Orthodox Church had been isolated from the West for centuries owing to the schism between Old Rome and New Rome and the rise of the Ottoman Empire. The Ecumenical Movement influenced the Orthodox Church, which opened up to the West, but it must be said that the Great Church of the East also influenced the Movement. The prominence of the liturgy within the Ecumenical Movement was one of the more influential themes, and it generated an interest in the Eastern Church.

In the 1960s, Alexander Schmemann, Dean of St. Vladimir's Orthodox Theological Seminary, launched a new paradigm, Liturgical Theology, which evolved across different denominations. Liturgical Theology highlighted the liturgy as Primary Theology, which was not "an object to observe or a resource to quarry from, or a milieu to work out of," but was instead seen as theology *par excellence*.[2] Schmemann inspired a generation of priests and scholars. His legacy continues today and has become a fundamental core in Eastern Christian theology.

The paradigm is however not without problems. I have encountered numerous orthodox priests and scholars who are convinced that the liturgy

---

1. For the Patriarchal Encyclicals and the Orthodox Churches' engagement in the World Council of Churches see Patelos, *Orthodox Church*.

2. Fagerberg, *Theologia Prima*, 73–80.

is more or less enough. This in turn leads to an idealized church, one which neglects the fact that parish schools and theological seminaries were closed due to oppression—within the ottoman Empire and the Soviet Union—and not due to a voluntary choice, which has lead to the ecclesiastical condition of *sola liturgia*.[3] The reduction of the church to the liturgy undermines the communicative act that is needed in "the liturgy after the liturgy," where linguistic communication is the medium by which we achieve mutual understanding and consensus. *Sola liturgia* also seems to be one of the more crucial problems for the Eastern Church in addressing the difficulties in the post-totalitarian society that have emerged after the fall of the Soviet Union.[4]

Furthermore, theology has largely remained a quest for wholeness with presumed Divine revelation as an underlying holistic vision that mostly requires a complete mediation of theory and practice. Liturgical theology is an offspring of this quest. By identifying the liturgical act with the Coming Kingdom, Alexander Schmemann aimed at uniting theory and practice, thereby securing a holistic vision. In my dissertation I use the emancipatory perspective of Jürgen Habermas to criticize Schmemann's attempt to create a holistic vision. I argue that a presumed holistic reality makes Schmemann's project ambivalent, where the individual becomes an object of his/her own vision and risks alienation.[5]

In this short article I will argue for a primary theology that takes into account the entire Church and not only the liturgy; I will call this *Primary Ecclesiology*, and it is a subset of contemporary Systematic Ecclesiology.

SYSTEMATIC ECCLESIOLOGY

The twentieth century witnessed a dramatic evolution in the field of ecclesiology, and yet we have just embarked on this journey. Brian Flanagan, in his 2011 thesis *Community, Diversity and Salvation*, describes this evolution as a reaction to the late nineteenth and early twentieth centuries' apologetic and legalistic ecclesiologies. In this early stage every denomination tried to support their own unique confessional structure at the expense of other confessions.[6] The Ecumenical Movement, which commenced after World

---

3. Dimitry Pospielovsky describes the dreadful state of the Russian Orthodox Church and its theological education just after the reopening of the schools in 1988 to 1995. See Pospielovsky, "Impressions."

4. By post-totalitarian I refer to a society oscillating between being open and democratic and being closed and totalitarian.

5. Hjälm, *Liberation*.

6. Flanagan, *Communion, Diversity*.

War II, made it virtually impossible to continue this competitive way of doing ecclesiology, especially after Vatican II. Instead, Flanagan argues, ecclesiology became *modeling*. Scholars either made use of primary normative models such as communion (*koinonia*), or tried to establish a balance by providing a plurality of models such as Avery Dulles's *Models of the Church* and Yves Congar's plurality of metaphors.[7]

When scholars abandoned the structural defense of the single confession, it opened the way for a shared ecclesial imagination that transcended different confessions. The language used in this modeling was more akin to poetic discourse, Flanagan continues, than systematic theology more similar to scientific discourse. This *pre-systematic* modeling of the twentieth century has two shortcomings according to Flanagan.[8] First, these models are not self-evident. Even though "everything seems possible and everything seems permissible," as Henry Rikhof argues, they depend on implicit assumptions to shape the development, discussion, and assessment.[9]

Secondly these models overemphasize the non-empirical factors of ecclesiology, factors such as grace and eschatology. This enables beautiful descriptions of the Church and the flowering of ideal images, but these images are difficult to attach to a particular church community. Flanagan instead argues for a systematic ecclesiology that "investigate[s] the church methodically, critically, and constructively, in contrast to catechetical and pastoral exercises in theological communication and academic religious studies approaches to religious phenomena." Systematic ecclesiology attempts to provide relevant questions and work out appropriate systems for conceptualization and remove inconsistencies, thus providing an insight or understanding of the Church as spiritual matter. At the same time Flanagan shares the same view as Joseph Komonchak, who argued that the ecclesiology produced in the more confessionalist era had one advantage. In the nineteenth and early twentieth centuries scholars doing ecclesiology made use of the social theory available at that time. Therefore, Flanagan and Komonchak argue, any contemporary systematic ecclesiology has to appreciate not only the theories about the Church but also the social reality in which the Church exists.[10]

The outcome of this juxtaposition of systematic theology and social theory is Systematic Ecclesiology. The integration of the social sciences with

---

7. Dulles, *Models*; "Half Century."
8. Flanagan, *Communion, Diversity*, 11–12.
9. Rikhof, *Concept of Church*.
10. Cf. Flanagan, *Communion, Diversity*, 17–18; Komonchak, *Foundations*; and *Lumen Gentium*, especially chapter 27.

theology is a delicate question. Most scholars would agree that systematic ecclesiology has to avoid two extremes. The first is the reduction of ecclesiology to social science, which would more or less be a regression to the early confessionalist ecclesiologies. These ecclesiologies neglected the Church's graced reality under the pretense of scientific progress. The other extreme is the rejection of modern social sciences due to a suspicion that they have an atheistic pedigree.

The effort of avoiding these extremes has developed as a major exertion among contemporary scholars of ecclesiology. Different approaches to this dilemma have been presented. Roger Haight prefers to speak about a theology from below, beginning in the social reality.[11] Stanley Hauerwas, taking a similar-yet-different stance, defines the Church out of the theories that operate within practices.[12] Neil Ormerod advocates a perspective of dialectics, and Nicholas Healy propagates a hermeneutic of suspicion.[13] Though different, these approaches all operate on the same axis—the reconciliation of theory and practice.

THE CRITIQUE OF THE PRESUMED MEDIATION OF THEORY AND PRACTICE

The reconciliation of theory and practice goes all the way back to the fifth century when Boethius presented the image of the bride, who had a *Theta* attached to the top of her dress and a *Pi* attached to the bottom, as a symbol of how theory (*theoria*) and practice (*praxis*) are attached to the same continuum yet distinct from each other. The problem with this image in contemporary social sciences is the superiority of theory. Though, it should be noted that Boethius propagated a theology from below, which is seen in the image of the bride with a ladder on her dress, with practice ascending toward theory. The ultimate goal was nevertheless to mediate between theory and practice.[14]

The idea of reconciling theory and practice acquired new strength in the nineteenth century with the publication of Friedrich Hegel's *Phänomenologie des Geistes* (1807). Hegel postulated a complete union between these two as the most desirable achievement and therefore saw reality as an organic whole of spirit and nature.[15] The idea of the union of theory and practice was prevalent during the nineteenth and much of the twentieth

---

11. Madar, "Roger Haight's Contribution."
12. Thomson, *Ecclesiology of Stanley Hauerwas*.
13. Ormerod, "Dialectical Engagement"; Healy, *Church, World*.
14. Boethius, *Consolation*, 12.
15. Hegel, *Phänomenologie*.

century. Within several philosophical schools, the mediation between these variables was the very meaning of philosophy and formed the foundation of the Marxist ideology with its holistic ambition.[16]

During the second half of the twentieth century, an increasing number of philosophers and thinkers criticized the effort of the overall mediation of theory and practice and the desire to achieve "wholeness." One of these was Jürgen Habermas who possessed a holistic ambition in the beginning of his career and argued for a necessary unity between theory and practice. Nevertheless, from the 1970s onwards he gradually distanced himself from his earlier belief in the possibility of reconciling these variables. Finally, he came to the point of thinking a complete mediation of theory and practice is not even desirable.[17] This led Habermas adhere to Theodor Adorno's understanding that philosophy needs to learn "to renounce the question of totality" and the idea of the particular representing the universal, which subsequently became a characteristic of the Frankfurt School.[18]

PRIMARY ECCLESIOLOGY: WORKING WITH KNOWLEDGE—INTERESTS

The general problem in mediating between theory and practice is simply that they will not stay together without a human agent—individually or collectively. This implies that the ones safeguarding the mediation between theory and practice cannot avoid constituting an authority. To avoid making arbitrary choices they need to refer the authority to something outside themselves—an objective standpoint for how to mediate between theory and practice. When they make that move they tend to forget the more important thing; what made them initiate mediation in the first place? The forgetfulness of this first move is a surrender of human responsibility for the sake of objective authority. Habermas identifies this initial move as human interests and the second move as a quest for knowledge. Together they constitute a knowledge-interest (*Erkenntnisinteresse*).[19] The attempts of reconciling theory and practice in contemporary ecclesiology are more or less concerned with the second move of referring ecclesiology to an objective standpoint. This implies working out an appropriate system of concepts and removing inconsistencies through the juxtaposition of social theory and systematic theology.

---

16. Kitching, *Karl Marx*.
17. Dahms, *Vitality*.
18. Adorno, "Actuality of Philosophy."
19. Habermas, *Knowledge*, 315.

Therefore, following Habermas, contemporary systematic ecclesiology cannot satisfy itself with achieving knowledge but also has to be concerned with the interests in the first move of mediating between theory and practice. Dealing with the first move constitutes what I would call Primary ecclesiology. Primary ecclesiology intends to reveal the interests involved in the process of mediation, then work with them, and finally act with regard to these interests. This demands different methods from those generally applied within ecclesiology. First of all we have to realize that it is not knowledge that guides interest, but rather interest that guides knowledge. This implies that we have to move the reference point from the objective world to the subject. When we move in this direction there is a risk that "ought" and "is" lose their distinction. Therefore, the move has to be followed, according to Habermas, by a distinction of "ought" and "is." Human interactions otherwise become suppressed by the ontology of the factual, by those facts that seem to bestow an appearance of immediacy on what is really mediated in a symbolical reproduction. These facts of immediacy foster an abstraction that both creates indifference toward what is other and, in the end, neutralizes the relation to the other. Instead of being contested validity claims, they are presented as irrefutable facts.[20]

Through the differentiation between "ought" and "is," reciprocal recognition of difference and otherness is possible, which in turn fosters communicative freedom. Habermas explains this phenomenon by making yet another differentiation, that between *knowledge* and *interest*. Knowledge, according to Habermas, is guided by interests, which are deeply embedded in the social existence of human beings. Different ways of knowing are shaped qualitatively by different interests. Habermas makes a distinction between the interest of the "empirical-analytical sciences," aimed at acquiring technical control of their objects, and the hermeneutic sciences, aimed at "the preservation and expansion of the intersubjectivity of possible action-orienting mutual understanding."[21]

This does not mean that knowledge serves interest, but rather, according to Habermas, the two are in a dialectical relation. In this inter-action between knowledge and interests, the self-reflective being stands forth guided by the more foundational interest of emancipation. Self-reflection in this sense is emancipatory in two ways, according to Peter Dews. First it enables us to access the world as definite for us but not of us. Secondly this enables us to use explanation and understanding in order to free ourselves.

---

20. Cf. McCarthy's "Introduction" in Habermas, *Theory*, vii–xvi; Habermas, "Communicative Freedom," 95.

21. Habermas, *Knowledge*, 310.

Habermas is eager to emphasize the importance of the primacy of the emancipatory interest. Even though it is possible to predict and control human behavior we have to be careful that we don't suppress the role of its object as a potential partner in a dialogue through such knowledge.[22]

EMANCIPATION AS THE PRIMARY INTEREST IN ECCLESIOLOGY

The juxtaposition of systematic theology and social theory (with the latter as understood by Habermas) implies a choice of perspective regarding interests. If we make the same choice as Habermas and make the emancipational interest our primary departure, it will qualitatively shape our way of knowing. If we return to the image of the bride, with theory on top and practice at the bottom, theory from on high will fall down and will take part in the inter-subjective play between human agents in their effort of realizing their primary interest of emancipation. Beginning in the initial move for emancipation conveys a systematic ecclesiology shaped in a different manner with a new set of questions. The primary question is not "What makes the Church?" but "What makes people active in the Church?" From a theological standpoint, the change of perspective is justified by the view that the human beings cannot be used for any higher purpose than being with God. This is also what the Gospel proclaims when Mary of Bethany washes the feet of Christ, and Jude, standing beside her, questions the purpose of her act. What good comes from this act? Why did she not give the money to the poor instead? Yes, what is the purpose of her act? What is the purpose of weeping, praying and extending such a love? The answer is simply that there is no outer purpose greater than loving God and our fellow human being. When every righteous act has been fulfilled and every agreement has been finalized, the act of Mary remains, and everything else fades away.[23]

In order to reveal the emancipatory interest that shapes knowing, we need to move the reference point from the objective world to the subject engaged in that world. This move, according to Habermas, implies moving from a subject-centered understanding of reason and rationality to an inter-subjective understanding, where language is the main medium of

---

22. Dews, *Habermas*, 8–9.

23. In Eastern Christian tradition the three events of anointing the feet of Christ (divided into four textual passages) are referred to as three separate events with three different women. Mary of Bethany is identified with John 12:1–8. The other passages are Luke 7:36–50; Mark 14:3–9; and Matthew 26:6–13. The act of Mary transcends every kind of legislation, which instead is identified with a change of mind, *metanoia*, a new mentality, and as such she becomes an icon of an ecclesial ethos going beyond the sinful tragedy of human errors.

communication. Consciousness then becomes inter-subjective and emerges through mutual understanding.[24] In the context of systematic ecclesiology this would mean that we have to change our parameters. In a world where practice is the consequence of a presumed revelation (or the act of realizing the ideal Church) there ecclesial life could be understood as a finite game, similar to a game of soccer. In a finite game there are certain rules that have been established before the play begins, and the game has certain objectives with an already established end. This is precisely why a game of soccer is a finite form of play. In an ecclesial context a finite game means that the ultimate goal is salvation, and God sets the rules for this through revelation delivered in the Church. Revelation here is understood as a set of rules that is given in advance. Ecclesiastical orders, canons, liturgical protocol, and the like are there for maintaining the purpose of the game and achieving the ultimate goal.

When emancipation becomes the primary interest, we instead enter into an infinite game. An infinite game is unbounded, and all are potential players. The rules and theories and even the truths are changing in an infinite game because the purpose is to keep playing, continue with life, and continue with an endless life of prayer. In this context the play itself is the objective, a goal in itself, or as Aristotle formulates it, an *entelecheia*. An infinite game is open with many differences working through nonlinear relations, which creates an exponential network where every player has several relations. For the Church this means that salvation or truth is not the ultimate goal. The ultimate goal is instead love—a category that cannot be instrumentalized or used for any higher purpose. This love is contained in the play itself and cannot be separated from the game. You cannot deduce this love from the game or induce it into the game. Love is the game. Revelation in this sense is given in the game, which manifests a love that the believing Christian identifies as Divine. Ecclesiastical orders, canons and liturgical protocols, and the Bible are there for maintaining the game.

Systematic ecclesiology, understood as the process of providing relevant questions, working out appropriate systems for conceptualization and removing inconsistencies, seems too narrow, from the perspective of primary ecclesiology. Instead we have to understand ecclesial life from a different angle. The teachings of the apostles should not be understood as a package that the apostles received from Christ but as a game expanding through time with Christ in the midst. Tradition is the maintenance of the game where more and more people are involved. Those working with systematic

---

24. For a communicative rationality, see Habermas, *Theory. Volume One*, 11, 75, 140, 397–99.

ecclesiology as primary ecclesiology work with the human resource in the Church, while those working with secondary ecclesiology, the second move toward knowledge, work with the structures generated from the game.

PRIMARY ECCLESIOLOGY AS A DYNAMIC ECCLESIOLOGY

Working with the human resource of the Church, with the emancipational interest as the point of departure, should be considered as a central part of systematic ecclesiology. On a macro-level I would label this Political Ecclesiology, where we try to find patterns of meaning in the inter-action between different cultures or between Church and Society. On a micro-level I would consider it simply as Primary Ecclesiology. The point of departure in primary ecclesiology is the game itself and not the outcome of the game. Even though we use the same sources in primary ecclesiology as with secondary ecclesiology, e.g. liturgical books, collections of canons, the Scriptures, or the summaries of teachings among the fathers and mothers of the Church, we use them in a different manner. In primary ecclesiology we use them in order to reveal the game itself. The aim is not primarily to eliminate or expose inconsistencies but to track down patterns of meaning and change.

In a game of soccer rules are changed in a predetermined, controlled manner. Otherwise the very meaning of playing soccer would be lost. If for example the player during the game suddenly decided that it should be allowed to use hands and pick up the ball, it would not be soccer anymore. Life does not function in that way. Instead rules are changed constantly. The same goes with ecclesial life. Rules are stretched, changed, and abandoned, but more importantly the play expands in an unforeseen way. The play becomes so big that it is hard or even impossible to see the edges. There are too many perspectives, everything changes faster than a single human being can survey, and the resources seem to be lacking. We enter into a history of frustration, and we feel that solutions to different problems will not remain valid.[25] The problem with the primary interest of emancipation is simply that it expands into oblivion if it is not restrained. The later Habermas became more and more occupied with this perspective, and in the 1980s he developed the Theory of Communicative Action (TCA), which he altered several times.[26]

In TCA Habermas argues that when more and more people are released from the bondage of being observers or observables and begin to be transformed into participators, there is a heightened risk of dissensus. Therefore there is a need of mediatisation. For the Church this would mean

---

25. Cf. Eoyang, *Voices*.
26. Habermas, *Theory*, vol. 1; ibid., *Theory*, vol. 2.

that power is used as a system-media, substituting mutual understanding and consensus, with the intention of unburdening the responsible actors of the demanding requirements of communicative inter-action. This generates yet another risk, colonization, i.e. evolving pathological patterns, which is an effect when the system-medias used are not anchored in ordinary life and therefore are not felt as a relief but rather as suppression, e.g. clericalism and alienation among the people. Colonization may also cause theories to evolve completely independent of life. In order to avoid this, the use of system-media has to equal the level of rationalization, i.e. the ability of differentiating between various truths in life, acquiring what the Greeks called *phronesis*.[27] In a primary ecclesiology, focus is given to the interaction between evolving ecclesial systems and rationalization in the effort of maintaining ecclesial life.

Primary ecclesiology provides a dynamic ecclesiology where we study how the Church constantly adapts to change through ecclesial system dynamics, and especially how the Church as a community avoids dissensus and/or colonization. Contemporary social science identifies this as adaptive action, with three basic steps: 1) Finding the patterns of what is happening. 2) Making sense of what is happening through inter-subjective communication and mutual understanding. 3) Taking action as a result of the inter-subjective meaning. The third step creates a change that will start the process all over again.[28] The scholar working within the field of primary ecclesiology has to maintain the perspective of the participant. The scholar has to observe the other as a potential partner in achieving, sustaining, and renewing mutual understanding and consensus, which rest on the inter-subjective recognition of different criticizable validity claims.[29]

If the potential partner is reduced to an object, unity and totalization will be enforced instead of a communicative freedom that cultivates reciprocal recognition of difference and otherness. This does not mean that primary ecclesiology necessarily becomes arbitrary. Instead a communicatively achieved agreement must, in the end, be based on reason. By employing communicative reason, grounded in the emancipatory interest,

---

27. Cf. Habermas, *Theory. Volume One*, 345–99; ibid., *Theory*, vol. 2, 119–52, 332–73. In *Nicomachean Ethics*, Book 6, Aristotle deals with phronesis and argues that it is concerned with particulars, which is the ability to recognize difference in handling a particular situation. According to Habermas, making use of rationality simply means acquiring the competence to differentiate between different truths and different realities. System-medias are structures that are detached from ordinary inter-subjective communication, where decisions and actions instead have a tendency to be found within the structure itself, e.g. organizations, financial systems, or communicative systems.

28. Cf. Eoyang, *Voices*.

29. Cf. Habermas, *Theory*, vol. 1, 17

participants seek a justified consensus, which cannot be reached without reciprocal recognition of the other and of difference.[30]

THE CRITIQUE OF HABERMAS VIEWED AS A POSITIVE APPROACH TO DISCLOSURE

Habermas was working out his Theory of Communicative Action in the wake of Nazi-Germany and in the shadow of the rise of the Soviet Union. This made him defensive toward difference outside the boundaries of inter-subjective discourse. He was especially critical toward disclosure.[31] Several scholars have criticized him for this, and one of the more decisive critical assessments has been made by Nikolas Kompridis.[32] In short, one could say that inter-subjective relations within an infinite game sustain a self-organizing system that expands beyond inter-subjective discourse basically because no single individual can overview the play. This then leaves room for a disclosure of new possibilities and new discoveries that cannot be traced to an individual or group of individuals but evolves from within the play.

These disclosures are instead to be understood as basic for patterns of change constituting the events needed for the continuation of the game. In ecclesiology they are revealed as patterns that alter the course of ecclesial life. Basically they can be grouped into three categories: static change, dynamic change, and a combination of the two. August Comte was one of the first that defined the difference between static and dynamic change. In the first category we have those patterns of social systems that resist change. Comte believed, for example, that religion compensates the weaknesses of language by binding the society on the basis of a few common beliefs. Furthermore, religion ties the society by morality, keeping it from falling apart because of the disparities among people, and provides the guidance for behavior as the root of social order. Dynamic change, according to Comte, was instead seen as a process of progressive evolution in which people become cumulatively more intelligent and in which altruism eventually triumphs over egoism. This process is one that people can modify or accelerate, but in the end the laws of progressive development dictate the development of society.[33]

The distinction between social statics and social dynamics is a lasting contribution by Comte in contemporary social science, but today we also have a combination of both. Evolutionary dynamics follows a defined pattern that can be frozen in a moment and still reveals a direction toward

---

30. Cf. ibid., 18.
31. Cf. Bohman, "Two Versions."
32. Kompridis, *Critique*.
33. Comte, *Social Statics*.

the future. Primary ecclesiology works with these patterns of change within inter-subjective communications and actions. The Ecumenical Movement, for example, provided new patterns in ecclesiology based on the need for peace and reconciliation in post-war Europe.

The question that arises after describing these patterns of change is the meaning that people attach to these changes. Still residing in primary ecclesiology, the scholar does not infer any meaning from outside the play. Instead the scholar is a partner in dialogue who assists the community by describing these changes and reveals hidden intentions based in an emancipatory interest. Meaning evolves when the community makes use of the cultural background, i.e. revelation or tradition, in assessing these patterns of change. The theologians of Vatican II, for example, identified changed patterns in the wake of the Ecumenical Movement, and by making use of the Roman Catholic tradition they attached meaning to these changes.[34]

The sense of meaning was however not generated arbitrarily. Karl Rahner for example had to merge the cultural background of the Roman Catholic Church with contemporary settings of the Ecumenical Movement.[35] In this attempt Rahner is considered a primary theologian working directly with the patterns of change. A secondary theologian works with the outcome of Rahner's work, providing relevant questions and working out appropriate systems for conceptualization and the removal of inconsistencies, thus advancing an insight or understanding of the Church as spiritual matter. The major difference between a primary theologian and a secondary theologian in this second step of primary ecclesiology is the concept of truth. A secondary theologian works mainly with objective truths—such as facts and explanatory theories—while the primary theologian works with various truths. Besides the objective truths that he or she receives from the cultural background, the primary theologian also works with social and subjective truths. Social truths are achieved through mutual understanding and consensus, and subjective truths depend on the individual choice of perspective, such as, for instance, choosing the perspective of emancipation or artistic authenticity.

The scholars of Vatican II did not satisfy themselves with merely attaching meaning to patterns of change. They also took action and suggested a change in structures and resources. Rahner was most active in adapting the Church to new forms of life, because meaning implies change in primary ecclesiology—even though those working with the meaning could be different from those working with the result of the structural and social changes.

---

34. See for example Sullivan, *Road to Vatican II*.
35. See for example Lennan, *Ecclesiology of Karl Rahner*.

Secondary theologians work with the outcome of the deliberations of these changes by asking if these new patterns are stable, emergent, or unstable.

CONCLUSION

In conclusion, I would argue that systematic ecclesiology in the twenty-first century needs to work as well with primary ecclesiology as with secondary ecclesiology. The separation between them tends to develop a forgetfulness of the initial move, which involves the desired interests and foremost the emancipatory interest. This in turn bears the risk that potential partners are reduced to objects that enforce unity and totalization, where scholars impose a theory of ecclesiology without the participation of those involved in the game of ecclesial life itself.

4

To Compare or Not to Compare, That is the Question

Some Thoughts on Comparative Method in Ecclesiology

TIIT PÄDAM

> **EDITORS' INTRODUCTION**
>
> In the following chapter, Tiit Pädam takes us into his research worksite where comparative methods in ecclesiology are created and used. Here he shares and reflects upon experiences from studying the understanding of diaconal ministry in ten Anglican and Lutheran churches within the *Porvoo Communion.* At the center of his attention are ordination rites. The research approach is shaped by an understanding of ecclesiology as a mosaic of various dimensions of the factors that constitute church.
>
> He presents the steps he took when he developed an analytical model. The model made it possible to discern characteristic features without violating the understanding of the particular churches' identities. Pädam's narrative challenges abstract and idealized understandings of comparative ecclesiology. With clear parallels to the approach of Engdahl, he opts for using complimentary methods — such as a qualitative and a quantitative method—in the process of analysis.
>
> Pädam's research is an example of the threefold understanding of ecclesiology presented by Sven-Erik Brodd in chapter 1. That is, ecclesiology as a tool for analysis, the object of the study and the result that comes out of the study. As Brodd also mentions, the kind

of systematic ecclesiology research presented by Pädam also points to clear parallels between the work in the research seminar and the process in ecumenical dialogues.

Tiit Pädam (born 1958) is minister in the Estonian Evangelical-Lutheran Church in Stockholm and a lecturer at Uppsala University. His dissertation, *Ordination of Deacons in the Churches of the Porvoo Communion: A Comparative Investigation in Ecclesiology*, is a study of the diaconate in ten Anglican and Lutheran churches. Pädam received his doctoral degree at Uppsala University 2011. An overview of methods and hermeneutics from his research on the diaconate in the Porvoo Communion is presented in an article in *International Journal for the Study of the Christian Church*, 18 December 2013.

There are many things in our everyday life that we do without reflecting on very deeply why or what is really taking place as a result of our action. One of these things is the act of comparison. We compare ourselves with other people, and we compare things and events with one another. By doing so we presuppose receiving new knowledge not only about the state of affairs but also about ourselves. To compare something with something else is so natural that we hardly reflect about how we proceed or whether the comparison is really justified and gives us something adequate or useful. Thus, comparison is a common feature in reflective human life.

In the same way, comparison and comparative methods are often used in all fields of science. They serve as useful tools or means in dealing with various scientific problems. We presuppose that comparative methods allow the researchers to find out whether the studied phenomena or cases only characterize certain local circumstances or whether they have a wider meaning and influence a wider spectrum of significant phenomena in our world. In this way the comparison also seems to help scientists to test or develop their theories and achieve new knowledge, which may help people in various circumstances. However, designing the scientific research around comparative methods is not free from some specific problems, which presents researchers with a challenge to identify the weaknesses and dangers of this method.

Every field of scientific research has certainly some specific features, which must be considered when using comparison as scientific method, but according to my mind there are also some common characteristics and grounds. When I began to carry out one of my theological research projects, I understood that all the churches must be considered in a wider spectrum.

My general aim was to find out whether there is a common understanding of the diaconal ministry in ten different churches.[1] I had to make weighty decision: which method would be most effective helping me to answer the question. All the churches studied were actively involved in the work of their respective societies. They all practiced an ecclesial act: ordination as the way of receiving new deacons into the ministry of the Church. Their deacons were engaged in serving people in local communities. Therefore I decided to analyze their rites of ordination to the diaconal ministry as adequate expressions of the churches' ecclesiologies, which receive their expression in the serving engagement of people.

Thereafter I had to choose whether the analysis would be carried out with the help of comparison or by selecting some other method in order to get satisfying results. I decided to use comparison in order to answer the main research question. I immediately faced a number of different kinds of difficulties. In this paper I shall discuss the use of comparison as method in order to find out the respective profile of the churches studied with respect to each church's rite of ordination and to common understanding of diaconal ministry.

WHAT IS COMPARATIVE ECCLESIOLOGY?

Ecclesiology is a term frequently used in theological discussions on matters relating to the Church.[2] However, already the meaning of this term is ambiguous. Different uses of the term are evident not only between theologians from different confessional traditions but also within the traditions.[3] The term is often used to describe the theory of the "characteristic marks"

---

1. In 1996 ten Anglican and Lutheran churches in the British Isles, the Nordic countries, and Baltic countries agreed upon an ecumenical agreement known as the *Porvoo Common Statement* (PCS). This document was part of the wider ecumenical report, *Together in Mission and Ministry*, which the churches had drawn up between 1989 and 1992. The wording is used in the PCS 1993, para 58 b (vii): "to work towards a common understanding of diaconal ministry" is one of the commitments of the common goal.

2. In the text a distinction is made between the Church and the church. Although the distinction is not always easy to clarify in the context, the "Church" denotes the universal Church of Christ, characterized by the words of the Nicaeo-Constantinopolitan Creed as One, Holy, Catholic, and Apostolic. The latter term "church" refers to a particular local church which could be identified geographically and by its institutional structures. The local church is considered always as part of the Church and, at the same time, as the embodiment of the whole Church on the local level.

3. Cf. Pannenberg, *Systematic Theology*, 21–27; Avis, "Anglican Ecclesiology," 202–6; Saarinen, "Lutheran Ecclesiology," 170–73; Lennan, "Roman Catholic ecclesiology," 234–37; Kärkkäinen, *An Introduction to Ecclesiology*, 9–16; *The Gift of the Church*, 23–158.

that make a Christian Church genuine.[4] Ecclesiology is identified as the study and analysis of church organization and governance and is used as a doctrinal basis for the organization, liturgical life, sacraments, and ministry of the Church (including the description of the relationship between the Church and civil society). Sometimes ecclesiology also is used as an apologetic means to defend the Church with the help of a system of doctrinal statements and argumentation.

All these connotations have a common denominator: they refer to what dogmatically constitutes the Church as Church. This includes teaching on the nature of the Church, normative concepts, and a vision of what the Church will become. Ecclesiology may also be defined as a way of integrating dogmatic understanding into a wider framework where ecclesiology is not merely "confined to a *locus* in dogmatics but includes also the study of ecclesial practices. Dogma and empirical data are kept together and the spiritual is not conceived as a parallel to the material but held together in an incarnational perspective when trying to understand what church is."[5] This means that the Church could be studied adequately in the perspective of ecclesiology when a number of different kinds of dimensions, not only dogmatic, are taken into consideration.[6]

This way of understanding ecclesiology does not exclude dogmatic aspects but studies them in connection with other dimensions that are characteristically significant to the Church in the world—such as the historical, cultural, social and political. It also makes it possible to keep different variables together when considering different expressions of the Church. Ecclesiology is thus a mosaic, consisting of various elements, which only together constitute a whole. The comparison of these churchly mosaics may be called comparative ecclesiology. After having understood ecclesiology in the way described above, I had to acknowledge immediately that not only the meaning and the content of ecclesiology but also the way one tries to compare the great variety of expressions in ecclesiology is both complex and complicated.

One of the spokesmen of comparative ecclesiology, Roger Haight writes: "Comparative ecclesiology consists in analyzing and portraying in

---

4. The most commonly acknowledged marks of the church are unity, holiness, apostolicity, and catholicity.

5. Brodd, "Theological Focus," xix.

6. Cf. Mannion and Mudge's definition of ecclesiology: "Ecclesiology looks at the churches' forms of governance, liturgical life and corporate witness as primary instruments by which the gospel is lived and communicated. Ecclesiology becomes the normative study of communities which make social and symbolic space in the world for workings of grace." *The Routledge Companion*, 3.

an organized or systematic way two or more different ecclesiologies so that they can be compared."[7] He proposes that common patterns may be used in order to carry out comparison of different ecclesiologies:

> A [. . .] feature of comparative ecclesiology consists in the strategy of organizing and presenting the thought of different theologians according to a common pattern of template [. . .]. This pattern serves as a bridge for comparison and contrast, even when that task is not undertaken formally and methodically.[8]

This interpretation was seriously challenged by a Finnish theologian Minna Hietamäki:

> Even a mere comparison with the help of common template assumes that, in the best scenario, the template is in a way applicable to the ecclesiology. In a less good case the ecclesiology starts to fit the template. [. . .] Does this not assume that the differences are some kind of decorative surface covering a common form or structure? Can it not be that ecclesiologies are different beyond comparison?[9]

In Haight's definition, as well as in his proposed way to apply the theory, one might identify several weaknesses. One may ask whether it is possible to create a "common pattern of template" that sensitively manages to discern characteristic features of different ecclesiologies without violating their own understandings and interpretations. Composing a common neutral template is without doubt a complicated, if not an impossible task. Several outstanding theologians question the possibility of creating such a kind of template.[10]

One of the serious problems, as I saw it, was the de-contextualization of these kinds of templates from the great diversity of ecclesiastical traditions. The diversity of ecclesiologies is too great and embraces too many different cultural and ecclesial paradigms. Nevertheless, when focusing on the comparison of the ecclesiologies, I became convinced that it is possible to create a comparative ecclesiological model that enables one to discern characteristic features whenever and wherever ecclesial structures exist and to do so without violating the churches' own identity.

---

7. Haight, *Christian Community in History*, 4.
8. Ibid., 6.
9. Hietamäki, "Is Comparative Ecclesiology Enough," 90.
10. For example Dalferth, "Representing God's Presence," 237–56.

HOW I PREPARED A COMPARISON

There were some basic questions that I had to address before addressing the basic character of an imagined template or model. The first was the problem of pluralism as a challenge for the comparative ecclesiology. The fundamental differences between ecclesiological traditions are often seen as serious obstacles for the possibility of comparison. But, I discovered, contrary to my expectations, a kind of paradox with pluralism.

Analysis of the practices showed me that in spite of the potentially confusing differences between totally different ecclesiologies, it is much easier to discover their similarities and common characteristic features than compared with seemingly similar ecclesiologies and ecclesial practices. This is due to the possibility that when hypothetic relationships exist between numbers of characteristic features across a large number of ecclesiologies, a characteristic link between chosen variables may be assumed. It means that in the act of comparison, the departure should take place from the perspective of the relationships or inter-church level rather than from the intrinsic level of local ecclesiologies or churches.

I put this aspect into practice by using documents from the ecumenical negotiations on ministry in order to create the analytical tool. In addition, I assumed that this tool included necessary and sufficient aspects for the analysis of the diaconal ministry in the churches studied. In order to proceed, I discerned characteristic motifs, biblical images, terms and specific features from these documents and later ordered them together systematically as a tool for close reading and analyzing the ordination rites.

This tool also served later on as a means to carry out the comparison of the rites and helped me to discern what the rites of ordination say characteristically about the diaconate in the particular church. While the characteristic motifs, biblical images, terms, and specific features in the rites (i.e. language of symbols and practices) cannot, in my mind, be translated directly from one tradition to another without disconnecting them from their context, I used an analytical instrument, which in its character transcended the limits of local ecclesiologies in the respective rites.

Applying this instrument to different ecclesiological phenomena enabled me to carry out comparison without violating the basic identity of the ecclesiology studied. Having said this, one still has to admit that the result of such kind of comparison is always a reduction of the object-of-study's real state of affairs, but this is a methodical reduction that does not diminish the studied reality but consciously acknowledges the limits of the comparative method.

DIFFERENT STRATEGIES OF COMPARATIVE METHOD

Quite often one hears researchers who use comparative method say: "all other things being equal." This saying characterizes the problematic side of the comparative methods. There is nothing, according to my experiences, that remains equal when one of the characteristic features or variables in a certain ecclesiology is changed. Nor are there identical ecclesiological practices that could be compared with each other without paying attention to the limits of the comparative method. There exists always a so-called "third variable" outside the researcher's proposed theoretical framework for comparison, which may cause changes and influence the characteristic features of the ecclesiologies being compared.

One way to identify the basic characteristic features is to choose consciously the possible strategies of comparison. I have identified at least two main strategies for using the comparative methods.

Quantitative Comparative Analysis

The first strategy is quantitative comparative analysis, i.e. to focus mainly on quantitative data and to consider the existence and extent of some chosen variables across a larger number of ecclesiologies. This way of proceeding helps to discover the existence of common features of the ecclesiologies studied but does not pay very much attention to the differences.

Due to the strategy of proceeding across the various contexts, this method does not take into consideration the particular context of each of the ecclesiologies. The nature of this strategy made me choose the characteristic features which could be amended in the quantitative analysis. This may lead to the choice of empirical variables that are not adequately applicable on the research question.

In my research on diaconal ministry I have chosen to use the texts of the rites of ordination to the diaconate of ten churches as presented in the ordinals used in Porvoo churches between 1989 and 2009.[11] This selected textual material also included introductions and commentaries, which have been presented together with the ordinals by the legal authorities of the churches and complemented by contextual material that might have helped in the analysis of the ecclesiology and practices of the churches studied.

---

11. The Porvoo churches consist of four Anglican Churches and six Nordic and Baltic Lutheran Churches who have all accepted and signed the Porvoo Agreement: the Church of England, the Church of Ireland, the Church in Wales, the Episcopal Church of Scotland, the Church of Norway, the Church of Sweden, and the Evangelical-Lutheran Churches of Estonia, Finland, Iceland, and Lithuania.

The rites of ordination in all the churches form an integral whole. However, in order to create a common pattern for analysis and to carry out the comparison, the rites were methodically divided into three structural parts. The central part was the act of ordination with prayer and laying-on of hands. The first part, which precedes it, began, in most of the cases studied, with the introduction and presentation of the candidates. In various forms this part of the rite includes biblical readings, declarations, and prayers. The concluding part, following the act of ordination, consisted often of words of dismissal and the welcoming of the newly ordained deacons.

This methodical structuring helped to describe, compare, and analyze the rites of ordination. The special emphasis on some parts or the absence of others, as well as the balance between these structural parts, was significant for the ecclesiological understanding of the role and meaning of the rite as well as of the ministry. Nevertheless, the aspects named above cannot give answers to all relevant questions on ordination to the diaconate. In order to arrive at a more comprehensive understanding of the diaconal ministry, I complemented my analysis, in a limited way, with a consideration of the educational requirements for ordination and the social context of ecclesial relationships within the society in which the church is working.

Qualitative Comparative Analysis

The second strategy, qualitative comparative analysis, focuses on a smaller number of aspects studied and enables on, in a larger extent, to discern and analyze characteristic features from rather different ecclesiologies. The strategy offered me a greater reliability in generalizations but at the same time limited their scope. The qualitative strategy enabled me to study the ecclesiologies within their contexts and to consider the ecclesiological phenomena as a complex of various significant variables with their combined effects. In my study it also helped me to create an adequate relationship between complicated ecclesiological phenomena and proposed theory.

I used two kinds of qualitative comparative analysis. First, theological analysis, based on the analytical tool and rationale from the initial parts of the study. Second, an analytical reflection, which aimed to give meaning to the results of the analysis in the context of the Porvoo churches. The analysis focused on the ecclesiological themes that were articulated in ecumenical negotiations as essential for ordination theology and involved questions about direct and sequential ordination: whether the ordination was understood as temporal or permanent, how the rites were related to baptism and the Eucharist, and what difference ordination made for those who are involved in ordination to the diaconate.

A multifaceted picture of the ordination rites and their meaning for the communion of the Porvoo churches required the comparison of the characteristic traits—either through the choice of biblical readings or the images that are used in the texts of the rites. The analysis also included the examination of constitutive elements in the rites, namely how the different elements and their order in the rites created the meaning that expressed the churches' understanding of the diaconate.

The basic structuring elements were vocation, ordination, and sending. These three, common to the majority of the rites studied, helped me to carry out a qualitative comparative analysis. In addition, theological aspects that were identified as relevant in studying the ecumenical texts—i.e. Christological, pneumatological and eschatological—were also used in this qualitative analysis of the rites' texts. Each of these parts of qualitative comparative analysis indicated ecclesiologically important and characteristic features of the churches' understanding of the deacons' ministry. Thereafter I again placed results in a wider ecumenical context.

By doing this, the qualitative comparative analysis created a way to both a more general ecclesiological theory and to more complex explanations. The use of the analytical tool, mentioned above, played a crucial role studying the ordination rites and contributed in several ways to the purpose of the study. First, in this way the analysis managed to reflect the churches' ecclesiological position and self-understanding in a way that seriously considered the churches' intrinsic relationships. Second, the analysis considered the churches' openness to other churches. Finally, the tool that was created out of ecumenical premises was sensitive in analyzing the churches' consciously addressed issues and their practical implementation of their diaconal ministry.

Still, there are several dangers that I became conscious of and had to consider. With both strategies described above, the issue of the validity of generalizations appeared. For example, this question: when theoretical relationships between chosen characteristic features and the ecclesiologies studied really exist, are these features still relevant for the particular study-question? It is possible that the meaning of certain characteristic features of a particular ecclesiology have not been specified carefully enough. There was a risk that, due to incorrect or careless choices, a problem of the validity of the theoretical conclusions might later appear.

Due to the risks and limitations, I used the combination of quantitative and qualitative strategies in comparison. These strategies complemented one another in a constructive way in my comparative research and provided necessary and organized material for my further analysis. In the following analysis I used this data but complemented it with data that I have identified when describing the wider background and context of the diaconal ministry in the churches studied.

Proposed Character of the Comparative Model

As already indicated, one of the most complicated tasks associated with the comparative method is how to identify the characteristic features that may adequately help to compare the ecclesiologies or ecclesiological phenomena. Out of my experiences I suggest that the choices should begin with studying shared ecumenical experiences. What I mean by this is that the identification of the characteristic issues must be approved as characteristic before beginning the particular research.

In my case, when studying the ordained diaconal ministry, it was not enough to rely only on the comparative research on the experiences of a particular church. Rather, this needed to be supplemented by the issues, which have been identified by several churches together in their discussions, negotiations, or even agreements. Proceeding in this way there appears a realistic possibility of contributing something essential to the common understanding of the phenomena—without ignoring characteristic issues of the particular ecclesiology. In addition, it also helps to see the limited understanding of one's own tradition through fresh eyes.

I propose to create a dynamic model, which considers at least three or four variables that are interwoven with each other and should not be considered without taking into account the influence of the other. Based on my theory, these chosen variables do not have the same significance or value in the research; rather, one has to discern a certain hierarchy between them. The analysis itself takes place in the space of tension, constituted by a triangle, the angles of which consist of characteristic variables.

Besides variables from the quantitative and qualitative analysis, the context of the study-objects should be one of the variables considered. To a certain extent, the content of these variables overlap. Together they constitute both the structure and the meaning of the ecclesiology and become the object of research. The dynamic template-model creates the possibility for comparing ecclesiological models instead of comparing some independent ecclesiologies in different contexts.

SPECIFIC PROBLEMS WITH COMPARATIVE LANGUAGE

When using comparison, researches will always be constrained not only by the complexity of problems with various kinds of data but also by the complexity of language—and not only by their own skills in languages but also by the variety of meanings of ecclesiological terms in different languages. For example, in this article the English language is used as a tool enabling me to describe the use of comparison in different ecclesiologies and contexts. M. Middlemiss Lé Mon has pointed to the problems that might "ensue if it is assumed that the English language transcends cultural context."[12]

There are several difficulties concerning the use of terms from one language in the context of the other cultural sphere. M. Middlemiss Lé Mon points to the first linguistic challenges of international comparative projects and claims that two aspects should be taken into consideration: "First, contextualization and dangers of domestication, both linguistic and conceptual, and, secondly, universalization and problems raised by a search for universal models."[13] Both of these problems are, according to my experiences, real and must be seriously considered. Being conscious of such complications makes it possible to manage the role of translator and interpreter when working with the theologically complicated matters from different cultural and social contexts. In doing so, one has to "abandon ideas of achieving full and accurate reproductions and rather see language as a tool which can assist in the cross cultural mapping."[14]

Theo Hermans has developed the concept of "thick translation," an approach which "tries to avoid imposing categories derived from one tradition on another and in making the translator or author's subject position visible removes the illusion of neutrality which is otherwise a danger."[15] Therefore, established, fixed models—around which one carries out objective comparison—are not used. Instead, I have used the languages and concepts as analysis tools that reflect the practices of different churches.

The second group of difficulties, relevant to the act of comparison, is the theological character of ecclesiological terminology—because there is always some dialectic between theology and terminology.[16] For example, the churches that signed the PCS agreed "to work towards a common understanding of diaconal ministry."[17] But already the English term "diaconal ministry" is ambiguous and may be used to refer either to "the deacon's ministry" or to a more general kind of lay ministry of a diaconal type. It will be even more difficult to decide on how the churches that do not use English as their first language should translate "diaconal ministry" into their own

---

12. Middlemiss, "Divided by a common language," 12.
13. Ibid., 14.
14. Ibid., 16.
15. Ibid., 16; She quotes Hermans, "Cross-cultural," 387.
16. Iversen, "Purpose, Background," 25.
17. "The Porvoo Common Statement," paragraph 58 b (vii).

languages. This kind of specification helped to avoid unnecessary confusion in the analysis.

There are similar problems involved in the terminology of ordination and even the term ecclesiology. Although there may be some convergent theology behind the different terms used in different ecclesiologies in the churches, this cannot be taken for granted. The dialectic in question is partly caused by the fact that churches have come to the certain wording and formulations through a process influenced by their particular historical background, the confessional circumstances in their respective countries, relationships between different actors involved in the processes, their theological preferences, and results of ecumenical dialogues.

CLOSING REMARK: TO COMPARE OR NOT TO COMPARE?

In my comparative research described above, I received great help from using the method of comparison in order to find answers to my research question. The comparative method was a means by which I was able to formulate and later confirm the scientific generalization of my initial theories. But when working with the comparative method and using the strategies described above, I also learned that the comparative method presupposes not only knowledge and theory about the comparative objects, subjects, or circumstances, the method also additionally means a serious way to construct theory for the use of the comparative method.

When, as a theologian, I intended to provide explanations of specific problems in ecclesiology with the help of the comparative method, the validity of possible explanations always depended on the sensitivity of cultural complexity and on the adequate analysis of the results of comparison, which had to be confronted by analytical studies and respective theories.

5

Reflections on Understanding Ecclesiology

HARALD HEGSTAD

> **Harald Hegstad** (born 1959) is a Norwegian Lutheran theologian. He is Professor of Systematic Theology at MF Norwegian School of Theology, Oslo, Norway. His research in ecclesiology includes empirical studies in the area of congregational studies, as well as publications within systematic and practical theology. In the book *Real Church: An Ecclesiology of the Visible* (2013) Hegstad argues that the church we believe in is not, and cannot be, anything other than the church we live within and experience. He is currently a member of the General Synod of the Church of Norway.

INTRODUCTION: TWO METHODOLOGICAL APPROACHES

Under the leadership of Professor Sven-Erik Brodd, the ecclesiology department at Uppsala University has produced a variety of interesting research related to the Christian church. The contribution lies not least of all in the broad approach to the field and in the ability to combine different approaches in the same context. The growing interest in ecclesiology internationally has led to various efforts to understand the Christian church. To some extent this research has been either theologically or empirically based.

On the one hand, there has been a broad discussion of theological ideas about the church within the context of systematic theology. Methodologically this research has mainly involved analyzing theological texts from church bodies and individual theologians. On the other hand, there has been a growing engagement with the practices and social structure of the church. This type of research has been taking place within sociology of religion, and to some extent, within practical theology. Methodologically this research has made use of empirical methods.

The important contribution of the Uppsala milieu has been to combine these two methodological approaches: engaging theologically with the church as it is empirically available in a theological perspective. The work of Uppsala scholars has been an inspiration for scholars elsewhere that have made similar attempts to combine these two approaches to ecclesiology.

As far as I can understand, this research has not been very methodologically standardized; rather, individual researchers have been allowed to follow different approaches. This tolerant attitude and open approach has led to a variety of results. However, it has also opened up methodological and theoretical questions that have not been answered. Some of these issues are visible in the three articles I am commenting upon, written by Michael Hjälm, Hans Engdahl, and Tiit Pädam. In the following I will raise some of these issues and make some reflections from my own perspective.

EMPIRICAL METHODOLOGY AND SOCIAL SCIENTIFIC PERSPECTIVES IN ECCLESIOLOGY

The use of an empirical methodology borrowed from the social sciences is a recent development in theology in general and in theological ecclesiology in particular. The use of such methodology has been controversial due to its roots in the social sciences. The relationship between sociology and theology has historically been full of tensions, mainly due to a reductionist tendency in the social sciences that reduces religion to a purely social phenomenon. The negative evaluation of the social sciences from theologians like John Milbank and others is a reminiscence of this history.[1]

It seems that the relationship between theology and the social sciences has become less hostile in the last decades, owing among other factors to the less positivistic attitude in sociology. This has raised the question of how theology should make use of empirical methodology. We see that theological researchers are employing different models. According to one of the pioneers in this field, Dutch practical theologian and advocate for an "empirical theology" Johannes A. van der Ven, we might distinguish between

---

1. Pointed to by Engdahl in this volume, 35–36.

the models of monodisciplinarity, multidisciplinarity, interdisciplinarity, and intradisciplinarity.

While in the monodisciplinary model the theologian relates directly to praxis—without the use of scientific methods—in the multidisciplinary model the social scientist offers the empirical description and analysis and the theologian subsequently develops a theological reflection. The interdisciplinary model then adds an element of cooperation and interaction between social scientists and theologians. In the intradisciplinary model, recommended by van der Ven, the theologian takes up the empirical methods and techniques developed within other social sciences and makes use of them within his or her own work. This is in principle not different from what theologians have done in other areas throughout history, when including, for instance, methods and perspectives from historical science, philosophy, literary criticism, and so forth.[2]

The research done by the Uppsala ecclesiologists shows that the intradisciplinary model has found acceptance within theology. Even if this is a positive development, one should be aware of the danger of theological isolation. The inclusion of empirical methodology in theology does not exclude the possibility and necessity for interdisciplinary collaboration with social scientists who are not themselves theologians. Theologians should also make use of insights and results from the general social sciences and empirical research that are not in themselves theological. It is also important that theologians do not develop less stringent methodological standards than those generally upheld by the social sciences.

WHAT IS THEOLOGICAL ABOUT ECCLESIOLOGY?

The use of empirical methodology in theology raises fundamental questions regarding the theological dimension of this research. There is no need of a theology that, in Michael Hjälm's words, is reduced to social science.[3] So what then might be theological about empirical research? Traditionally, theology has pointed to the non-empirical as its primary subject matter, not least the reality of God. However, there are theological reasons for arguing that such an approach is insufficient. Even if God is not part of empirical reality, God's acts in the world are. This becomes especially clear in the case of ecclesiology.

Traditionally, ecclesiology has been marked by a tendency of talking about "the church" in two ways: on the one hand the church as a human reality in the social realm, on the other hand the church in a theological

---

2. van der Ven, *Practical Theology*, 89–92.
3. Hjälm in this volume, 53.

spiritual sense. In Protestant theology this duality has often been linked to the distinction between the visible and invisible church. While the former has been left to the social sciences and to practical theology, the latter has been the theme of systematic theology. However, there are strong theological reasons for leaving such a duality behind. In recent years, ecclesiologists have argued for a "concrete ecclesiology," that is, making the empirical church the main object for theological reflection.[4]

In a recent book I have argued for a similar approach, anchoring my case in a dogmatic reflection on the identity of the Christian church.[5] My main thesis is that the church in the theological sense is the church as it is experienced in the world, as a fellowship of people. The church as it exists in the world is, in a theological sense, the only church and the real church. This does not mean that a theological understanding of the church collapses into a subset of sociology. Theology has more to say about the church than what can be said from a purely empirical point of view.

The difference between a sociological and a theological understanding of the church is not that they refer to different objects, sociology to the visible fellowship of people, theology to the invisible object of faith. Rather, the theological perspective means that the same (visible and empirical) object is understood in its relation to God in Christ, to both his presence now and his coming in the *eschaton*. As Hans Engdahl rightly points out, theology is an enterprise with a truth claim.[6] Confessing faith in the church (as it is done in the Nicene and Apostolic creeds) means believing that Jesus is speaking truthfully when he promises, "where two or three are gathered in my name, I am there among them" (Matt 18:20).

ECCLESIOLOGY BETWEEN LOCAL AND DOCTRINAL THEOLOGY

Engaging theologically with the concrete church means that theological research has to engage with the church as it *de facto* is, in all its various versions and expressions. This insight seems to lie behind Michael Hjälm's concept of "primary ecclesiology," which in his view "provides a dynamic ecclesiology where we study how the Church constantly adapts to change through ecclesial system dynamics."[7]

---

4. One important contribution in this line of thought was Healy's *Church, World*. This has been followed up by various contributions, e.g., in the Ecclesiology and Ethnography network, cf. Ward, *Perspectives*; Scharen, *Explorations*.

5. Hegstad, *Real Church*.

6. Engdahl in this volume, 43.

7. Hjälm in this volume, 59.

The insight that ecclesiology has to deal with the church in all its various local forms might lead to a critique of the tradition of working with abstract and general "models" of church.[8] This tradition is also criticized by Nicholas M. Healy, who points out that it has idealized the church, rather than dealt with the church in its concrete and sinful reality. According to Healy, the aim of ecclesiology should be a reflection of the concrete identity of the church rather than the formulation of general statements concerning the *nature* of the church.[9]

While I do agree with the concerns that ecclesiology should relate to the concrete church, I disagree that ecclesiology should never attempt to formulate general statements concerning the basic identity of the church. In its consequence this position would render a systematic-theological or a doctrinal approach to the church impossible. Or rather: a doctrine of the church would have to be developed with regard to every local church and not to the church in general.

There are, however, important theological reasons detracting from such a conclusion, reasons found in the understanding of church as *one and catholic*, as expressed in the Nicene Creed. This idea of the singularity and unity of the church is grounded in the belief in the one God and the one Christ. If there is only one "body of Christ" in the world, the investigation of local churches should not only look for their specific traits, but should also ask how they might be understood as expressions of the "one, holy, catholic and apostolic church." This might also represent critical perspectives on various local forms of church, perspectives that are not necessary found in the local churches themselves.

It is obvious that we can never arrive at a final or non-contextual formulation of the church's identity. Furthermore, both the Bible and Christian tradition are so rich and varied that *any* attempt at formulating what the church is, in more general terms, will clearly represent an incomplete and one-sided picture. However, this is not undermining the necessity of such a project, but instead it is a continual reminder that all theological constructs are works in process and imperfect. I believe we should distinguish between different stages of a theological and ecclesiological work, as for example proposed by Don Browning in his model of four phases in theological works as part of a comprehensive "fundamental practical theology": descriptive theology, historical theology, systematic theology, and strategic practical theology.[10]

---

8. This is for example the case in Dulles, *Models*.
9. Healy, *Church, World*.
10. Browning, *A Fundamental*.

This model might be applied to ecclesiology: While a descriptive ecclesiology is primarily an examination of the church at a given point in time and space, systematic (or dogmatic) ecclesiology is an attempt to formulate a valid understanding of the church that cuts across time and space (without becoming decontextualized). An ecclesiology that only deals with the church in a specific context is problematic, especially when we consider the theological conviction that the church is the one church of Christ that exists in different places and at different times. Yet a theology that only deals with the church in a general, abstract sense,—not relating the general to the concrete—is obviously insufficient. This means that for dogmatic ecclesiology, all work regarding ecclesiological ideas should be considered with an awareness of what these ideas refer to, namely the concrete, empirical church.

In a methodological sense, this points to the need for a comparative approach. In his article, Tiit Pädam anchors such an approach in an understanding of ecclesiology that "does not exclude dogmatic aspects but studies them in connection with other dimensions that are characteristically significant to the Church in the world—such as historical, cultural, social and political."[11] In order to study phenomena in a comparative perspective, an idea of what keeps them together is necessary for understanding the relevance of their differences.

This is an area where a sociological perspective might differ from a theological one. For sociology, the interest lies in studying religious groups and communities as social reality, and there is in principle no difference between churches and other religious groups. For theological ecclesiology, the assumption that a certain group or community is "church" in a qualitative sense is an important key to researching and understanding such groups and communities—and also to comparing them in a meaningful way. My own experience in this field lies primarily in comparisons of different types of congregations in a Norwegian folk church setting, trying to describe the social reality from an empirical perspective, as well as trying to interpret this reality as church in a qualified theological sense.[12]

THE QUESTION OF NORMATIVITY

The task of a theological interpretation of the empirical reality of the church also raises the question of normativity.[13] Theological ecclesiology is not just a descriptive enterprise but should also have a critical and constructive task.

---

11. Pädam in this volume, 66.
12. Hegstad, "Minority."
13. Cf. Hegstad, "Normativity."

According to Michael Hjälm, love, as well as revelation, is immanent in the ecclesial "game" itself and should not be induced from the outside.[14]

I agree with Hjälm that normative perspectives in ecclesiological research have to be rooted in the church's self-understanding. According to Karl Barth, "dogmatics is the scientific self-examination of the Christian Church with respect to the content of its distinctive talk about God."[15] On the one hand this means that theology is done on behalf of the church, investigating the content of its faith and doctrine—and we should add: its practice. What at the same time makes it a *critical* enterprise is that the church's faith, doctrine and practice have an external reference. Theology is not simply reproduction and defence of what the church thinks and does; it is also a critical enterprise. The criterion for such criticism is given in the *object* of theology: God.

Christian doctrine of God does not primarily refer to timeless truths of God's being, but rather to God as God is acting in the world. A critical, normatively-based question for a practical theology analyzing the practice of the church would then be whether this practice can be understood as participating in God's acts in and for the world. John Swinton and Harriet Mowat give textbook definition of practical theology that seems to be in line what this: "Practical Theology is critical, theological reflection on the practices of the Church as they interact with the practices of the world, with a view to ensuring and enabling faithful participation in God's redemptive practices in, to and for the world."[16] This might be applied to ecclesiology as well.

THE CONSTRUCTIVE TASK OF ECCLESIOLOGY

In Don Browning's four-phase model of theological work, the last phase is what he understands to be practical theology in its real sense, namely "strategic practical theology." On the basis of empirical analysis and theoretical reflection, strategic practical theology asks both what should be the practice in the given situation and what means and strategies could be used.[17]

This moves the question of normativity in ecclesiological research one step further: It is not only a question of understanding what is going on in the field or evaluating the empirical findings on the basis of theoretical and theological insights, but it is also a question of how ecclesiology may influence ecclesial practice, i.e. having a constructive function.

---

14. Hjälm in this volume, 57.
15. Barth, *Church*, 3.
16. Swinton and Mowat, *Practical Theology*, 6.
17. Browning, *A Fundamental*, 55–56.

While ecclesiology and ecclesial practice are related to each other, it is necessary to distinguish the two from each other. There is thus a basic distinction between ecclesial practice in its primary sense and ecclesiology as theory of ecclesial practice (and as such, of course, a practice in itself, but on a secondary level). The normative task of ecclesiology as an academic discipline is not to regulate concrete practice, even if it should contribute with criticism and constructive proposals. The decisions in such cases have to be taken by the reflective practitioner him- or herself, or by the group or community of practitioners. Such decisions cannot be made just on the basis of theoretical consideration alone; it also demands a certain practical wisdom and a sense for the uniqueness in the situation.

This also means that the relation between ecclesiology as an academic discipline and the field of ecclesial practice should have a dialogical and discursive character. Ecclesiology is conducting its influence not by prescribing concrete solutions, but rather through offering plausible theoretical interpretations of empirical phenomena, giving frames for understanding, and pointing to alternatives. The decision of how to use these perspectives and frames for understanding should be left to the practitioner.

An alternative, or supplementary, approach for practical theological research to simply reflect on the basis of collected empirical data is to be engaged in the field through an "action research" strategy. In "action research," the researcher is actively involved in changing a situation in a desired direction. In this type of research the researcher is not only a practitioner, but utilizes his/her theoretical insights and methodological skills. An important aspect of action research is the fact that the researcher is working with the people affected by the changes. Action research is not primarily research on people, but with people. It is "a practice of participation, engaging those who might otherwise be subjects of research or recipients of interventions to a greater or less extent as inquiring co-researchers."[18]

This type of research is also used in theological and ecclesial contexts, even if few projects have been labeled as such. Research on the church with church members fits well an understanding of theology as something done by and for the church. An interesting ongoing example is a British project called Theological Action Research (TAR).[19] In a process initiated in congregations from various denominational contexts, congregational experience and practice is shared and reflected upon in conversations between researchers and practitioners. These reflections are aimed at suggesting both renewed action and theology.

---

18. Reason and Bradbury, *Sage Handbook*, 1.
19. Cameron et al., *Talking About God*.

One basic characteristic of this process is that the researchers are not put in a privileged position compared to the practitioners; the process is a shared reflection and conversation process between researchers and practitioners. The researchers taking part in the process do not act normatively in the way that they provide the "answers" or make decisions. The normative element is rather understood as a framework, represented by the theological character of the project. By insisting that practice should be understood and interpreted theologically, the projects create a certain normative framework, even if the consequences of this framework are the subject of joint reflection.

Since 2008, I have been leading a similar project called "Congregational Development in the Folk Church" at MF Norwegian School of Theology. In this project, researchers work together with practitioners in a process of analysis and reflection. In the first phase of a three-year cycle in each congregation, empirical data about the congregation and the local community are collected. In order to secure the reflective use of the data, practitioners are involved in the data gathering. The data is then used as a basis for a reflective process in the congregation about their situation and identity. On the basis of a renewed self-understanding, the congregation is invited to discuss strategies for the future.

The normative element of the process is also here primarily represented by the framing of the process, as the practitioners are challenged to interpret their practice and their experience in an ecclesiological framework. The project does not supply a defined ecclesiology, leaving the congregations themselves to define their ecclesiology. The normative contribution of the researchers is rather to insist that theological questions should be asked and provide some theological frameworks for these questions, rather than to give the answers. In the project we labelled this approach a "soft normativity."[20]

CONCLUDING REMARK

Ecclesiology is a subject that cuts through all the traditional theological sub-disciplines. It is empirical studies of congregations and churches and their role in society. Ecclesiology is a dimension of biblical exegesis. The discipline of church history may be understood as ecclesiology in a historical mode.

Ecclesiology is done as part of systematic theological reflection, and ecclesiology is part of constructive practical theology. Ecclesiology therefore requires interdisciplinary efforts, both within the theological sub-disciplines

---

20. Birkedal et al., *Menighetsutvikling*.

and in relation to non-theological disciplines. Important questions regarding methodology and normativity become urgent in unique ways. At the same time this is a field under development. That makes ecclesiology an area of research and reflection well worth following and engaging.

PART TWO

Empirical Ecclesiology under Construction

In Part Two of this volume, each author is studying empirical data from both history and the present time. Their struggle has been to integrate empirical data into an ecclesiological frame and theory, or maybe it can be described as an attempt to cross-fertilize fields that tend to be separated in the humanities. The following chapters are good examples of how historical and ethnographic theories and methods become integrative parts of ecclesiology. Then, this approach can be read as the counter to the thesis that ecclesiology essentially is systematic theology (Part One). Here is the antithesis a matter of doing ecclesiology on the basis of empirical data.

Data comes here from various forms of ecclesial practices, such as preaching, singing in choir, visiting the sick, and practicing the liturgy. From this follows that the data is of different types. Fahlgren has established data from the recordings of sermons, Fallberg Sundmark from artifacts and images, and Ideström from participating in observations and interviews.

Sven-Erik Brodd claims that the main challenge for Ecclesiology is keeping doctrine and practice together. The authors in Part Two show that this challenge is met "in the trenches," in the ongoing conversation they have with theories, theology, and data. These reflections can sometimes result in reconstructing or slightly altering the theories, or they might open up for new theological perspectives. Regardless, such dynamic conversations create deeper understanding of the study object.

The following three chapters are examples of how ecclesiology—according to Brodd (p. 13)—can be conceptualized into three meanings:

(1) it is the object of the study,

(2) it is the way of studying something, and

(3) it is the result of the study.

Fahlgren, Fallberg Sundmark, and Ideström are all doing ecclesiological investigations (1), and they prefer to call it ecclesiology because the study objects are manifestations of church. The way (2) they accomplish their studies is through traditional historical, sociological and ethnographic methods respectively, but these methods are informed and shaped by the ecclesial conditions.

The result (3) is the outcome of analysis and that is also ecclesiology, but it is often qualified in a way that reflects a certain perspective. Fahlgren calls the result *Communication Theory Ecclesiology*, Fallberg Sundmark calls it *Operative Ecclesiology*, and Ideström *Implicit Ecclesiology*.

One of the characteristics of the three studies is their high level of materiality. Here is ecclesiology densely incarnated in social bodies, in practices, in space, and in what is heard and touched.

At the end of Part Two professor Claire Watkins reflects on empirical ecclesiology from her experiences of studying the ecclesiology that Churches in urban contexts are practicing.

6

Studying Fundamental Ecclesial Practices

SUNE FAHLGREN

EDITORS' INTRODUCTION

In *Communio Sanctorum* (1927) the young Dietrich Bonhoeffer reflects upon the church as a sociological reality. Others have followed over the years and Sune Fahlgren's chapter can be read in relation to this conversation within ecclesiology. If data from the reality of the lived church is absent in Bonhoeffers dissertation, the opposite can be said about Fahlgren's research. For him, the questions of how to use empirical data in ecclesiology are drawn to the center of attention.

In the following chapter we are invited to reflect on how to use a social practice approach in ecclesiology. Fahlgren argues that research on ecclesial practices can give important knowledge on the very identity and self-understanding of churches. The data he uses comes from Free Church traditions in Sweden.

Since there is an absence of written material of traditional creedal character in those traditions, he discovers new ways to create knowledge about Free Church ecclesiologies. Fahlgren's chapter is also an example of how empirical ecclesiology can discern changes over time in a tradition. As for Sundmark Fallberg, he interprets historical data.

In this chapter he gives an account of the development of *preachership* and *choirship* as theoretical concepts for studying and interpreting ecclesial practice. Here one can see clear parallels with Ideström's work with developing theories and methods for studying ecclesial identity. Revisiting his own doctoral project, Fahlgren presents a draft for so-called communication ecclesiology, which is in sharp contrast to traditional communication theories. In this way, argues Fahlgren, it is possible to expand the ecclesiological understanding on how the church comes into being continually through communicative practices.

Sune Fahlgren (born 1952) is Associate professor at Stockholm School of Theology, where he teaches Practical Theology. His dissertation *Predikantskap och församling* [Preachership and church] is an empirical and historical study of preachership as a fundamental ecclesial practice within the Free Church traditions in Sweden.

Fahlgren took his doctoral degree at University of Uppsala in 2006, and he has also worked as director of the Swedish Christian Study Center in Jerusalem, 2008–2011. His preachership concept is discussed and evaluated in an article in *International Journal for The Study of the Christian Church* (6/2006). Fahlgren is a minister in the Uniting Church in Sweden. He is editor and co-author of *Shalom Inshallah: Encountering Jews, Christians, and Muslims* (2013).

TWO INTRODUCTORY CASES

The Pentecostal minister Lewi Pethrus is preaching for approximately three thousand people at the Sunday Service in Filadelfia Church, a church building with functionalistic architecture in the center of Stockholm, next to the Rörstrand Palace from the 1630s. Today is Easter Sunday. The year is 1931. Most of the attendants in the church are working-class people.

The preaching event is the peak of the service. Rev. Pethrus's sermon is narrative in form, integrating the Bible paraphrase with metaphorical stories and applications. The language has short sentences and no difficult words. Pethrus's message about the angels at the empty tomb, where Christ's body had been buried, also has ecclesiological references: an invisible heavenly presence is connected to the vibrant fellowship in the congregation. The angels participate "with us." Thus, the listeners are a part of a larger ecclesial communion.[1]

---

1. The sermon was published in a sermon collection 1932, celebrating the first year in the new Filadelfia Church. See Pethrus, *Gud*. Members in the Church who were skilled in shorthand had written down the sermons.

Studying Fundamental Ecclesial Practices   89

Figure 1. **Rev. Lewi Pethrus (1884-1974).**

From the pulpit, with the name JESUS written on its front, the preacher also expresses an understanding of "Christendom" similar to the influential liberal thoughts of the German theologian and Church historian Adolf von Harnack (1851-1930). He communicates, for instance, that the Christian faith is principally an interior, personal experience.[2] The external, the bodily, could support this "essence of Christendom," but it is not a part of the nature of faith; it cannot mediate God's salvation to mankind.

On the basis of data from this historical occasion, from the ministry of Lewi Pethrus (1884-1974), and from five other case studies, I have constructed in my dissertation a category of social practices that I named *preachership*.[3] Because it is a category of practice with distinctive characteristics from a specific social body—the church—it was qualified as an *ecclesial* practice. A further clarification in my study of this category of practice is *fundamental*, meaning here that a church and an ecclesial practice reciprocally create and presuppose one another. Thus, an *ecclesial fundamental practice* is expressing and creating identity and self-understanding

---

2. Harnack, *Wesen*. See Fahlgren, *Predikantskap*, 253–54.

3. Fahlgren, *Predikantskap*; I have also studied the implicit and explicit understandings of preaching and preachership in the new Swedish textbooks in Homiletics. See Fahlgren, "Preacher."

as church—a kind of iterative re-production of a being Christian in communion in a specific context.[4]

Figure 2. **Sanctury in Filadelfia Church, 1931.**

The preachership I constructed in this case study at Filadelfia Church goes beyond the traditional understandings of ministry in Pentecostal congregations. The operant ecclesiologies embedded in it are far more diverse than the official teaching of these congregations,[5] since preachership is seen as an expression of a church's event dimension (German: *Ereignis*) more than its structural dimension (German: *Struktur*).[6]

In this article, I will present some of my theoretical considerations, as well as the tools I have used, in my studies of ecclesial fundamental practices. The specific methodological challenges that I met when I was working with the rich field of data from historical archives and from field studies are discussed thoroughly in two other articles in this book.[7] Here I will concentrate on the research approach, the choice of perspective, and the construction of theory. Before I invite the reader to my research worksite, I

---

4. Regarding my use of church in small and capital letters, with definite and indefinite article; see Brodd in this volume, 13, 16, 19.

5. For example, one ecclesiological "model" is here called *mobilization* and is related to the zeal of the pastoral ministry to mobilize members in evangelism and social work. Another one is called *intensifying* and represents the listeners' church and Lewi Pethrus as a revival preacher.

6. Iserloh, *Kirche*. ("Struktur" is here "Institution"); Cavanaugh, *Torture*, 269–70.

7. For historical data, see Fallberg Sundmark in this volume, chapter 7. See also Fallberg Sundmark, *Sjukbesök*. For data from field studies, see Ideström in this volume, 133–35. See also Ideström, *Lokal*.

would like to introduce the modern Filadelfia Church in comparison to its counterpart of the 1930s. The architecture style and the pews are the same as in 1931, but the chancel (or "stage" area) is different.[8] There is no longer a pulpit in the center of the church and no longer a special place for the choir and musicians. The new chancel has several stage lights, like those used at a theater, and a big screen in the front of the chancel gives information about the Church and its programs. Among the attendees, the middle-class is the majority, and very few immigrants are present, although currently almost one third of the population in Stockholm has an immigrant background.

Figure 3. **The stage area in Filadelfia Church.**

The 2013 Easter Day service begins when a young "worship team" enters the brightly lit stage. As in 1931, the preaching is still central in Filadelfia Church, but the way of singing songs together and the choir's role in the service has gone through a major shift. In 1931 there was a lot of communal singing from the hymnbook, accompanied by organ or string instruments, and several kinds of choirs were singing—string band, mixed choirs (singing SATB),[9] and other song groups—plus the solo singers. In 1931 the most renowned vocalist was Einar Ekberg (1905–1961), a Swedish-American baritone singer.

At present the texts for the communal songs are projected on the screen in the front of the sanctuary. This new technology enables greater physical freedom and less downtime between songs. The lyrics reflect the Neo-Pentecostal theology of modern movements such as Hillsong and

---

8. In Fahlgren, "Rum för möten," there is a study on what kind of social practices that are forbidden in the Free Church sanctuaries.

9. An initialism for soprano, alto, tenor, and bass, defining the voices required by a *choir* to perform a particular musical work.

Vineyard. Stylistically, the songs are similar to pop music and are frequently referred to as "worship songs," led by a "worship team" in front of the congregation. This group of musicians has a more exclusive or professional role in the liturgy than the previous types of choirs in this congregation. The leader of the worship team, in particular, has become the conductor of the service, and "worship" is the new concept for communal singing.

What this choir in the Filadelfia Church and similar groups in other churches are performing can also be interpreted as an ecclesial fundamental practice, like preachership. In ecclesiological studies I have conceptualized it as *choirship* and have given examples of the interaction between different choirships and operant ecclesiologies in the congregations where the choirs were active.[10] Both preachership and choirship are analytical tools that have been constructed to give a deeper understanding of the lived reality of the church. Studies of choirship have also highlighted spirituality as an ecclesial dimension. This is in itself an invitation for further research.[11]

Thus, my dissertation is essentially a social practice approach. What follows in the next section is an outline of my research trajectory in terms of influences, decisive choices, and collecting and understanding data, which was particularly in focus during the first phase of my study process.

HOW ECCLESIAL PRACTICES CAME TO THE FOREFRONT

The point of the departure for my interest in social practices related to the Church was not a discovery of the importance of practices for Christian faith, or an ambition to initiate a new approach to the study of the living church.[12] The major concern for me was to create more knowledge about the concrete, lived ecclesiologies in the many Free Church traditions in Sweden, including both the historic Free Churches and their modern counterparts.

The first problem I faced was data. The textual material usually used in ecclesiological studies of the Church of Sweden and other mainline Churches—creeds, canons, liturgical books, etc.—are often absent, or at the very least rarely present, in the Free Churches.[13] In general, these churches are

---

10. Fahlgren, "Från blandad kör." A church choir can also be seen as a kind of *ecclesiola in ecclesia*. For church "as music," see Brodd, "Ecclesiology."

11. Fahlgren, *Predikantskap*, 288–302; Fahlgren, "Från blandad kör," 42–48; cf. Fahlgren and Joö, "Baptismens spiriutalitet." The organization and the discipline of a choir are expressing specific spiritualties. Cf. Brodd, in this volume, 14, for ecclesiality as an interpretative tool in ecclesiology.

12. For the discussion on practices in relation to Ecclesiology at the same time, see Bexell, "Om kyrkans."

13. For a brief introduction to the Free Church traditions in Sweden, see Fahlgren "Loss."

so called non-credal, in the sense that they do not have written documents of a credal character, and when they do exist, there is no guarantee that the congregations are following them.

The non-credal churches have strong oral traditions, and they focus more on actions and commitment than on formulating their beliefs and self-understanding in creeds and canons. Maybe these circumstances can explain why very little "theologizing" has been done about their ecclesiology. But this explanation cannot hide the neglect; instead it displays the underlying incorrect assumption that there is no theology in praxis and pragmatism or that praxis is theologically irrelevant.

How, then, is it possible to create ecclesiological knowledge about the Free Churches? In the historical archives of the Free Churches,[14] there has been immense material collected from the congregations' daily life, material about what the members and the leaders of the Free Churches have been doing and reflecting upon. The archives contain weekly papers and magazines, periodicals for choir leaders and Sunday school teachers, letters, annual reports, minutes from meetings, tapes with sermons, the spiritual books they were reading or pamphlets they spread, instruments, hymnbooks, songbooks for string band, photos, artifacts, etc.

These kinds of data challenge the traditional idealistic approach to the Church because here we find the struggles that are involved in being church and the frustrations of dealing with things that are not at all perfect. Perhaps this is a reason that theology has overlooked the theological importance of the lived reality of the Church and has hesitated to interpret the results of empirical research.[15]

How can such data of historical, sociological, ethnographic, and theological character be used for ecclesiological studies? One of the first and most helpful hints came when I was reading William T. Cavanaugh's dissertation, *Torture and Eucharist* (1998), in which he shows how social practices embody and enact ideology/theology. Cavanaugh has examined the Catholic Church's response to the torture practices under the Chilean dictatorship of General Augusto Pinochet, who took power in a coup d'état in September 1973. Even if the distance between Sweden and Chile is huge, both geographically and culturally, the history Cavanaugh presents helped

---

14. Well-organized archives can be found both on local and national level in the free churches in Sweden. In each county in Sweden there are also Popular Movements Archives. These collections consist of historical material from the popular movements in Sweden, including the older free churches, starting with the local associations and their functions.

15. Healy, *Church, World*, 37. See also footnote 24, below.

me to see the role of the Church in the society and how this role relates to the connection between practices and ecclesiology.

After taking power, Pinochet's regime intimidated, killed, and tortured rivals and those not supportive of his government. The state literally possessed the "body" of its people. Through the fear of disappearance and pain, society began to lose its social connections. The end result was the total fragmentation of the society and the elimination of everything, except broken individuals who had lost the ability to voice their pain, their connections with others, and even their ability to feel. The net effect in Chile was the loss of any social body that could rival the regime, including the church.

Cavanaugh discusses in his dissertation why the church was also lost in this sense, and therefore slow to respond to the practice of torture. According to Cavanaugh, the loss and slowness had to do with bad ecclesiology.[16] The realm of the soul had become the church's area, which meant that the body was the property of the state. Eventually, the church began to gather itself and recover its ability to resist the evil power of the regime. Cavanaugh argues that it did so only when it broke with the ecclesiological dichotomy between spiritual and temporal and became "the true body of Christ." The ability to recover the Eucharist as a bodily practice was central to this renewed self-perception of the church. Cavanaugh perceives torture and Eucharist as opposing social practices.[17]

In my studies of the Free Churches in Sweden I have found a similar unaware conformity with the modern society that has to do with the loss of opposing social practices and theological visions.[18] In the past, "Free" in "Free church" meant free from any coercion from external human authorities. Today these churches hesitate to act in public if they do not behave in line with the secular-rational status quo.

The Catholic Church in Chile became efficiently political when it discovered the meaning of its own manifestation in the Eucharist, and this discovery included the right to lay claim to bodies in the name of Christ. The Eucharistic practice was an operant and widespread imagination of the church. In this way, Cavanaugh contends that the "church does not simply perform the Eucharist, the Eucharist performs the church,"[19] and that the church built a social body capable of resisting the regime.

---

16. The theological influence on this ecclesiological dichotomy came to Chile from the French theologian Jacques Maratain. Cavanaugh, *Torture*, 151–97.

17. "Where torture is an anti-liturgy for the realization of the state's power on the bodies of others, Eucharist is the realization of Christ's suffering and redemptive body in the bodies of His followers." Ibid, 206.

18. Fahlgren, "Loss," 63–66. Cf. Cavanaugh, *Theopolitical*.

19. Cavanaugh, *Torture*, 235. See also Cavanaugh, *Migrations*.

This understanding of the church as both a subject and an object eventually also became a point of departure in my ecclesiological studies—as did the fact that practices are both expressions of church as an acting and receiving body. In Chile, as a direct consequence of the development of the church as a social body, the church established three practices that were particularly relevant and effective in resisting the politics of the regime. Those practices were excommunication for all of those who were involved in torture, the Vicariate of Solidarity (which provided legal, medical, and relief services), and the Sebastian Acevedo Movement against torture.[20]

Cavanaugh's approach fascinated me, and so I adopted it for the study of the Free Churches. His study of torture and Eucharist as social, bodily practices is based on a rich field of data that we usually do not find in a theological book. He refers frequently to political, sociological, anthropological, legal material, and interviews. With the support of such data he also *constructs* the national and ecclesial practices of torture and Eucharist in Chile, embedded as they are with political ideology and theology.

A REVISION OF ECCLESIOLOGY

Cavanaugh's dissertation *Torture and Eucharist* can be reckoned as seminal in the turn to the concrete in ecclesiology. I am just one of several researchers that learned from his groundbreaking ecclesiological study, in which there is a juxtaposition of ecclesiology with the broader field of the social science.[21] Qualified by theology, the empirical and non-empirical materials used from the other sciences are analyzed from an ecclesiological perspective. Eventually, this also became my methodology.

Cavanaugh extended ecclesiology from the systematic study of historical and contemporary faith-systems and philosophical assumptions to the subjects that natural science, economy, psychology, and social sciences are studying. This is an example of the revision of church and theology that have taken place since the 1990s and which has also been a concern in the research seminar in Ecclesiology in Uppsala—as reflected in this anthology. In the seminar, I received support to understand and develop these new perspectives and this new methodology in ecclesiological studies and to discuss their potential pitfalls and dead ends.

The revision is especially relevant in the post-secular West, where church and theology tend to be reduced to the spiritual or other internal/private dimensions apart from the public and secular world. There are many prior understandings and stereotypes embedded in this dichotomy

---

20. The three practices are discussed at length in Cavanaugh, *Torture*, chapter 6.

21. For more on this, see Ideström in this volume, chapter 8.

and dualistic thinking that must be questioned and problematized.²² One of the major concerns for the revision of ecclesiology is to reclaim the Church as a historical and sociological reality, and for this direction towards the "concrete Church," new approaches and methods are necessary.²³ They are influenced by and located in the lived experience of people. In the postsecular West the context for the Church has also become significantly pluralistic, culturally and religiously, which is another reason for the revision of theology and church.

It is clear to me now that the data question I faced is about the major concerns in this revision of ecclesiology. The existing data about the noncredal churches in the archives and the data from field studies are from the concrete history and life of these churches, which can be seen as the lived faith of the churches.²⁴ The data set is from a rich field of data that incorporates persons, their actions and decisions, the shift of cultures, as well as realizations and failures of the mission of the churches throughout history. Thus, the data turned my dissertation into a study of what was *coming to be* the Free Churches, not what is said about them.

The rich field of data I found in archives made it possible to write "thick descriptions"²⁵ of my study objects, which proved to be very important for the focus on practices.²⁶ The descriptions, narratives, and photos are therefore a substantial part of my dissertation, but how do we move the

---

22. Reading John Howard Yoder was one of my first encounters with a theological response to this dualistic thinking; see for example Yoder, *Politics*.

23. Beside William Cavanaugh, there are several other renowned international theologians working along this trajectory, including: Graham Ward, Miroslov Volf, Clare Watkins, Stanley Hauerwas, Sarah Coakley, and Pete Ward.

24. Joseph A. Komonchak refers such data to the "concrete self-realizations of the Church" (p. 53). In his book *Foundations in Ecclesiology*, he explains ecclesiology as "Church-talk" and discusses the dialectics between the church as a human product and the church's transcendent origin, nature, and goal. In Komonchak's book I also found an understanding of ecclesiology as a kind of social theory (cf. John Milbank's understanding of "theology as social science" and "first and foremost an *ecclesiology*," see Milbank, *Theology*, 320).

25. The influential cultural anthropologist Clifford J. Geertz (1926–2006) established this essential concept in empirical research in social sciences and beyond. A "thick description" explains not just the human behavior, but its context as well, such that the behavior becomes meaningful to an outsider. Geertz, "Thick Description."

26. Already in 1996, Nicholas Healey proposed narrative descriptions as an ecclesiological method in his critique of "ecclesiological models" (Healy, "Some observations"). He saw this method as a way to get beyond the idealized theologies of the Church, which he called the "blue print ecclesiologies" (Healy, *Church, World*). Following from this, Healy argues for a church *in via* shaped by a discursive search for truth (ibid., 107–8). Eventually, he became critical to the idealistic use of the practice concept in ecclesiological studies. See Healy, "Practices;" Healy, "Ecclesiology."

study beyond traditional church historical results? I could use an inductive method to establish texts of ecclesial practices, but how could they be analyzed ecclesiologically?

Since the practice approach stems from social sciences, I realized that my ecclesiological study had to come to grips with social theory in order to move beyond description into explanation. It became a long-term move beyond common sense into the realm of theory. And no specific social theory or any other hermeneutical tool was ready, waiting for me in order to make the study ecclesiological. Therefore, development of theory became a necessary part of my project.

Ecclesiology as a Kind of Social Theory

Different forms of liberation and feminist theology have opened the door for social theories in ecclesiology.[27] These theological movements have in common the striving for new ways of doing theology. One of their keywords is *praxis*,[28] and they made theology into a practical theory. A good theology (theory) is related to the liberating or empowering actions (praxis) in the society, which means that praxis is seen as a part of the conditions for the theology (theory).[29] Thus, the theology (theory) and the praxis cannot be separated from one another. This differs from a traditional understanding of praxis as an applied theology (theory).

In contemporary liturgical studies, there is a similar turn to praxis as the "primary theology."[30] In addition, other theological disciplines pay attention to the social and bodily dimensions of faith. Thus, significant for the revision of theology and church is the striving for understanding from the inside (called "emic knowledge" by culture anthropologists), for example the ambition of understanding a certain belief in its original ecclesial context.

The revisioning has also given attention to particularities. It is not the Church in general that is studied. It is specific Christian communities, in specific contexts and from specific perspectives, that gives church a corollary of an empirical and authentic pluralism.[31] In the introductory

---

27. For an example, see Edgardh in this volume, chapter 12.

28. Praxis was then a concept in fashion, both in political movements, e.g. marxism, and in interdisciplinary developments of social theories, e.g. in the Frankfurt School.

29. Sven-Erik Brodd expressed this view on the relations between praxis and theory when he became professor for the research seminar in Ecclesiology in Uppsala. See Brodd, "Ecklesiologi," 114.

30. See Oljelund in this volume, chapter 10. On primary and secondary theology, see the influential work by Kavanagh, *On Liturgical*.

31. Such a culturally integrative and practically oriented approach to particularity

cases I examined, I found, with the help of the categories preachership and choirship, various kinds of ecclesiologies in Filadelfia Church. In their daily practices, the congregation represents multiple ways of being Christian in communion, of being church, even if the official identity is more uniform or standardized.

As is apparent from this brief exposition, social theory and theology using social theory have two key concepts that both relate to social acting: *praxis* and *practice*.[32] The concept of praxis is mainly used in liberation theology and other theological movements with roots in resistance against colonialism and other oppressing structures. The concept of practice is mainly used in theologies that focus on the ecclesial context to understand the life and the mission of the Church for the sake of the world. The similarities between the two alternatives are more important than the differences; both are interested in lived faith on a grassroots level and both are contextual.[33]

That I picked out the practice concept in my dissertation and in my ongoing ecclesiological studies is due to the social/ecclesiological theory I constructed; it is not due to any standpoint in theological methodology that has been related to each of the concepts.[34] Methodological discussions have made it clear that there are always theological presuppositions in the study of social practices/praxis and in the understanding of the context and structures in which they take place.[35] It is reasonable to assume that methods and theories are not neutral in relation to presuppositions and postulates.

---

is spelled out in the work of Lieven Boeve. The quest of radical pluralism is at the center of his theological method; see Boeve, *God Interrupts*.

32. There is no linguistic difference between these terms, which makes it a bit difficult to establish the conceptual difference as analytical tools.

33. The divergence of theory and practice in theology has often been treated as if each forms the basis of a completely separate type of theology, with little interaction between them. It has even been claimed as an unbridgeable gap between correlation method (*praxis*) on one side and post-liberalism and cultural-linguistic theology (*practice*) on the other. A book by Kathryn Tanner challenged me not to exaggerate the differences (Tanner, *Theories*).

34. The impact of this discussion about theological methodology can be seen, for example, in the way David Tracy's anti-correlation school has shaped Thomas Groome's use of "shared *praxis*" in his program of Christian religious education, and in how George Lindbeck's performative hermeneutic school has shaped Bass and Dykstra's use of "Christian *practice*" in their educational program. Yet both Groome and Bass and Dykstra are emphasizing the appropriation of faith.

35. Cf. John Milbank's influential book *Theology*, in which he claims that social science is not a neutral, secular vantage point. In response, he wishes to develop a theological social theory that takes questions about virtues such as worship and desire as essential to understand the society.

A THEOLOGICAL UNDERSTANDING OF SOCIAL PRACTICES

Definitions of practice have been established in several disciplines, but when the concept is used in ecclesiological studies, references are usually given to Alasdair MacIntyre and his book *After Virtue: A Study in Moral Theory* (1984).

According to MacIntyre, a kind of social grammar exists in all types of communities, and this grammar consists of the following three components: *convictions* ("goods"), *social practices*, and *reflections*. These internal components make social bodies such as churches identical and coherent over the span of time. Among these components, the practices have a special character because they give shape to convictions and cause reflections of various kinds. MacIntyre claims that the goods of practices can be identified and known "by the experience of participating in the practice in question."[36]

Spelled out in another way, social practices are not just a means to achieve something. They have their own meaning for those participating in them. If anybody does not know how to take part, it can be learned from more experienced participants in the practice. Thus, convictions and reflections are embedded in the practice.

MacIntyre's definition has been discussed and applied in several ways in modern ecclesiology. His approach is related to the classic moral philosophy of Aristotle and Thomas Aquinas. Dorothy C. Bass and Craig Dykstra have shortened MacIntyre's definition and emphasized the external dimension of "Christian practices." Their definition is theological and thus understood not only internally, but also through the responsive relationships of ecclesial practices to God. Thus, when Bass and Dykstra refer to ecclesial practices, they have something normative and theological in mind. The participants in ecclesial practices are "taking part in God's work of creation and new creation, and thereby growing into a deeper knowledge of God and of creation."[37] Here is their definition:

> By "Christian practices" we mean things Christian people do together over time to address fundamental human needs in response to and in the light of God's active presence for the life of the world.[38]

---

36. MacIntyre, *After Virtue*, 187.

37. Bass and Dykstra, "Theological Understanding," 21. For a fundamental theology, see also Brodd in this volume, 19.

38. Ibid., 18. On pp. 19–26 is an explanation of this definition. Dorothy Bass has developed the definition towards everyday practices, which relate to elementary human needs.

The current theological reflections on practice show that there are several approaches to practice. Bård E. Hallesby Norheim concludes that the practice paradigm has evolved in a context where "more and more theologians agree that church and society exist in a post-Christendom climate."[39] But what makes a practice ecclesial or Christian? Dykstra tries to move beyond MacIntyre's moral dimension of practices or practice as just any activity. A practice can also have a sacramental dimension, in the sense that through it we may become aware of certain realities, which outside of a certain practice are beyond our ken.[40] This epistemological weight is also related to the fact that such practices have distinctive roots in The Christian Canon. Several theologians such as Miroslav Volf stress that Christian practices are part of a mutually interpretive pattern, in the way that beliefs shape practices and vice versa.[41]

In my research I have categorized two basic types of ecclesial practices: preachership and choirship. Preachership and choirship are examples of *fundamental practices* that create identity and describe church as a whole, respectively. They belong to the "DNA of the Church."[42] Such a significant practice is in turn constructed by *sub-practices*. Preachership includes, for example, such sub practices as ordination, sermons, and meetings. From another perspective in the study, a sub practice, such as ordination, may be a fundamental practice in a church.

How to Establish a Text of Preachership

The ecclesial DNA-metaphor assumes that fundamental practices such as preachership are structuring factors in being church and in the constant reproduction of church. In order to study and interpret such practices, a text must be established, but first the empirical factors that are constructing and characterizing the practice must be defined.

I understand preachership as a social interplay between someone preaching and the listeners to the spoken word. The interplay is affected by and is emanating from the room they share, the message, the wider context, the preparations for the event, and other factors—all of which are held together and integrated into the social practice.

---

39. Hallesby Norheim, *Practicing*, 16. His history of the theological development of this paradigm is valuable; see chapter 2.

40. Dykstra, "Reconceiving Practice," 170–82.

41. Volf, "Theology for a Waly of Life," 248–51. Volf also makes a distinction between practices and sacraments related to normativity. For a theological reflection on what constitutes the presence of Christ in Christian/Ecclesial practices, see Hallesby Norheim, *Practicing*, chapter 3.

42. This analogy is developed in my dissertation; see Fahlgren, *Predikantskap*, 41.

When I established the text for preachership, I focused on the following four components: sermon, preacher, listener, and situation. Each component was named in such a way that it related to the stipulated definition of an ecclesial practice. The public speech activity was called a "message" in order to stress the convictions and practical application in what was said. The main actor in the speech event was given the conventional name "preacher," and in the text I stressed his or her identity and legitimacy as a preacher. The analytical concept for the listeners became "congregation," not in its formal meaning but in the sense of the prerequisite for the event and the outcome of it. One of the results of each case study was to answer the question "what is a congregation?"

The fourth component, which the preachership integrates, is called a "performative situation," that is to say all the other things that are underlying the preachership: meeting, room, the time, the purpose for the meeting, and other contextual factors, such as politics, economy, culture, religion, and history. "Performative" means that the act and the situation produce results or real consequences, including the result of constructing reality itself.[43]

This brief review of my work process shows that the established text had intentionally analytical concepts, which made the textual description into a part of the hermeneutical process of understanding and analyzing preachership as an expression of being church.

PERILS IN THE STUDY OF ECCLESIAL PRACTICES

As the two introductory cases imply, the study of ecclesial practices can give knowledge about a specific congregation and its operative theology and ecclesiological imagination. If several fundamental practices are studied in a congregation, an understanding of its "ecclesial DNA" can appear.

From outside it might look very easy to study a practice in a church and read its theology, but the study needs awareness of things that may go wrong or may cause problems.[44] The first pitfall of studying a practice in the church is to think that one already understand the practice of one's study, or to be convinced that one's theology is the only way to interpret what the practice "really" means.

If data comes from a field study of a practice, it is very important that the theologian doing the study is well trained in field study methodology, such as participant observations and qualitative interviews, and is aware

---

43. Here I refer to theories about performative rites; see Richard Schechner, Victor Turner, and others.

44. Ideström's self-reflective text in this volume is an excellent example of theologian struggling with he dilemmas in field studies; see Ideström in this volume, chapter 8.

of the possibilities and limitations of these methods. It is also important to see the meta-narratives that are operative both in the researcher's understanding and in the data that the researcher collects from participants of an ecclesial practice in a given context.

A specific pitfall is the search for *one* ecclesiology or *the* real theology in an ecclesial practice.[45] Studies of practices often display multiple convictions, imaginations, and theologies. This causes, explicitly or implicitly, a critique of deified or simplified ecclesiology.

Finally, the practice approach is not a polemic against the importance of the sacraments and their significant place in the Church. It is the wider sacramentality of the Church that the practice study is focusing on in terms of social relations and actions in a specific Christian community.[46] In several of the dissertations from the research seminar in Uppsala, the whole life of the church is interpreted as a bodily dimension of faith, an expression of the sacramentality of the Church's life and mission in the world. Ecclesial practices are seen as signs and instruments for the Kingdom of God.[47]

Becoming aware of these perils, I made the study process into a constant interplay between the data I collected and the ecclesiological theory I had tentatively constructed. So, in practice, the dissertation has an abductive method, even if the approach looks thoroughly inductive. In addition, I tried to use not only different ecclesiological perspectives (such as church traditions, ecumenical, and sacramental), but also perspectives from other disciplines (such as economy, human rights, and rhetoric), in order to open a deeper understanding of the study object and avoid the pitfalls of trusting in the first impressions and other kinds of fast thinking.

REVISITED: ECCLESIOLOGY FOR A COMMUNICATIVE COMMUNITY

Finally, I will reflect over the re-reading of my dissertation eight years after it was finalized. The revisit made me discover that the ecclesial practice approach can be seen as subordinated to another approach—the communication approach. The result of my study firmly emphasizes the communication character of preachership. Perhaps I was so busy during the study process

---

45. See Healy, "Ecclesiology." See also above, footnote 26.

46. An influential thinker for this way of understanding the ecclesial practices is John Howard Yoder. The little booklet *Body Politics* is a collection of "occasional papers" he wrote on the sacramentality of ecclesial practices. Recursively, he writes that "in, with and under" these human practices is God at work, and it is signs that the world can see and grasp.

47. Fallberg-Sundmark in this volume, 111–19.

in following up the initial impulses to study ecclesial practice and to use social theory that I did not the see the potential in communication theory as a kind of ecclesiology, in the sense of an analytical tool in ecclesiological studies. A communication ecclesiology is in sharp contrast to traditional communication theories with the components sender, receiver, message, medium, and feedback.

Preachership and choirship are obviously communicative practices in the Church. In the interaction between data and theory (theology), I constructed a sketch of a communication theory ecclesiology. This theory assumes that there are different kind of communication systems in Christian communities—both verbal and non-verbal, both interactive and simplex. These systems contribute to creating, to maintaining, and to structuring the communities, since they are embedded in ecclesial communication practices.[48]

A communication theory ecclesiology relates to a significant number of theological expressions of church as communicative. A type of speech and singing (!) is assumed that makes church come to exist in reality. This communicative beginning is theologically described in many ways, for instance in 1 John 1:1-4 as the hearing and receiving the proclamation of the gospel of Jesus.[49] In reflexive terms, the Christian communities have in Church history understood themselves as *ecclesia creatura verbi* and *ecclesia ex auditu*—a community created by the Word, and a community of listeners and receivers of the Word.[50] And the messenger has in some traditions been given the title VDM, *verbi divini minister*, the minister of the divine word. To this category also belongs self-presentations as being a school, *coetus scholasticus*, kept together by a teaching ministry (*magisterium*).[51]

In all these examples of theological concepts and reflections, a church is understood as a communicating community. And this communicative beginning did not happen once and forever. Church comes into being continually through "listening" (cf. *Shema!*) and from singing (Col 3:16; cf. Eph 5:18-20). Not only does faith come from what is heard—the message (Rom 10:17)—church also comes from listening and singing, and the condition that makes this possible is communicative practice embedded in the church.

---

48. Kress, *Church*; Döring, *Grundriss*; Brodd, "Kyrkan som kommunikativ"; Fahlgren, *Predikantskap*.

49. The reference to the old Jewish confession, the *Shema* (Hear, Israel. . .) is evident. The duty of the People of God is to listen, learn, think, and "do" the Word of God.

50. The protestant churches stress either the message or the receiving. The Lutheran tradition has emphasized the objective, the preaching of the Word. The reformed tradition has focused on the subjective receiving of the Word.

51. Brodd, "Einige Bemerkungen."

In my studies I have examined preachership and choirship. The following theoretical model is constructed to explain what happens "in, with, and under" the communicative processes (Fig. 4).

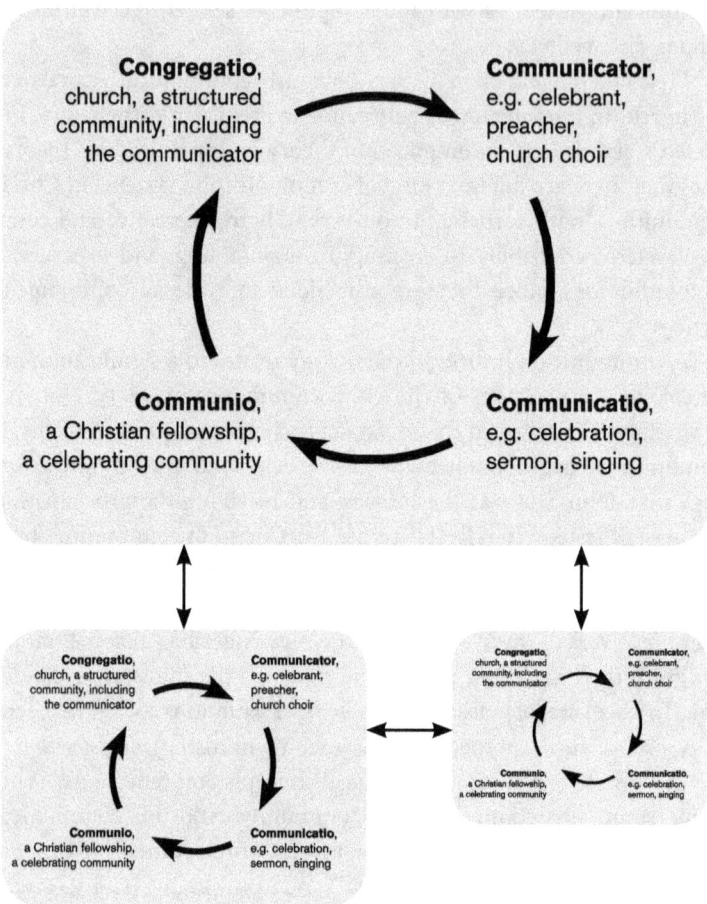

Figure 4. Ecclesiology based on a communication theory. Each "body" is also interrelated to others in time and space.

The components are, firstly, preacherchip/choirship, which are the performative event, the communication practice (Latin: *Communicatio*); secondly, the ecclesial fellowship (Latin: *Communio*), which is the result of the communication—and also a condition for it; thirdly, if the temporary fellowship becomes a structured community, it will be a congregation (Latin: *Congregatio*). Fourthly, the person or group that communicates (Latin: *Communicator*) becomes a structure in the congregation.

The study of ecclesial fundamental practices contributes to an understanding of the process by which the Church reproduces itself as a distinct human community for the life of the world. The study also reflects a threefold understanding of ecclesiology in the process of research—which is in accord with the Uppsala perspective presented in this book.[52] Firstly, the study object is a practice-expressed ecclesiology, what my colleague Michael Hjälm here calls *primary ecclesiology*.[53] For the purpose of interpreting data from ecclesial practices, we need, secondly, *analysis ecclesiology*. I constructed the "preachership concept" and the "communication theory ecclesiology" as such analytical tools. Thirdly, ecclesiologies are also understood as the result of academic studies of ecclesial practices. Maybe this third category can be called *secondary ecclesiology*?

The ecclesiology I disclosed, for example, in my study of the itinerant preachership of Carl Gustaf Hjelm is beyond the radical Congregationalist claims of his denomination. Hjelm's preachership created churches as a "School" (*coetus scholasticus*) with a living magisterium and churches as "Pilgrimage," with pilgrims waiting for the moment when they will be transformed, i.e. experience the bodily resurrection.[54] This result of my studies is secondary to the confessed ecclesiology of the study object, but as the operative ecclesiology it can also be seen as primary.

---

52. For ecclesiology as study object, means and result, see Sven-Erik Brodd in this volume, 12–14.

53. Hjälm in this volume, chapter 3.

54. Fahlgren, *Predikantskap*, chapter 9.

7

The Active and Concrete Church

Operative Ecclesiologies in the Visitation of the Sick in the Middle Ages and Reformation

STINA FALLBERG SUNDMARK

EDITORS' INTRODUCTION

The liturgy and the pius life of the church are to a large extent material and bodily. For Stina Fallberg Sundmark this is an important point of departure for her historical study of the visitation of the sick in medieval Sweden. In her research it becomes crucial to supplement liturgical texts with other data and sources from various genres.

Looking at her reflections gives a clear sense of a both fascinating and frustrating journey of investigation and analysis. Using images and artifacts she adds important dimensions to the liturgical texts. These data makes it possible to include other actors than the priest in the analysis. But the fact that there are relatively few sources available makes the work difficult.

One of the challenges she faces is how to deal with tensions between what is ideal and what is real in the data she analyzes. As with Fahlgren and Ideström, this is an example of how data of material and bodily manifestations of the church are brought into the ecclesiological analysis. It is a study of how ecclesiology and theology are operative or implicit in ecclesial practices. And as with Fahlgren, Fallberg Sundmark works with historical material and her chapter gives an interesting insight of how the pius life of the church was affected by the reformation in Sweden.

Stina Fallberg Sundmark (born 1977) is a senior-lecturer in Church and Mission Studies at Department of Theology, Uppsala University. She has finished a three-year research project on a Theology for Practical Use in Medieval Sweden (2014). Fallberg Sundmark took her doctoral degree at Uppsala University 2008. Her dissertation, *Sjukbesök och dödsberedelse. Sockenbudet i svensk medeltida och reformatorisk tradition* [The Visitation of the Sick in Swedish Medieval and Reformation Traditions] is a study of the liturgy of the visitation of the sick in medieval Sweden. She also has a MA in the History of Arts.

Her studies on liturgical images and artifacts are also documented in "The Rosary and the Wounds of Christ: Devotional Images in Relation to Late Medieval Liturgy and Piety" in *Images and Objects in Ritual Practices in Medieval and Early Modern Northern and Central Europe* (2013).

INTRODUCTION

It is 1485, and in a small parish in what is now Sweden, a woman lies dying in her cottage. She is not alone but surrounded by her family and neighbors. The woman is weak so her son decides to send for the priest. It is wintertime, and it has started to snow. The man takes his horse and rides two kilometers to the priest, who is fortunately at home. He does not need to say much before the priest understands the gravity of the situation and goes to the church to get the receptacle with consecrated hosts and the chrismatory with the oils and chrism. Getting his horse, he starts the journey in company with the woman's son. The snow is falling heavier now, and they have problems finding the way. Will they arrive in time to the deathbed, and will the woman's soul be saved by the reception of the sacraments?

This central part of religious life during the Middle Ages and the Reformation in Swedish parishes is the focus of my doctoral thesis.[1] I will here present the aim, questions, material and method that I used. With this as context and point of departure I will go one step further and analyze how

---

1. *Sjukbesök och dödsberedelse. Sockenbudet i svensk medeltida och reformatorisk tradition* (The Visitation of the Sick in Swedish Medieval and Reformation Traditions), Fallberg Sundmark, *Sjukbesök*.

the Church[2] as community was expressed through the liturgy and piety related to the priest's visitation of the sick and dying people in his parish.

POINT OF DEPARTURE

The basic point of departure of my study was to try to get to know people of the past through the pastoral care. It was this sense of the dramatic described above in the fictive but realistic story that first caught my interest and made me fascinated of that particular agency of the Church, namely the priest's visitation of sick and dying people in their homes.

I decided to study mainly three aspects of the visitation. Firstly, the liturgy of the visitation came to function as a foundation for the whole study. To have stopped there would have been to conduct only a liturgical study, which could have resulted in a study that mostly reproduced what was given in the liturgical sources. Since those sources were written for the priest, a solely liturgical perspective would have led to a study in which the priest was in absolute focus. The priest was no doubt an indispensable actor in the ecclesial practice of the visitation, but there were also other important actors, namely the sick or dying person and also other lay folk such as relatives, friends, and neighbors. With a narrow liturgical perspective, these actors would have been forgotten.[3] To be able to incorporate these people I needed to add another perspective: the actions related to piety.[4]

These two perspectives on the visitation are interesting, but alone they posed the risk of focusing solely on acting and doing. Therefore it became necessary to add a third perspective, the theological, to question the function and meaning of what took place. This aspect deepened the two others since it gave additional focus to the purpose of the acting and doing.[5]

Thus, one of the principal questions posed in the doctoral thesis was how the visitation of the sick or dying was supposed to be performed and what function and meaning it possessed.[6]

---

2. Since the Church was a normative entity during the Middle Ages I have chosen here to use "the Church." For more on this, see Brodd in this volume, 13.

3. Fallberg Sundmark, *Sjukbesök*, 23, 26. For a slightly more inclusive view of liturgy, see Fallberg Sundmark, " Rosary," 53. For the visitation of the sick as ecclesial practice, see Fahlgren in this volume, 99–105.

4. Fallberg Sundmark, *Sjukbesök*, 45–49.

5. Ibid., 22.

6. Ibid.

MATERIAL AND METHOD

To conduct research with a historical focus is sometimes fascinating and sometimes frustrating. Among the fascinating aspects is the effort to ascertain how people at a certain time and location lived, acted and thought. In this quest, history comes to life, so to speak. It can be equally frustrating, though, to have ones research bound to a certain time and geographical location from which many sources have not been preserved.

This combination of fascination and frustration became driving forces during my work with my doctoral thesis. This because I choose to study the pastoral practice of the priest's visitation of the sick and dying during the Middle Ages in the Church province of Uppsala, and in the same geographical area during the Reformation. The sources for these periods and areas are scarce. Earlier research has underlined the alleged impossibility of studying the priest's visitation of the sick or dying in Medieval Sweden. These arguments suggested that the Swedish sources are poor, and that the preserved sources only reflect continental sources and circumstances not applicable on Swedish ground.[7] It is true that there are no preserved extensive eyewitness accounts of a visitation of the sick from this time, which could tell us both how individual people reacted to what they saw and heard and what they thought about it. It is equally true that many of the sources relate to the continent, but this does not mean that it is impossible to carry out such a study. It is more a question of combining sources of different genres. I found it interesting enough to, through the prescriptions, try to draw reasonable conclusions of what actually could or would take place.

For this to be possible, I would need to discuss the issue of the ideal and the real. It is, on the one hand, often impossible to decide whether the different prescriptions of the canonical law really were followed and if they therefore can be seen to reflect the ecclesial practice in Church life, since they can have their point of departure in abuse and perhaps do not always reflect the normal circumstances. On the other hand, the actual circumstances might have led to the actual formulation of the prescriptions. In my study I looked upon the prescriptions concerning the visitation of the sick as some kind of ideal since it is not possible to get an exact knowledge from the sources of how the visitations were actually performed. Components such as the priest on duty, the distance from the church to the home of the sick, the physical and mental status of the sick person, and periods of plague made each performance of the visitation different. Through the extraction of as much relevant information as possible from the sources and by using

---

7. On the question of processions to the sick or dying, see Johansson, *Hemsjömanualet*, 154; Johansson, *Bidrag*, 24, 26; Fallberg Sundmark, *Sjukbesök*, 92, n 2.

this information in a way that is not too generalizing, it was possible to increase the knowledge and understanding of how a visitation of the sick was actually performed.[8]

The question of the possibility of studying the visitation of the sick is also a question of what sources one decides to investigate.[9] In historical studies it is still very common to merely use scriptural sources. Those are of course necessary and can be categorized into many different genres. I used several different textual sources such as liturgical texts in manuals, statutes both from different dioceses and from the church province as whole, and pastoral aids for preaching and teaching.[10]

One certain kind of source material is not, however, related to just one single discipline of research but can be used in many contexts, all depending on the sort of questions posed to the material. For instance, a liturgical phenomenon in historic times does not need to be limited to studies of texts but can also include images. It is however still relatively uncommon to use images as sources in a study of a historical phenomenon, and if images are used it is mostly to confirm and visualize the content of the scriptural sources of the study. During my work, I understood that I would need to investigate more than just texts if I was to be able to come a bit further than a repetition what was said in the ideal prescriptions.

With my previous studies in art history I found it interesting to look for illustrations showing certain moments of the visitation of the sick. What fascinated me was that these images did not merely come to work as sources that, in a visual way, would confirm what was said in the prescriptions in the textual sources. The images were in themselves important sources, and I was able to show how they could give information about which the textual sources were silent.[11] As an example, the *ordo* of the visitation of the sick or dying was written to give instructions for the priest. That means that such a text gives information on how the priest would perform the liturgy but relates hardly anything on how other people would act. Through the images it became for instance possible to study how the relatives could be active at the bedside of the sick or dying.[12]

---

8. Fallberg Sundmark, *Sjukbesök*, 28. For more on this, see Idestrӧm in this volume, chapter 8.

9. For other examples of difficulties in studying ecclesial practices, see Fahlgren in this volume, chapter 6.

10. Fallberg Sundmark, *Sjukbesök*, 29–36.

11. For reflections on the use of images as sources for the visitation of the sick, see Fallberg Sundmark, *Sjukbesök*, 36–37, fig. 8, 10–22; Fallberg Sundmark, "Bilden," especially 9–10.

12. Fallberg Sundmark, *Sjukbesök*, 26.

One basic problem with using images to investigate the visitation of the sick within a Swedish context is that there are just a few images with relevant motifs that have been preserved. In addition, these preserved images were produced abroad or are copies of foreign originals. Therefore these images could not be used as "proofs" of a certain praxis on Swedish ground. On the other hand they could—together with images from Germany, England, and the Netherlands—complement the Swedish scriptural sources.[13]

Together, the texts and the images led me to studies of equipment and vessels used in the visitation of the sick in different periods. Concerning the medieval period, these artifacts helped me to approach the medieval liturgy and pious life as something that was not only about abstract theology but was also something very much material and bodily. The materiality of the Christian life, expressed through both the actions of all agents involved and all the equipment and vessels, was something that opened my eyes to the theology of the visitation of the sick and vice versa.[14] To combine texts and material expressions are very rare in studies of medieval liturgy, piety, and theology, and I realized that I was on track of something fairly new.

ECCLESIOLOGIES OPERATIVE IN THE VISITATION OF THE SICK

In the emergent Sweden, the Reformation ideas were presented during the 1520s, but the changes were realized very slowly and in varying degrees in different parts of the country. The adoption of these new ideas and liturgy could depend on the attitudes of the priest as well as those of the parishioners. In some parishes, the Reformation might have taken root early while in others the medieval liturgy and theology could remain for several decades during the sixteenth century. Therefore I will talk about the medieval tradition and the Reformation tradition. The question is how did the implementation of Reformation ideas affect the liturgy and piety related to the visitation of the sick. Was there both continuity and discontinuity, and did that mean any changes in the way the Church was expressed in doctrine as well as in ecclesial practice?[15]

In the following I will show how I have continued the study of the visitation of the sick since the publication of my doctoral thesis.[16] Through focusing

---

13. Ibid., 36–37; Fallberg Sundmark, "Bilden."
14. Fallberg Sundmark, *Sjukbesök*, 38, 69–83, fig. 1–7, 9.
15. To keep doctrine and ecclesial practice as a unit, see also Brodd in this volume, 12–14.
16. For a developing article including the genre of Ars moriendi, see also Fallberg Sundmark, "Om konsten."

on certain moments in the liturgy of the visitation of the sick, I will analyze in what ways the active and concrete Church manifested itself as a community.

Expressions of the Church as Community

The Church during the Middle Ages would not let a sick or dying person suffer or die alone; however, the relatives had to send for the priest, and the priest was obliged to respond and make a visit.[17] Even though it is not expressed in the sources, it could be stated that in that situation the Church, through the laity as well as the priest, played the role of caring mother towards her suffering children.[18] Also the Reformation sources emphasize the relationships of mutual support and caring in the parish when a person was sick or dying.[19]

One important conclusion of the thesis is that it was not only important what was performed in the sickroom but it was also important what happened on the way. The priest could make his way to the sick or dying in the form of a procession. He could walk on his own, but the synodal and provincial statutes prescribe that an assistant would precede him. These sources also speak of a crowd of people coming after the priest. The aim of such a procession was to carry the Host, believed to be the body of Christ, in a solemn way. As the priest walked, his assistant would ring a small hand bell to draw people's attention to the sacramentally present Christ in the receptacle carried by the priest. People would then, according to the prescriptions, physically respond to the ringing of the bell through kneeling, folding of hands, bowing of heads, and beating of chests. The procession with the sacramentally present Christ was carried through the parish and passed people's homes and their work in the fields or in the woods. Because of the sacramentally present Christ, the way to the sick person's house was not merely a question of transport from one point to another but a solemn service.[20]

The church building, where the procession started, was consecrated by the bishop. The building was aimed to facilitate the encounter between God and humans, which was perhaps most obvious when Christ became sacramentally present in every Mass. When the Host was carried through the parish, the walls of that church building were, metaphorically speaking, smashed and the sacred entered into people's everyday area. One could argue that, unlike in

---

17. Fallberg Sundmark, *Sjukbesök*, 55–68.

18. On Mary as mother of all Christians, see Härdelin, *Världen*, 407, 413–14, 425–26, 428. For an overview over how medieval theologians handle the title *mater ecclesiae*, see Dittrich, *Mater*, 76–277.

19. Fallberg Sundmark, *Sjukbesök*, 57–58, 62.

20. Ibid., 91–126.

the modern West, during the Middle Ages no absolute division was made between the sacred and the profane. This meant that also the world outside the church building was in some sense seen as sacred, as a part of God's creation. But since the church building was consecrated, that building was probably seen as more holy than the fields and woods through which the procession passed. In this context the Church was expressed as visible and concrete in different ways outside the church building: as institution, represented by the priest, and as the people of God, represented by the parishioners.

Figure 5. **A procession with priest, assistants and attending parishioners on their way from the church to the sick. Part of altarscreen, Basilica di S. Lorenzo Maggiore, Milano, fifteenth century.**

People were exhorted to gather in the procession. Those who participated showed that the Church was represented not only by the priest and his assistant but also by ordinary people. In the procession people would show reverence towards the sacramentally present Christ. But they would also likely respond to the seven penitential psalms and the litany of saints that the priest would recite. Through that and through their own individual prayers they could pray for the recovering of the sick or for the soul of the dying person. Thus, the medieval society was a caring community that showed solidarity between people.[21]

The Middle Ages was a period of concretion. So the medieval Church was not just an abstract idea or a piece of theology; her different expressions of liturgy and piety were characterized by being visual and concrete, bodily and materialized. The church room was so to say scene for the liturgy performed, and mural paintings, sculpture, liturgical vessels and textiles all cooperated with the liturgy performed and people's private meditation. Images and liturgical vessels could also express certain theological ideas and much of the theology was converted into concrete matter. Behind all bodily expressions there was always a system of abstract thoughts and theology. Not the least for ordinary people with no education, theological or otherwise, the tangible and corporeal became important ways to try to grasp the holy.[22]

There were many components in the procession to the sick which focused on the body and the senses. The different actors that formed the procession expressed in a visual way the community of the Church mentioned above. The Church visualized through the procession was also audible through the ringing, recitation, and praying. The people around would respond to what they saw and heard through gestures and bodily expressions. It was the body of Christ in itself which motivated and conjured up this corporeal expression of the Church, and the sacramental procession emphasized how the Church was one body with many different members.[23]

None of the sources of the Reformation tradition contain any prescriptions concerning the carrying-through of the journey. In spite of that, it is

---

21. Fallberg Sundmark, *Sjukbesök*, 92, 103, 106–7, 110–22. For the expression "communion of solidarity," see Piltz, "Communicantes," 29–31, 42–43. On the procession to the sick as an expression of solidarity from the whole fellowship in the parish to the sick person, see Avril, "Pastorale," 106. On the presence of the holy outside the church building in connection with a procession with the sacrament, see Felbecker, *Prozession*, 440–43. For the relevance of "Church as community" in a discussion on ecclesiology, see Blückert, *Church as Nation*, 122–23.

22. On concrete and bodily expression in the Church, see Marks, *Image*; Walker Bynum, *Christian*.

23. On the Church as the body of Christ, see Chodorow, *Christian*, 65–8; Flanagin, "Extra," 340–41. On the body of Christ as an expression for the unity of the Church, see Congar, *L'ecclésiologie*, 69–71, 76–77, 81–90; Chodorow, *Christian*, 83–85, 93. The central idea in medieval theology of a strong unity between the body of Christ—the Church—and the body of Christ in the Eucharist, is thoroughly handled by de Lubac, *Corpus*, especially 19–43, 89–137. See also Tavard, "Church"; Prusak, *Church*, 196–97.

possible to draw certain conclusions. In the Reformation tradition the priest could bring an already consecrated Host. If he did so, he might have carried and handled the Host according to medieval praxis, which entails placing it in a ciborium or pyx and treating it with great reverence. If the priest on the contrary consecrated at the sickbed, he brought unconsecrated bread and wine. If this was the case, he would also carry a smaller communion set.[24]

Proponents of the Reformation held that there would be no use of the consecrated elements outside the Eucharist, which means uses of the Host and wine that did not relate to the actual communion. The result was that the priest never would consecrate more wafers than the number that would be needed during Holy Communion. All consecrated wafers had to be consumed and nothing could be reserved for communion at the sickbed, since no adoration outside the Eucharistic use was allowed.[25] As a result the priest carried unconsecrated bread and wine to the sick. Then there was no real presence of Christ to adore and as a consequence, no reason to walk in a procession. In addition there was no reason for the people to show expressions of piety when the priest passed on his way to the sick.[26]

The Anglican *Book of Common Prayer* from 1552 prescribes that the priest would prevent all kinds of reverence of the bread and wine when it was brought to the sick for consecration.[27] This shows that people acted as they and their ancestors always had done when the priest was on his way to a sick person. They worshipped and showed reverence, no matter if Christ was sacramentally present or not. It was simply a part of their inherited way of acting and was a part of their world of belief.[28]

When the priest went with unconsecrated bread and wine and consecrated them at the sickbed, it had strong consequences for the laity's piety. Earlier in history, Christ had been present on the roads in their own parish, passed their everyday milieu and as such, the people had been able to encounter the holiness.[29] A procession expressed fellowship as the people moved in the same direction, with the same purpose.[30] Now there was no sacramental presence to revere or worship during the journey. This meant that people were left without the opportunity of expressing this togetherness and the possibility

---

24. Fallberg Sundmark, *Sjukbesök*, 98.
25. On adoration within the use of Mass, see Ahlberg, *Laurentius*, 214–15. Fallberg Sundmark, *Sjukbesök*, 123–24.
26. Fallberg Sundmark, *Sjukbesök*, 124.
27. Duffy, *Stripping*, 474.
28. Fallberg Sundmark, *Sjukbesök*, 124.
29. Ibid., 124–25.
30. Flanigan, "The moving subject," 39.

of adoration in their own milieu, which reasonably must have meant that a part of their previous everyday piety was limited in a radical way. A sense of emptiness may have pervaded the parish, and the people may have been inactive. This is an example of how the Reformation tradition changed liturgy and piety and marked clear break with medieval tradition.[31]

With those changes, earlier expressions for the Church as a concrete and visual community were lost. In that sense the Church became less vocal and not as visual as before, and the way to the sick and dying was no longer seen as a solemn service but merely a way of transport.

Expressions of the Active and Concrete Church

In the Middle Ages, the Church was clearly expressed at the sickbed. One can just imagine the transformation that took place in a poor and rather dark cottage with a low ceiling, no bright colors, and few or no pictures at all. The priest, perhaps together with his assistant and friends and neighbors, entered the house of the sick or dying person wearing the white and perhaps colored vestments and holding a golden container of the Host. There would have been one or more lights shining, a bell ringing, and the sound of the solemn liturgy being recited. Even if the Middle Ages did not draw an absolute line between the holy and non-holy, one could say that the ritual and its elements made the ordinary room and home holy, at least as long as Christ was sacramentally present there. Through all this the Church became present, visible, and concrete in the everyday setting.

The sacraments were at center of the liturgy in the sickroom. Through the three sacraments of penance, communion, and extreme unction the person was made ready to die and prepared for salvation. It is clear that salvation was only accessible through the Church—*extra ecclesiam nulla salus*.[32]

The sacraments all spoke to the senses in various ways. The penance aimed at cleaning the sick person from sin to prevent him or her from the risk of damnation at the moment of death. The penance was also a prerequisite to receive the communion and unction.[33] When the sick had expressed remorse and confessed, the priest placed, according to images, his hand on the head of that person and gave the absolution.[34]

---

31. For Reformation changes for the laity in England, which in various ways probably might be comparable to Swedish circumstances, see Scarisbrick, *Reformation*, 163. Fallberg Sundmark, *Sjukbesök*, 125.

32. See e.g. Flanagin, *Extra*, 335–37.

33. Fallberg Sundmark, *Sjukbesök*, 153–64.

34. Ibid., 151.

The communion also aimed at cleansing from sin. In addition it was thought to bring eternal life. The communion was called *viaticum*, which means that it was seen as food on the road to Heaven. Another side of this was that the communion was seen as protection against the devil.[35]

Much of what happened in the liturgy of communion in the sickroom had clear relations to the liturgy of Mass. During the Middle Ages, with an increasing respect and reverence towards the sacrament of the altar, an idea emerged that the devotional grace of the consecrated elements could function as a substitute for the concrete communion. The result was that the congregation normally did not receive the Host more often than at Easter. Instead the people beheld the sacramentally present Christ when the priest lifted up the Host and the chalice at the elevation. Then people were thought to receive spiritual communion.[36] Thereby the priest's communion was seen as a substitute for the congregation.

Figure 6. **The priest gives communion to the sick. Woodcut from *Ars moriendi* printed by Konrad Kachelofen, Leizig 1493.**

---

35. Ibid., 187.

36. For spiritual communion, see Duffy *Stripping*, 95–102; Fallberg Sundmark, *Sjukbesök*, 175.

The ideal was that the sick person would receive a concrete communion, which means being able to consume a Host. When the sick person was in a weak state and could not receive concrete communion, he or she was given spiritual communion when the priest showed a Host. At the same time, the others in the room also received spiritual communion, which was an expression of togetherness in the Church. At the elevation during Mass, people would kneel, fold their hands, and bow or behold the sacramentally present Christ. Since Christ was present in the same way in the sickroom, we have to believe that people present could act in the same way as in church.[37] Irrespective of setting and context the parishioners would show reverence to the sacramentally present Christ through different kinds of outer bodily expressions.

In the medieval tradition the anointing of the sick, or the extreme unction, was seen as giving forgiveness for sins committed through the five senses. It was also thought to bring salvation, and health for the body as well as for the soul. In addition, it gave protection against evil spirits.[38] At the anointing, the sick person experienced the tactile contact when the priest applied oil on the skin.

Figure 7. **The priest anoints the feet of the sick. Woodcut from** *L'art de bien vivre et de bien mourir,* **Paris 1492.**

---

37. Fallberg Sundmark, *Sjukbesök*, 185.
38. Ibid., 220–23.

What we have seen here is the Church directed towards the material, the bodily, and the senses. There are no contradictions between the holy and the material, but the holy is rather experienced and reached with the body and the material as instruments. Also, in the sickroom the community of the Church came to clear expression as the people were gathered and participated actively through liturgy and piety.

According to the prescriptions in Reformation tradition, the visitation of the sick included a moment of confession. Also in this tradition confession had the function of purifying and preparing for the other sacraments. Only someone who was free from sin through genuine remorse, confession, and absolution was allowed to take communion and receive unction.[39]

After confession and absolution, the communion of the sick would follow. This would be prepared by putting a cloth, candles, the chalice, and paten on a table, thereby creating an altar in the house. The actual act of communion was preceded by the priest's exhortation and readings from the Holy Scripture. The verbal expressions and explanations of the texts were central. The study shows that it seems as though the priest, at least in an early phase of the Reformation tradition, could choose between bringing a consecrated Host and consecrating it by the sickbed. When the latter alternative was chosen, the priest would give the sick person both consecrated bread and wine. According to that tradition, the relatives were also given the opportunity to receive communion.[40] This must be interpreted as a strong image for the community of the concrete Church when everyone—both sick and healthy—was included in the act of Eucharistic communion.

In the Reformation tradition, the anointing was not to prepare someone for death but to bring that person back to health. According to the early Reformation tradition, extreme unction was voluntary and not necessary. Later on it was thought that the sacrament ought to be abolished since Christ did not institute it. However, anointing was retained in the earliest rules governing the visitation of the sick, but it was voluntary. Not to be allowed to receive extreme unction must have been seen as a major break with previous tradition.[41]

CONTINUITY OR CHANGE?

During the revisitation of my doctoral thesis, I experienced even more strongly than earlier that at the visitation of the sick both the medieval Church and the Church of the Reformation were clearly expressed as

---

39. Ibid., 144–47, 154, 163–64.
40. Ibid., 173, 190–98.
41. Ibid., 207, 223–29.

community, albeit in different ways and moments according to the different traditions. Through the procession and the sacramental liturgy in the sickroom, the sick and dying—and in some ways also the people attending—experienced the concrete, active, and bodily Church through the senses of sight, hearing, taste, and feeling, and they could respond to the present holiness in an active, concrete, and physical way through gestures and body language. This was mostly the case during the Middle Ages, while the Church of the Reformation was more moderate regarding those kinds of expressions and more oriented towards the Word.

Medieval liturgy and piety focused on the senses, for the laity's part not least of all on the sight. As we have seen, people's ability of viewing the sacramentally present Christ in the consecrated Eucharistic elements—especially the Host—was in focus at Mass, during the procession to the sick, and at the communion by the sickbed. The priest had the role of mediating the holy. Through the consecration and the following elevation at Mass or the showing of the Host at communion of the sick, the priest presented the holy to the congregation in a visual, concrete, and material way, and people responded to what they saw.

If medieval liturgy and piety had the visual and tangible, the senses and the heart, in focus, the Reformation tradition centered on the audible and the intellectual. We have seen how the priest at the visitation of the sick would give exhortations and consolations and read biblical texts to the sick person and others in the sickroom. Here, the priest became in some sense a teacher and the people his pupils. As pupils, the role of the people was mainly to listen. This meant a big change from the medieval tradition where people were more physically active.

The Church of the Reformation remained concrete, but it was not visual in the same way in parish life without a procession to the sick as in the earlier tradition, and it did not manifest the bodily, and material expressions in relation to the holy. The sense of community did not become manifest on the way to the sick but was on the other hand clearly expressed when everybody attending at the sickbed received consecrated bread and wine with the sick or dying at communion.

With the liturgy and piety of the priest's visitation of the sick as a case, it has become clear that the Church of the medieval tradition remained in some respects unchanged, while in others it was radically altered during the Reformation.

8

Implicit Ecclesiology and Local Church Identity

Dealing with Dilemmas of Empirical Ecclesiology

JONAS IDESTRÖM

EDITORS' INTRODUCTION

In a network of scholars in Ecclesiology and Ethnography researchers attempt to address the gap between empirical and theological analysis of the church. The first volume in a series of cross-disciplinary studies that has come out of this work is *Perspectives on Ecclesiology and Ethnography* (2012). The author of the following chapter, Jonas Ideström, participates in this network. He reflects here on his dissertation, which is an empirical study of local church ecclesiology with a wide range of theories from Sociology and Organization Theory.

As in Sune Fahlgren's chapter, ecclesial practices are used as a theoretical concept. But here it is one of several other components in a theoretical model. The model is developed in order to make a thoroughly holistic approach in the study of a local church possible and disclose so-called implicit ecclesiology. An ongoing discussion among the scholars of Ecclesiology in Uppsala revolves around the differences and similarities between "implicit" and "operative" ecclesiology (used in the foregoing chapter by Fallberg Sundmark; cf. Brodd in this volume, 13–14).

Above all, inspiration for Ideström's development of his research approach comes from Sven-Erik Brodd, Charles Taylor, and Niklas Luhman.

In comparison with the other two chapters in Part Two, the study here is on the present-day church. This creates certain methodological and theoretical dilemmas. The solution Ideström finds on these dilemmas is not a formula but a way of doing research that is characterized by virtues that enable conversation, relation, and hermeneutical processes. This highlights indirectly the questions on what kind of practice ecclesiological studies is, and what virtues are needed for the scholars in this discipline.

Jonas Ideström (born 1968). Since 2012, he has worked at the Research Unit at the Church of Sweden on a project concerning parishes in rural areas. The study is presented in *Spåren i snön* [Tracks in the Snow], 2015. His dissertation, *Lokal kyrklig identitet* [Local Church Identity], is a field study on the implicit ecclesiology in a suburban parish in Stockholm.

Ideström received his doctoral degree from University of Uppsala in 2009. Between 2010–2012, he lectured in Ecclesiology at the University. He is also a minister in Church of Sweden. One of his recent publications is the article "What is So Great of Being Different: A Folk Church Response to Exceptionalism" in *Between Eucharist and the State* (2014).

INTRODUCTION

"What did you find?" That is a question I tend to get when I tell people about a research project I have conducted. I tend to hesitate in responding. A reason for my hesitation is that behind the question I often sense a mechanistic view on research that I find problematic: a detached and objective researcher who asks a distinct question at one end, uses appropriate methods and theories, and then comes out with an answer and new findings at the other end. Such a view misses fundamental dimensions of the actual research processes and the character of new knowledge they add. This goes for all forms of science, as sociologist Bruno Latour has shown with his studies of laboratories where scientific results are created. Results and findings in academic research are created through complex processes and networks of relations between people, theories, methods, practices, and artifacts.¹ Research presupposes ethics, morals, loyalty, curiosity, faith, and engagement. Naturally this also goes for various forms of ecclesiology.

A clear trend in contemporary ecclesiology is a turn to the empirical. Observations and material from the concrete life of the church are brought into the very heart of ecclesiological reflection and reasoning. One expression of this trend is a growing interest in qualitative methods from disciplines such as ethnography and anthropology.² This adds new components and actors to the relational networks of ecclesiological research, and the use of such methods are now at a point where it is possible to see patterns and raise fundamental ecclesiological questions in relation to how these patterns have developed. A cluster of questions that keep reoccurring in the ongoing conversations on empirical ecclesiology has to do with how theology and social theory are defined and related to one another as well as with the role doctrinal and normative aspects in ecclesiology are to play in empirical ecclesiology.³ I find it fruitful to treat these clusters of questions as dilemmas rather than questions that can be answered definitively. The overall argument of this article stresses the need for studies in empirical ecclesiology to be shaped by an ongoing reflection concerning these dilemmas in relation to theory, method, and the realities of the field. As I will argue towards the end of the chapter, this is due both to the contingency and uniqueness of each ecclesial phenomenon and situation and to a Trinitarian understanding of reality.

My contribution in relation to the dilemmas is to share reflections based on experiences from a research project I conducted in a suburban parish within the Church of Sweden, a project that resulted in my dissertation.⁴ I give a thick description of my work in the ecclesiological "laboratory"—or "trenches"—dealing with issues of local church identity. I focus on the theoretical dimensions of the research process, and I share and reflect upon the decisive steps of developing an analytical model to be used in the analysis of material from the field studies. Based on these experiences, I argue for an approach to empirical ecclesiology where the research process is shaped by an ongoing conversation between theology and social theory in relation to

---

1. Latour, "Thou shall not," 35–37; Latour, *Science*, 3.

2. For a brief charting of the ethnographic turn in theology and ecclesiology see Phillips, "Charting." For an overview and analysis of recent concrete approaches to ecclesiology, see Hawksley, *What is*; See also Hawksley, "Metaphor."

3. I use empirical ecclesiology as an umbrella term to collect various forms of ecclesiological research based on empirical material. The focus in my research has been on material generated by ethnographic methods.

4. Ideström, *Lokal kyrklig*.

the empirical realities of the field. This I will define as an *expressive* character of empirical ecclesiology.

I begin with a short description of the ecclesial context of the local church in Flemingsberg as a way of contextualizing the questions that guided the research project. In the following paragraphs, I describe and reflect upon the overall approach and the steps I took in developing the analytical model. A central concept in the story I am telling is *implicit ecclesiology*. As the argument will show, the concept is used as a theoretical frame for the various theoretical components in the analytical model. Based on the descriptions, I reflect upon the expressive character of empirical ecclesiology in relation to work by Geir Afdal and Paul Fiddes.

POINT OF DEPARTURE—CHURCH OF SWEDEN IN FLEMINGSBERG AND THE ECCLESIOLOGICAL QUESTIONS

Every research process starts in the middle of things—*in medias res*—both in relation to where the researcher is and what and where the study object is. In my project I set out to study the concrete or practical identity of a parish within the Evangelical-Lutheran Church of Sweden in a suburb to Stockholm.

Who is the church? What is the church? What role does the church play in relation to other social agents in the area? What is its mission? These were some of the questions that my reflections raised. The need for theological reflection in relation to these questions was generated by a sense that something needed to be addressed and transformed.[5] The identity and self-understanding of the Church of Sweden was challenged by the context of the suburb. In order to give some background to the research questions and my sense of need for reflection and transformation I begin by giving a short introduction to the field.

The Field

It takes twenty minutes to travel from Stockholm's Central station to Flemingsberg. The train tracks divide the suburb into two more or less separated

---

5. American theologian Mary McClintock Fulkerson points to the importance of raising the question why theological reflection is necessary at all. Her answer is that "[l]ike a wound, theological thinking is generated by a sometimes inchoate sense that something must be addressed. Such a process itself is defined by an a priori logic of transformation. More precisely, transformation is inherent in the image of the wound, for it invokes a sense of something wrong—of a fracture in things that should be joined or whole. The very sense of harm implies an impulse toward remedy—a kind of longing for it to be otherwise." See McClintock Fulkerson, *Places*, 13–14.

parts. The residential area that most people associate with Flemingsberg is situated on the western side a five-minute walk from the train station. The large apartment buildings were built during the 1960s and 1970s when millions of similar apartments were built in urban suburbs in Sweden. The neighborhood shares several of the characteristics of other similar areas in Sweden: an ethnically and religiously diverse population, fairly high rates of unemployment, and comparably low rates of membership in the Church of Sweden. Representatives for local government, companies, and organizations are struggling to change what they see as an unfairly negative and stigmatic image of Flemingsberg. In one end of the neighborhoods is the parish church building, which sits next to a small shopping mall. They were both designed by the same architect and built during the 1970s—at the same time as the apartment buildings.

Looking towards the south from the church entrance the western side of the suburb is divided once more, this time by a road. On the opposite side there are several large institutions including a university hospital and a college. There are no residential areas. The separation between these two parts is clearly visible when one follows the flow of people coming and leaving with the local trains from the station. A majority of the people coming to Flemingsberg takes the southern exit that leads them to the college and the hospital while a majority of the people living in the area where the church is take the train away from Flemingsberg. This division into separated areas is a fact that shapes Flemingsberg as well as the work and self-reflection of parish representatives.

The self-understanding of the Church of Sweden has to a large extend been shaped by close ties between church and state and the church and other central institutions in Swedish society.[6] In many places the church literary was, or is, in the center of the village or the city. Such ecclesial self-understandings are in many ways challenged in suburban contexts where the Church of Sweden is not at the center of the social life.[7] This was one main reason for me to locate my study where I did. As Swedish theologian Ola Sigurdson has frased it, the renegotiation of the informal contract between church and society has forced the Church of Sweden to rediscover its own body and reimagine its own identity.[8] Against this background the parish of Flemingsberg was an interesting object for a study on ecclesial identity in the contemporary life of the Church of Sweden.

---

6. For a short introduction in English to the modern history of Church of Sweden, see Ryman, *Church of Sweden*.

7. Ideström, *In Dialogue*, 75–77.

8. Sigurdson, *Return*, 125.

ECCLESIOLOGY AND IDENTITY—FRAMING THE RESEARCH QUESTIONS

How then could the concrete and practical identity, the embodiment of the local church, be analyzed and studied from an ecclesiological perspective and in relation to the wider context of the suburb? That was the theoretical and methodological question with which I was faced. *Ecclesiology* and *identity* were the central concepts around which my initial reflections evolved. My way of framing the research question was shaped by an understanding of ecclesiology that had been developed at the ecclesiology seminar at the University of Uppsala where the concept *operative ecclesiology* had been used for some time.[9] In focus were questions concerning which ecclesiology or ecclesiologies were embedded and operative in a various contexts and material. Using the concept made it possible to study understandings of church that were operative in certain expressions such as liturgy or music. Ecclesiology was understood and conducted not only as a locus within dogmatic theology but also as an approach for studying church as it comes to expression in various forms.[10]

My understanding of identity, on the other hand, was to a large extent influenced by the work of Canadian philosopher Charles Taylor who emphasized the narrative and moral dimensions of identity.[11] According to Taylor, human identity is shaped by a movement through time, but also by a quest, a movement towards a *telos*. From sociologists studying identity I had also adopted an understanding of the phenomenon of human identity as a configuration with a number of constituent parts such as experiences, self-understandings and roles. Identity was treated as a result of interactions between various parts and processes.[12] These understandings worked as cornerstones for my reflections on how to study the identity of a local church, though I was well aware of the fact that these theories primarily were concerned with the identities of persons and not collective entities.

Parallel to these theoretical reflections I was also methodologically influenced by the field of ethnography. Initially I struggled with the challenge of the broad character of the research questions. Standing in the middle of

---

9. See Brodd, "Themes," 124–25.

10. I use church without the definite article to make a distinction between a more dogmatically marked view of the study object (the church) and a broader and less defined understanding of ecclesial expressions (church). See Brodd in this volume, chapter 1.

11. It was primarily two of Charles Taylor's works that I had worked with: *Sources of the Self: the Making of Modern Identity* (1989) and *The Ethics of Authenticity* (1991).

12. See Stier, *Dimensions*.

things, not really knowing where to begin and where to end, I soon realized that, like a juggler, I had to keep several things in the air at the same time and to be patient before narrowing things down. How would I at an initial stage know what to leave out and what to focus on in relation to my questions? Based on what premises would I make such decisions? At this point I was faced with dilemmas, presented above, that demanded reflections and decisions. How was I to relate ecclesiology and identity to one another and based on which normative claims would I make my decisions and choices? I could not even formulate a relevant and useful research question without dealing with the dilemmas.

When reflecting upon my overall approach and guiding research question I realized that my choices were shaped by stronger or weaker normative claims from various fields in social theory and theology. There were fundamental ecclesiological presuppositions guiding me—e.g. that the Word of God and the sacraments of the Eucharist and Baptism are constitutive of the church—as well as fundamental theories on the "social" or the "collective" and how the various theories and fields relate or ought to relate to one another.

The Overall Approach

Eventually I defined my overall approach as *theologically reflective* and *abductive*. The framework of the study was *theological* in the sense that it concerned questions in relation to the divine revelation in Jesus from Nazareth and the role and identity of the church in relation to it. It is important to stress that I did not attend to "theology" and "social theory" as two distinct and qualitatively different phenomena. Rather the object of my study, the local church and its social embodiment, made me aware of the social dimensions of theology as well as the theological dimensions of social theory. Therefore I was forced into an ongoing hermeneutic process where I had to be aware of the fact that choices in the field of theology had consequences for what components and theories from the fields of social science I could use, and the other way around. Or in other words: I could not define church in isolation from my definitions of the field.

Reflectivity is an important aspect of ethnographic research and method, and it became an important part of my overall approach.[13] It had to do with both an ongoing reflection in relation to the dilemmas and with my

---

13. According to Scharen and Vigens "[r]eflexivity means that the researcher is willing to look honestly at one's self-location, biases, etc. Critical self-reflection involves taking a hard look at one's own assumptions." See Scharen and Vigen, "Ethnography," 19.

role as researcher in the process. The ecclesiological framing of the research questions raised questions in relation to the role of theory when creating, collecting, and interpreting the material from the field. Those questions also touched on the dilemmas. The ethnographic influence concerning method suggested an inductive method where theory was generated out of the material, as in different versions of grounded theory. But I did not enter the field, or conduct the field studies, without ecclesiological conceptions that shaped the study and the process of interpretation. Doctrines and theological claims on the nature of the church were not only components in the material I collected and created but also part of my overall approach. Therefore this was not a plain inductive approach. Neither was it deductive. Rather it was a dialectic process where theory shaped the empirical material at the same time as the growing corpus of material forced me to work on the theoretical components that I used. This is what I describe as *abductive*.[14]

Implicit Ecclesiology

As I developed a broader and more nuanced understanding of theories on human identity I also related this understanding to the ecclesiological framework I was using. At this stage I started questioning the relevance of using the concept of *operative ecclesiology* in my project.

Based on how the concept was used in our seminar I concluded that the purpose was to bring to the surface ecclesial self-understandings that were operative in forming and shaping embodiments and perceptions of church. In relation to the understanding of human identity as a configuration of several separate components I realized that the self-understanding of a subject, individual or collective, was just one of several components that, in relation to one another, formed a specific identity. If I wanted to understand and give a useful description of the identity of the local church in Flemingsberg it would not be enough to focus on the local church's self-understanding.

Therefore I needed a theological concept that was more holistic so that it would be possible to relate the self-understanding of the local church to other aspects and components. This is when I started working with the concept of *implicit ecclesiology*. Talking about something being implicit indicates that it is not accessible in an immediate way. Rather some act of interpretation is needed to make the implicit explicit and thereby accessible. In taking what amounted to a decisive step for the project, I put identity and ecclesiological theories on speaking terms with one another. The identity theories helped me see and articulate an aspect of an ecclesiological concept

---

14. Alvesson and Sköldeberg, *Tolkning*, 43.

that to my knowledge had not been spelled out earlier.[15] But my interest was not primarily to try to bring to the surface some hidden meaning. Rather, the concept of implicit ecclesiology made it possible to relate a variety of ecclesial expressions to one another and through such an act contribute to new views and angles on perceptions of the identity of the church.

In relation to the questions of embodiment and concrete identity of the local church in Flemingsberg it was possible to use the idea of implicit ecclesiology as a theoretical frame in which theories and interpretative tools on identity could be used and operationalized. Eventually I defined the concept implicit ecclesiology as an understanding of what it is to be church, an understanding that is illuminated by an act of interpretation and analysis on various manifestations of the concrete church. In that way the concept of implicit ecclesiology could contribute to a holistic approach.

---

15. Martin Percy uses the concept *implicit theology* and gives a brief etymological history of the word implicit: "'Implicit' is derived from the Latin implicitus, meaning to implicate—a term, in turn, that suggests involvement, interweaving, and entanglement. The Latin word implicitus expresses this, with plicare conveying the notion of 'folding'—in the sense of mixing and combining, rather as one might expect to 'fold' an ingredient into a recipe. Thus, 'implicit' means the meaningful folding together and close connecting of a variety of strands. Correspondingly, 'explicit' is the un-folding, un-ravelling of explaining of the miscible." See Percy, *Shaping*, 1-2. Percy uses the concept with the purpose of "[o]n the one hand [. . .] examining the basic-but-nascent theological habits (e.g., language, culture, worship, practice, etc)" and on the other "guessing at the hidden meanings in structures and practices that on the surface appear to be benign and innocent," (p. 12). He views implicit theology as something that can guide and direct ecclesiology in ways that are deeper than the formal propositions of explicit theology.

According to Percy "[i]mplicit theology pays attention to the normally neglected and often overlooked dimensions of ecclesial life that are constitutive for belief and practice. [. . .] The emerging task for implicit theology is not to distinguish between God and the world, but rather realize that in a new kind of 'natural theology,' even apparently innocuous and innocent beliefs and practices are in fact 'texts' that demand interpretation. This is because the shape of the church is partly brought about by the subliminal as much as by the liminal; and by the implicit as much as by the explicit;" Percy, *Shaping*, 171–72. Both examining theological habits and making hidden meanings accessible supposes some kind of theoretical framing. To make the implicit theology explicit one has to interpret a complex material and such an interpretation is not possible without definitions of what e.g. habits and culture are, definitions that will shape the acts and results of interpretation. In this general sense of framing the work of interpreting material from a field with the concept of *implicit*, my use of the concept is similar to Percy's. But there are important differences. First of all, I talk of implicit *ecclesiology* and not implicit *theology*, and secondly, I do not intend to bring to the surface some hidden meaning.

IN SEARCH FOR USEFUL COMPONENTS

Among all the various voices that shaped the process of working out a useful theoretical model, there were two that I more frequently was in conversation with than others. Charles Taylor's voice, as already mentioned, was one.[16] The other was that of Swedish theologian Sven-Erik Brodd and the work he had done on sacramental ecclesiological models.[17] The character of these voices was important in regard to how they could work as creative partners in the conversation. Taylor's emphasis on listening to and making sense of a subject's self-understanding and the fundamental incarnational aspects of Brodd's ecclesiological model were key on integrating the two.

Church as Social Body

The choice to view *identity* as a configuration of different aspects and components worked well, both in relation to Taylor's work on human identity and Brodd's use of ecclesiological models. Once in conversation with these two voices I became more hands-on in in my approach to collecting, creating, and interpreting the empirical material. This step once again brought questions concerning the dilemmas in to the very core of my reflections. Choices of tools had to be made in relation both to certain doctrinal considerations and to fields of social theory.

At this point I made a choice to use the body of Christ analogy from Paul as a cornerstone for my further reflections. This was done in conversation with Brodd's sacramental eccesiological model. The concept of social body became an important integrative concept. I saw it as clearly anchored in scripture with concepts such as Body of Christ, a temple of living stones and a holy priesthood, but it was also a concept that could work in dialogue with less biblical theories and concepts.

My definition of implicit ecclesiology made it possible to see the theoretical tools as being operationalized within an ecclesiologically framed model. The important question was which theories to use. What was useful for my purposes? How could I find useful tools to describe and analyze the identity of the social body of the local church in Flemingsberg? This is when I took an important step and chose to view the social body as an

---

16. In the end Taylor was not that visible in the dissertation since the reflective process required me use theological and ecclesiological works on identity. They clearly shared the basic understanding of the narrative and moral dimensions of identity that Taylor argued for, and by using them I could present a basic understanding of the identity of the church where theological and social theoretical dimensions were not separated but integrated into a whole.

17. Brodd, *Diakonatet*.

organization. I turned to the field of organization studies to find concepts and tools that could help me study the embodiments of the local church and its identity.

An Identity In-via

As I took this step forward I was now faced with new questions that needed to be answered. What theories of organizational identity was I to adopt? The field of organizational theory and studies is broad, and the process of choosing was complex. Parallel to my dive into that field I continued reflecting on ecclesial identity in relation to Brodd's sacramental ecclesiology based on the body of Christ analogy. According the Brodd the analogy points to the fact that the collective exists prior to the individual who is integrated into an organic communion with Christ himself. The church is, in that sense, understood as a corporative person.

Brodd's argument presupposed an understanding of the incarnation as a fundamental pattern for God's dealings with creation.[18] As in Christ, divine and human, material and spiritual, are held together as a whole without being mixed. In the same way, what Christ and the church *are* cannot be separated from what they *do*. Brodd used the concept of structure as a way of describing how separate parts and persons were integrated into a whole— a corporative person.[19] He then added a distinction between structure and organization where the latter is understood as the function or expression of the former. Structures that can be related to Christ himself (eg. Baptism, Eucharist, or Ministry) are defined as sacramental structures, while others are defined as non-sacramental.[20]

Inspired by other voices from various fields I saw aspects in Brodd's model that were problematic. One had to do with the idea of a singular integrating structure and the other with the distinction between sacramental and non-sacramental structures. American theologian Nicholas M. Healy's argument that the *in via* character of the actual church's identity meant that human and divine were mixed in a dangerous way was important since it challenged the idea that human and divine, as in Christ, were not mixed in the church.[21] Such an understanding made it impossible to make any clear distinctions between divine and human in the life of the church and its historical and social embodiments prior to the eschaton. Healy's understanding of ecclesial identity had clear connotations with Taylor's theories

---

18. Ibid., 90.
19. Ibid., 67.
20. Ibid., 81.
21. Healy, *Church, World*, 167.

on human identity. So while trying to find my way through listening to and interpreting these voices, I tried to get an overview of the field of organization studies. This is when I stumbled over the organization theories of Niklas Luhmann in the library of economic studies at Uppsala University.[22]

Organization as Social System

In addition to a functional/substantial understanding of organizational identity and a symbolist/inter-subjective understanding, Luhmann's system theory offered a third, and for me more constructive way.[23] Luhmann's system theory views the identity of the organization as something that is created, upheld, and changed through an ongoing cooperation between processes and structures. It's not primarily an explanatory theory but rather a therapeutic one. It does not explain how identity is created but offers a fruitful way of viewing and reflecting on the actual identity of an organization.

A central concept in Luhmann's theory is *autopoesis*. It is a self-generating process that constitutes the continuity of the organization through space and time and according to the theory social systems generate meaning through communicative events. In organizations such events are decisions.[24] Every decision that is taken by representatives of an organization relates to former decisions and thereby the process continues and the organization lives on. Luhmann's theory equipped me with two analytic concepts that became central in the research process: *identity structures* and *self-descriptions*.

---

22. The book that first introduced me to Luhmann's theories on organizations was Bakke and Hernes, *Autopoietic*.

23. In a functional/substantial understanding of organizational identity focus is primarily on mechanisms that hold the organization together and identity is perceived as something of which the organization can have less or more, while a symbolist/inter-subjective understanding tends to view identity as an inter-subjective construction. See Schultz, *Studying*, 15; Seidl, "Organizational," 124–25.

24. Luhmann, *Essays*, 3.

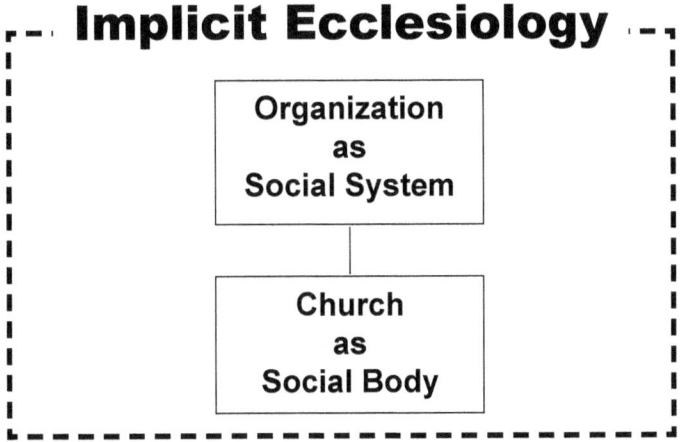

Figure 8. A theoretical model of implicit ecclesiology, part 1.

According to the theory, identity structures take shape over time through all the unique decisions taken by the organization; at the same time they gradually become important premises for the decisions that are taken.[25] The identity structures individualize the organization since the structures are shaped by the organization's specific history. This definition of structures worked well in relation to the research questions and the *in via* character of church identity that I had adopted. My purpose was not to decide a priori which structures were significant in the embodiment of the local church. Rather, I used the concept of structures as a way of making visible the actual embodiments of the local church.

According to the theory, *self-descriptions* were expressions used by the organization in its communication to describe itself as the totality of all its operations.[26] The self-descriptions worked like maps in relation to a terrain. When analyzing self-descriptions in different forms of communication in the organization, it was possible to draw conclusions concerning the social body that was described. Who was part of that body? What characterized it? As an initial act of analysis I started to analyze self-descriptions in various

---

25. According to Luhmann's theory, it is the organization's dependence on its own history that individualizes it and Seidl suggests that there are two ways of analyzing the individuality of an organization. Either you study and analyze a number of premises for a decision at a given moment, or you focus on a few but significantly stable structures that over time refer to several decisions. Seidl, *Organizational Identity*, 132. I chose the latter and named those structures *identity structures*.

26. Ibid., 133–35.

forms of material from the field studies.²⁷ That gave me a picture of how the social body of the local church could be seen and understood in relation to the church as a communicating and decision-making system. Based on such a picture I could also start discovering which the significant identity structures were. To a large extent the self-descriptions described a rather narrow social body consisting primarily of employees, board members, and a few others. But there were examples of how everyone living or staying within the territory of the geographical parish were described as being part of the social body.

Luhmann's system theory contributed with important components to the theoretical model that took shape. But I was well aware that I did not want to reduce the social body of the local church to a communicative system. That would give too abstract a picture of the local church and not give room for the practical and social embodiments. The model needed more components, and as I went on it turned out that the system theory was open for working in dialogue with other theories. I focused on the identity structures and decided to try to grasp how these structures were expressed concretely. In relation to the model that took shape I made a distinction between questions concerning *the shape and form of the social body* (a question less complicated when studying individual identity, where the shape and form of the body usually are more obvious) and *its movement and relationships to other agents*.

I brought a few more voices into the conversation, which resulted in two new concepts that I added to the theoretical model: *identity space* and *practices*. They worked as tools that helped me analyze how the social body took shape and came to expression in concrete situations and physical rooms. But these concepts also made it possible to analyze how the ecclesial body related to other agents and what it was striving towards.²⁸ The vari-

---

27. I analyzed self-descriptions in various forms of written material such as policy documents and minutes from meetings with the parish board. I also conducted group interviews with groups in the parish that I could see, in one way or another, were involved in making decisions (I had a broad definition of decisions including both formal and informal decisions). The group interviews gave me material where I could analyze the use of self-descriptions in oral communication. The self-descriptions gave me a picture of how the local church, as an organization, defined itself in relation to its surroundings. Even though the internal communication is an abstract dimension of the local church, the relation between communication and decisions in Luhmann's theory of social systems, also pointed to the fact that the analysis of the self-descriptions could say something about the organizational embodiment of the local church.

28. To develop the concept of identity space I used Henri Lefebvre's spatial triad. See Lefebvre, *Production*. His theories on production on space were also useful in relation to definitions of social practices. Lefebvre's theories could add important dimensions to Alistair McIntyre's widely spread theory on practices. For further reflections

ous components of the ecclesiological model used to study and analyze the implicit ecclesiology of the local church in relation to its embodiment can be summarized in the following picture.

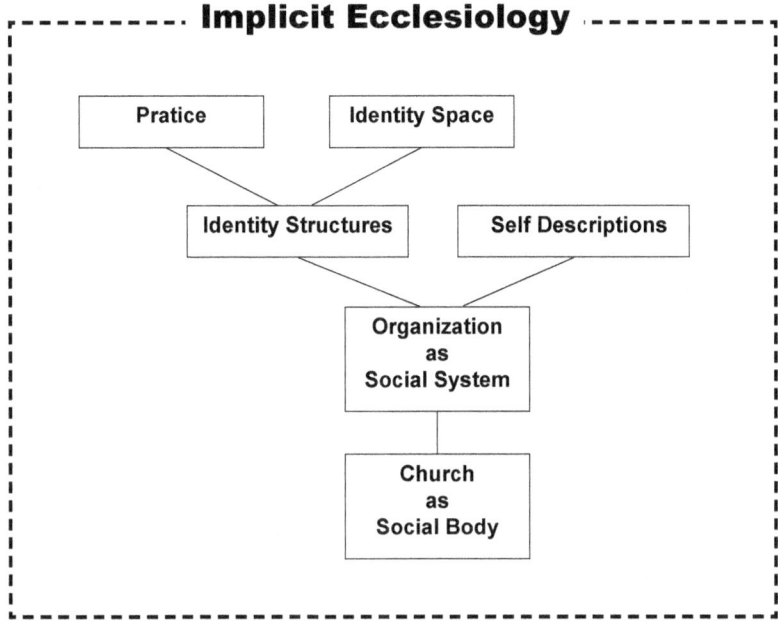

Figure 9. A theoretical model of Implicit ecclesiology, part 2.

In the description of my research process focus has thus far been on the theoretical dimensions of the project. The story could of course have been told from other perspectives. One such perspective is the continuous abductive process of moving between theoretical reflections and the establishment of empirical material. What I stumbled on in the field forced me to search for useful analytical tools just as the analytical tools and theoretical perspectives made me see things in the field that were significant for understanding the embodiment of the local church.

---

concerning social practices in ecclesiology see Fahlgren in this volume, chapter 6. To be able to add a more critical and analytical perspective to the analysis of how the local church as social body related to its surroundings I introduced a distinction between a *strategical* and a *tactical* approach. It was based on Michel de Certeau's definitions and had clear theological dimensions in relation to how time and space relate to one another. See de Certeau, *Everyday*, 36–37.

RESULTS

So what came out of my research? What was the implicit ecclesiology of the social embodiment of the local church in Flemingsberg? As my analysis of the rich material resulted in a holistic picture of the identity of the social body of the local church, I had to deal with a final question: how was I to frame my answer? What categories was I to use when putting words to the implicit ecclesiology? Was I to use ecclesiological typologies as e.g. Avery Dulles models or confessional ecclesial categories?

I chose a different path and treated ecclesiology as a narrative description of an understanding of the role the church plays in God's redemptive work in and through Christ. Through the ecclesiological analytical model that my reflective and abductive process generated I could analyze the rich material from the field and present a rather complex and non-homogenous picture of the identity of the social body of the local church. But it was still a picture of a body with certain characteristics. I could show three significant identity structures that gave shape to the body.

One created around the employees and their central role, another in relation to worship and the Eucharist, and a third in relation to the geographical borders of the territorial parish. The identity of the local church was in fundamental ways intertwined with identities of the local communities. It was in one sense a rather narrow social body, to a large extent represented by the employees, the parish board, and a few others. At the same time it was a body that was dislocated in ways that made it difficult to define it in relation to other social bodies such as the hospital.

The implicit ecclesiology that was illuminated by the analysis was dynamic. On one hand the role of the Church was seen as to make visible Christ, who was already present in Flemingsberg both within and without the church. On the other hand there were aspects of the implicit ecclesiology that seemed to imply that the church and its life were a prerequisite for the presence of Christ in Flemingsberg. Such aspects of the implicit ecclesiology were related to an understanding of the revelation of Christ as God's incarnation of fundamental patterns for establishing good relations that save people through communion with one another and with God. It was understood that the church, by stewarding the liturgy, participated in the work of upholding such patterns, and thereby making good relationships possible.

CONCLUDING REFLECTIONS

The purpose of this chapter has been to contribute with reflections in relation to dilemmas of empirical ecclesiology: How are theology and social theory to be defined and placed in relation to one another? What role are doctrinal and normative aspects in ecclesiology to play in empirical ecclesiology? So far I have given a thick description of the process of developing an ecclesiological model for analyzing material from field studies in a local church in a suburb of Stockholm, where I set out to study local church identity from an ecclesiological perspective. I have operationalized theories on organizational identity within the overall ecclesiological frame; therefore, I have been able to analyze the ecclesiology implicit in the concrete embodiments of the local church. As the description show, there has been an ongoing interpretative dialogue between various theological and social-theoretical components and perspectives. It is also clear from the descriptions that normative dimensions have been present in the process from start to finish but not only through doctrinal convictions. Rather the various steps of the process have been shaped by what could be defined as a soft normativity.

Expressive Character

The argument I want to make based on the reflective descriptions is that the dilemmas of empirical ecclesiology cannot be dealt with without attending to the concrete and unique realities of each field and research process. Questions concerning the relationship between theology and social theory, as well as the role and nature of doctrines need to be reflected upon in relation to each unique research process. Using the vocabulary of Norwegian theologian Geir Afdal I define this as an expressive character of empirical ecclesiology. Afdal makes a distinction between four types of theory: *descriptive*, *normative*, *prescriptive*, and *expressive*. Afdal uses the concept *expressive theory* to point to theories that are formed by means of an interpretative and dialogical approach and which are empirically informed.[29]

In relation to my experiences from the research process described here I want to argue that such an understanding corresponds well with how the work of developing an ecclesiological model actually was conducted. The process cannot be described as one shaped by correlation, where theology and social theory, as two more or less distinct fields, correlate one another. Rather the expressive character of the process shows that it is difficult to uphold any clear boundaries between theology and social theory within the framework of empirical ecclesiology when it comes to the actual work in the "laboratory" or the struggle in the "trenches."

Sacramental Understanding of Reality

As the descriptions of the research process have shown, this expressive character of empirical ecclesiology also relates to fundamental theological

---

29. Afdal, *Researching*, 74–75.

convictions concerning the identity of the church in relation to how cosmos and creation is understood. English theologian Paul Fiddes argues for a dynamic understanding of the relations between theology and other humanistic and social scientific disciplines within ecclesiology based on a sacramental understanding of reality. In a certain correspondense with Brodd's sacramental ecclesiology presented above he stresses the need to take incarnation seriously, which "means more than applying existing principles":

> God is encountered in an embodied way, through concrete realities, and not merely through ideas [. . .] God communicates God's own self through actions, relationships, and symbols in daily life, though this self-offering is fully expressed only in the person of Jesus. So we cannot simply impose a set of revealed truths on a situation.[30]

One conclusion Fiddes draws from this is that the theologian exploring the wordly forms in which faith is embodied also must draw on insights from various sciences. But, and this I would say corresponds well to the point I am trying to make in this chapter, "[t]he concern of the theologian working in ecclesiology is to find the theological dimensions within the wordly forms of community, be able to reflect on the presence, nature, purpose, and activity of the triune God."[31] Fiddes also argues for the need for the theologian to share models in a way that can contribute to the understanding of the expressive character of empirical ecclesiology articulated here. According to Fiddes, models from fields and sciences other than theology need to be used, but they also need to "interact with the models held in Christian story and belief. Out of a genuine dialogue and not a simple synthesis, both prediction and theory can emerge."[32]

I end where I started, in Bruno Latours description of research as a fundamentally relational practice where results are created through interactions between persons, artifacts, theories, methods, texts, models, and so on. But Latour's approach to research is founded on an ontology stressing the relational and materially heterogenous character of social life. In such approaches I see examples of creative conversation partner for empirical ecclesiology that gives room for theology and ecclesiology to participate in a constructive conversation concerning the challenges facing us all.[33]

---

30. Fiddes, "Ecclesiology," 19.
31. Ibid., 30.
32. Ibid.
33. See, e.g., the Gifford lectures held by Bruno Latour 2013.

9

Reflections on Particularity and Unity

CLARE WATKINS

> **Clare Watkins** (born 1963) is a Catholic theologian, teacher, and writer. Having completed doctorate studies in theology at Cambridge University, she has spent the last twenty years working in pastoral work and University teaching, as well as research and writing. She has researched, taught and published in the areas of ecclesiology, sacramental theology, and practical theology. Her book *Living Baptism: Called out of the Ordinary* (2006) integrates these pastoral and theological concerns in a way, which aims to help renew lay Christian living "in ordinary." Watkins was a member of the team developing Theological Action Research, and has published widely in this filed, as well as co-authoring the key text on the methodology: *Talking About God in Practice: Action Research and Practical Theology* (2010). She is currently a research fellow at Heythrop College University of London, and lecturer in Ministerial Theology at the University of Roehampton. University.

There is a good deal of suspicion and cynicism about the usefulness of theology—not only in contemporary western society as a whole, but even within the Christian churches. At a time of both unprecedented challenges and an increasingly unfamiliar set of contexts and demands, the church leaders want strategies and solutions, while many of the faithful look for something that will renew, nourish, and encourage their personal living of faith. Traditional academic theology often fails on both counts, with the result that ecclesiology can drift further and further from real church life, which, in turn, runs the risk of becoming increasingly weak in its theological underpinnings and sense of direction.

In part, theologians have themselves to blame for this. Too often the assumed demands of the academy leave us writing and thinking in ways that fail to connect with wider church life. We can hide ourselves in and behind our work, anxious that too personal a narrative, let alone a narrative of faith, might come across as unscholarly or academically unprofessional. When we do this, of course, we break with the longer traditions of theology in which prayer, faith, and pastoral purpose were major characteristics of the theologian's task.[1] What we have, however, in the three chapters presented in this cluster, is not only a vivid witness to careful scholarship, but also a self-disclosure from the scholars themselves, as each in turn narrates and reflects in some way on the processes of the ecclesiological research they have undertaken.

This self-awareness and reflexivity is being recognized and developed as a key part of practical theology. Here I welcome such a self-reflective voice for its recognition of that intractable tradition of the theologian as a person of faith, on a journey much like the rest of the faithful, through their "academic" vocation. But I am also encouraged as such a style highlights what is becoming a key area for concern and development in concrete ecclesiology, and in practical theology as a whole—the spirituality and formation of the practical-theological scholar. This is a theme to which I will return at the end of these reflections. For now, I note it as a fundamental question raised by the character of these chapters and allow it to begin to percolate through what follows. At the core of this ecclesiological work is a question about what is going on—spiritually, personally, and intellectually—when we do this kind of practical ecclesiological work, and what kind of initial and ongoing formation we need to carry out such work faithfully and in service to the church and God's mission in and for the world.

---

1. This longer tradition of a truly embodied practice of ecclesiology specifically and theology more generally is thankfully receiving more attention in recent years, in part in response to practical theology. At a time of the bifurcation of theology and practice, key thinkers such as Thomas Oden, Edward Farley, and, more recently, Ellen Charry have addressed this question in ways which enable the retrieval of a traditional (practical) theological approach. In particular Mark McIntosh *Divine Teaching* and *Mystical Theology* are important general texts in this regard.

A SELF-REFLEXIVE INTRODUCTION

In keeping with the self-reflexive tone of the chapters under discussion, I want to begin by describing something of my own context. In reading these essays I have been made conscious of a number of aspects not only of my own work, but also my own faith, which engage in particular ways with what has been described. In relation to my work, I come into the discussion with a pre-existing commitment to a methodological practice for ecclesiology, developed by myself and others, and described as *theological action research*.[2] This practical ecclesiological commitment heightens my sensitivity to certain questions around conversational methods, the relation of the researcher and the researched, and the complexity of sources and authorities for practical ecclesiology. My work with theological action research has employed a particular framework of reflection—*the four voices of theology*—which enables the struggle with this complexity to be held and engaged with constructively. Within this framework the particular questions around what, if anything, might count as *normative* sources (or voices) in the conversation has emerged as especially challenging.[3] Normativity presents itself in my reading of these chapters as a key question, which has, on the whole, yet to be grappled with in the wider field of practical theology with much success.

The significance of these developments in my own work will become more apparent below, as the specific engagements and mutual questioning of methods and understanding emerges. However, it must also be recognised at the start that there is a particular kind of ecumenical conversation being embarked upon here. I write as as a confessionally committed Roman Catholic theologian, whose ecclesiology, in particular, has been shaped by that faith tradition and lived out in practice, intellectually, pastorally, and domestically. At the same time, I have been involved some fifteen years or so in formal ecumenical dialogue, both on a national and international level, and would name such ecumenical engagement as an essential part of Catholic ecclesiology.[4] This specific set of ecclesial positionings has its own

---

2. The most accessible account of this methodology and its practice can be found in Cameron et al., *Talking About God in Practice*. Other examples of the work include Watkins and Cameron, "Epiphanic Sacramentaliyt;" Watkins and Cameron, "Challenge of 'Fresh Expression' in ecclesiology."

3. For an account of the four voices of theology, see Cameron et al., *Talking About God in Practice*, chapter 4.

4. So see the Second Vatican Council's Decree on Ecumenism, *Unitatis Redintegratio*, 5: "The attainment of union is the concern of the whole Church, faithful and shepherds alike. This concern extends to everyone, according to his talent, whether it be exercised in his daily Christian life or in his theological and historical research." See

effect on how I read the chapters form my Swedish colleagues. On the one hand, I am aware that they describe ecclesial practices—Free Church and Church of Sweden—which are shaped by theologies and histories different from my own church's; at the same time, my commitment to ecumenical conversations allows me to engage with this aware not only of difference, but also of mutual learning and receptivity.

This confessional and ecumenical formation has led me, in more recent years, to be especially concerned with the ways which Christian unity and common mission is likely to be, in the future, more enabled—*and disabled*—by the particularities of practices than by doctrinal disagreement. Dialogues between Christians of differing traditions is essential; but, equally, we know that very often we can leave the discussion table in peaceful agreement and yet remain alienated by each other's forms of worship, preaching and music styles, architecture and symbolism, and practices of mission. When I read about the specificity of practice in churches, I know, too, that I am reading about what might be the very things which keep Christians apart from each other, and unhelpfully apart from the world into whose service we are called. Practices raise questions of ecumenism and mission in sharp and often intractable ways.

Much of the significance of these contexts of self will become clear in what follows. In keeping with the self-reflective and self-disclosive style of my colleagues, I approach this chapter not so much as a commentator on my friends' papers, but more as a fellow thinker in the field, invited to join a *conversation*.

TWO FUNDAMENTAL AREAS OF QUESTION

The chapters under consideration, united as they are by a common commitment to practical ecclesiology and by their self-reflexive, narrative tone, are nonetheless rather different in their approaches and subject matter. Sune Fahlgren's empirical study of a particular church allows him to present us with a fascinating and concrete sense of "fundamental ecclesial practices," while Stina Fallberg Sundmark demonstrates the ways in which church history might have an important role to play in our practical ecclesiological accounts. For both Fahlgren and Sundmark there is a refreshing level of self-disclosure that enables the reader to glimpse something of the processes and "thought-journeys" involved in this kind of concrete ecclesiological work. It

---

also John Paul II's Encyclical *Ut Unum Sint* (1995) where the Catholic commitment to ecumenism is explicit as an essential quality of church life: "The Catholic Church embraces with hope the commitment to ecumenism as a duty of the Christian conscience enlightened by faith and guided by love."

is, after all, a particular kind of empirical and theological *discernment* which is at work, as the scholar works to "read" practices, past and present, with faithfulness and empathy.

Jonas Ideström's paper takes us further into what he describes as a "thick description of the process of developing an ecclesiological model."[5] Faced with the complexity of the variety of suitable disciplinary conversation partners for an authentic practice of ecclesiology, Ideström guides his reader on a compelling intellectual journey exploring different conversation partners and narrating how these "conversations" between disciplines are brought together through an "abductive" process. In the end, as I understand it, Ideström seeks to articulate a framework which will enable a reading of practice attested to by empirical data, which neither flattens the data into generalities, nor seeks to abstract from it some practice-transcending ecclesiological ideal, or "blueprint."[6]

In fact, for all three of these writers there is a strong and consistent sense of *incarnation as particularity* as a shaping theological theme. As Fahlgren puts it: "A specific pitfall is the search for *one* ecclesiology or *the* real theology in an ecclesial practice."[7] What is important for all is that incarnational instinct which resists the idea that there is some "hidden meaning" embodied in practices that needs to come to light.[8] Rather, what is sought is a clearer articulation of practices in all their particularity so as to better describe and relate them to one another constructively.[9] What we have as a result—as Ideström, drawing on Geir Afdal, so aptly puts it—is not anything approaching a normative or descriptive account of church; nor is it simply a descriptive exercise. That incarnational commitment to practice in all its particularity offers us, instead, an ecclesiology with an *expressive character*.[10]

---

5. See Ideström in this volume, 137.

6. The critique of much modern, twentieth century ecclesiology as "blueprint ecclesiologies" is now common among more empirically and practically orientated ecclesiologies, and draws much of its weight from the influential work of Healy, *Church, World and the Christian Life*. As we shall see, Healy's own shift in position in recent years is an important part of the conversation entered into by the authors in the present volume.

7. See Fahlgren in this volume, 102.

8. It is this instinct that differentiates Ideström's "implicit ecclesiology" from that of Martin Percy. See Ideström in this volume, 129.

9. This is particularly clear in Ideström's chapter, where he notes that "implicit ecclesiology made it possible to relate a variety of ecclesial expression to one another and through such an act contribute to new views and angles on perceptions of the identity of church." (p. 129).

10. See Ideström in this volume, 137.

This refusal to leave practice in the name of theology seems to me a common characteristic of these chapters, and it highlights a number of ways in which the contributors make a specific contribution to the wider field of practical ecclesiology. In doing so they also shine new light on a number of areas which can be highlighted as needing further reflection. In what follows I reflect on two such themes: the nature of "practices," and the Christian paradox of particularity and normativity. In conclusion, I will use these reflections as a basis for some tentative thoughts about what seems to me the next burning issue for practical theology: that is, the spirituality and formation that is called for in better enabling us as scholars in this complex and ecclesially crucial field of work.

1. The Sort of "Things" Practices Might Be

Practical theologians are concerned above all with practice. This is a recently asserted commonplace in all areas of practical theology today. However, the frequency with which it is asserted often fails to treat adequately the sheer complexity and difficulty of considering practices as both sources for and expressions of theology.[11] In fact, the move that the empirical ecclesiologist makes from the description and understanding of practical realities to theological articulation is highly problematic on an epistemological level; as soon as we have described a practice and selected the data, we have begun a hermeneutical process in which the empirically-based ecclesial practices under discussion have been left behind. All too often an articulated commitment to practice results in an intellectualization of themes and concepts, which may or may not then be dimly "applied" to practical living.

In part, it is awareness of this difficulty that lies behind Nicholas Healy's recent critical reflections on his own earlier call for ethnographic approaches to ethnography.[12] Whilst not despairing of the importance of empirical and broadly ethnographic approaches to church, Healy nonetheless seeks to alert us to the dangers of assuming that we can simply describe or translate the complexity of practice into language or concepts. In agreement with Frances Ward[13] that the writing up of congregational practices into a coherent text is, inevitably, an act of interpretation, he goes somewhat further to suggest that "ethnographic study can reveal how congregations

---

11. One of the few serious attempts to understand what is at stake in such a process philosophically is given in Murray, *Reason, Truth and*.

12. See footnote 6 above for Healy's original argument. This is critiqued in Healy, "Ecclesiology, Ethnography and God."

13. The article cited by Healy on p. 187 is Ward "The messiness of studying congregations."

are too complex to be described without some degree of distortion."[14] In fact, Healy argues that to remain rigorously true to empirical accounts of churches would mean remaining content with a high level of detailed description which ultimately defies conceptual analysis or the discovery of a hidden meaning or truth. Empirical reality is particular and detailed and not, as such, the bearer of some *one* "implicit ecclesiology" just waiting to be made explicit through careful analysis. Healy recognizes that there are certain characteristics "present in virtually all congregations, [but] the ethnographic view undermines the notion that they constitute the church as a 'community' or a moral person in a sufficiently rich and consistent way to work as a principle for theological or ecclesiological method. There is simply too much materially, that is not shared."[15]

This intractable particularity is uncompromisingly embraced by the chapters in this section of the present volume, as we have seen. Not only that, but they also seem to me to hint at a possible fresh response to this dilemma of practices and how we are to view practices in our ecclesiological study. What sort of "things" are practices? One common response, which is well articulated by Healy, is to insist that attention must be given, in a newly self-conscious way, to the manner in which our doctrinal and theological assumptions shape our reading of empirical material. As he expresses it: "We cannot, then, start with the church as it exists; everything slips between the fingers unless we cement and shape it according to our agenda, our construal of Christianity, and our formation within in our particular world."[16] It is to be concluded that ecclesiologists working with practices must make clear the interpretative framework in play for the shaping and articulating of how these practices are understood. This position clearly has implications for the training and formation of ecclesiologists for our task, in terms of self-awareness and self-disclosure in our work.

In my own work with theological action research a position broadly similar to Healy's more recent statements has been assumed from the beginning. As well as attending to the "voices" or theological authority of practices, we have sought to reflect upon them in the light of more traditional theological sources, which come under the headings of the normative and the formal voices of theology. The normative accounts of church might be understood broadly as those which are accepted as regulatory in some way for the community under discussion—the scriptures, certain church and traditional teachings, liturgies, and so forth. The "formal" voices are those

---

14. Healy, "Ecclesiology, Ethnography and God," 187.
15. Ibid., 189.
16. Ibid.

found in the academy, both contemporarily and historically, across relevant disciplines beyond the explicitly theological. The commitment of theological action research to *conversational methods* is an attempt to ensure that a space is kept open for the mutual engagement of these practical, normative, and academic authorities, and so enable theological disclosure from within that conversation of authorities to emerge. In theory, at least (and often in practice) the fruits of such a method are shaped neither by particular practices, nor by prior theological and ecclesial assumptions, but by the creative encounter of all these factors.

Both Healy's ideas and the worked methods of theological action research depend on a commitment to a certain kind of struggle to "balance" or mutually engage different theological sources. For both the assumption is that the process offers learning points for both systematic theology and ecclesial practice, and that these points can, ultimately, be articulated or written up in some way. It seems to me that the three chapters of the present volume under discussion hint at a somewhat different approach. In particular, the incarnational commitment to particularity enables a stronger resistance to the idea of coming to a particular conclusion about the practices studied. We have already commented on Fahlgren's refusal to fall into the "pitfall" of simply using the details of church practice to come up with an articulation of "the real ecclesiology" at play—a position which takes seriously Alasdair MacIntyre's non-instrumental reading of practices as having their own participative meaning of themselves.[17] And whilst Sundmark's historian's instincts echo this commitment to reflective description, Ideström's account makes clear the intention to let practice speak for itself, resulting in both an "expressive theory" of church and a framework for enabling an interaction of varied practices with one another.

Potentially this is a radical commitment to practice *qua* practice as an authority for ecclesiology and for theology more widely. It suggests that there is an authentic ecclesiological task in *narrating* church life in ways which are not simply descriptive, but rather enable communicative processes between practices of church living which are, themselves, transformative of practice and so formative of new ways of thinking. Embodied in such an approach I catch a glimpse, too, of a sense of practice itself as not so much a "thing" but as a *process* in which the researcher and thinker are called to participate in order to understand. There is a strong resonance here with Fahlgren's identification of "preachership" and "choirship" as fundamental factors in the communicative processes which make up church life: whilst there are specific "things" that contribute to these processes—not least of all

---

17. See Fahlgren in this volume, 102.

architectural setting and symbol—the practices are much better understood through MacIntyre's account as practiced expressions of meaning whose own meaning is essentially known through participation in their processes. For my own work this offers a striking fit, from a different Christian tradition, with my commitment to a process understanding of church as the locus of revelational discernment or progress, which I draw from the ecclesiology and fundamental theology of the Second Vatican Council.[18] The strong question that arises from this is, for me, how are the task and formation of the practical ecclesiologist to be conceived within such an understanding?

2. Particularity, Normativity and Christian Unity

Before moving to these central questions, I want to build a little on the reflections concerning the particularity of practice to which our authors are so vividly committed. Of especial concern here is how the incarnationally particular, contextual, and detailed can be understood within the normative traditions of Christianity. To extend the authors' use of incarnational metaphors, it is a question of how a universal salvific event can be articulated as effective and meaningful for all when it takes place within the sharp limitations of a particular time, place, and person. The "scandal of particularity" is potentially as troublesome for practical ecclesiologists as it is for christology.

As a Catholic ecclesiologist I am aware in a specific way about the place of normative voices in our understanding of church. The practice of theological action research in a Roman Catholic context requires the often-sensitive task of bringing voices from the places of ordinary Christian living into conversation with teachings of the authoritative magisterium, in ways which strive to get beyond simple agreement or disagreement and enable mutual understandings and formation.[19] For all that, there remains an intractable asymmetry between the "four voices of theology," given that the authority of the normative (notably magisterial) voices are already legitimated readings for tradition, whilst the operant and espoused voices from practice, and the formal voice of the academy are, at best, untested and as yet undiscerned expressions for the ongoing and lived out tradition—and at worst might be deeply flawed. It is, I suspect, this Catholic sensitivity to the significance of the normative that left me acutely aware of its absence (at least at an explicit level) in these chapters.

---

18. Something of this is set out in Watkins et al., "Practical Ecclesiology."

19. A particularly vivid example of this is given in Watkins, "Living marriage," where voices from marriage and family life are brought into dialogue with Catholic Church teaching.

Following the radical commitment to the particularity of practice just described, our authors here seem to suggest an approach that locates whatever normativity they wish to maintain within the practices themselves. So, for Fahlgren, what makes up the DNA of the church is not primarily to be understood in terms of doctrines, but rather as "ecclesial fundamental practices," which themselves account for the variety of sub-practices that populate the community at a given time and place.[20] Such a vision strongly suggests that, in order to understand the fundamental nature of the church, we should have recourse not to the academic study of traditional theological *texts*, but rather to an exploration of how the fundamental *practices* are lived out within a particular setting. The question remains, for me, whether this really does remove the problematic of the doctrinal as a normative voice. The identification of preachership, for example, as an ecclesial fundamental practice depends on a largely implicit ecclesiological assumption based, it might be supposed, on a reformed reading of the marks of the church. This is somewhat recognized by Fahlgren when he notes that, from another perspective (Roman Catholic, for example) it might be that ordination is seen as the ecclesial fundamental practice, with preaching as a dependent sub-practice.

If it is the case that these authors' commitment to practice as the content of ecclesiology tends to a weakening of the place of the normative in their accounts, then this presents a challenge, both to them, and, crucially, to more normatively explicit ecclesiologies such as my own. My challenge to this approach is related to Healy's observations about the limitations of ethnographic approaches, which ultimately, he argues, give us only highly detailed accounts of particular practices, which then need to be ordered and interpreted (he even uses the word "distorted") if they are to be theologically helpful. As I have indicated, my own reading of practice in theological action research depends on a conversational practice in which the authoritative place of the normative voices is recognized but does not go unchallenged. From such a position I want to enquire further into how the studies offered in these chapters can explicitly contribute to an articulated understanding of the nature of the church, in such a way as to help develop a common understanding of church that can form the basis of ecclesial unity and clarity of vision.

To eschew such an intellectual project entirely and strive to allow practices to speak for themselves would be to limit our notion of "practice" to the practical, the embodied, the non-articulated. Yet, as I have argued

---

20. See Fahlgren in this volume, 100.

elsewhere,[21] the academic and faithful intellectual activity of ecclesiology can, itself, be conceived as a particular kind of church practice. Just because it is a word-based practice doesn't stop theology being something that some of us "do," practically and on a day-to-day basis. Fundamentally, the explicit theological tradition, even with its "blueprint" tendencies, is an essential aspect of this practice of articulating ecclesiology. Whilst Jonas Ideström's helpful notion of the "abductive" as an appropriate practical ecclesiological response to data does imply some discursive role for formal and normative accounts of church, engaging with practice, I still would like to explore further with these authors how the more explicit inclusion of normativity in their reflections might work in ways that does not undermine their commitment to practice as such.

This last point is important. For, if it is the case that my own commitment to the normative leads me to challenging these chapters' accounts, it is also the case that their resolute incarnational particularity challenges me in a number of ways. On a straightforward level, the incarnational emphasis, allows a compelling understanding of the practical details of church, militating against Healy's disillusion with what ethnographic accounts can offer ecclesiology. The central "scandal" of God becoming a particular person, in a particular context affirms the significance of the detailed particularity of practical studies of church. More arrestingly still, for me, is the ecumenical significance of such resolution to let practices speak for themselves.

There can be little doubt that the real study of the ecumenical documents between churches in the last sixty or so years attests to a remarkable level of agreement or convergence having been reached in doctrinal matters.[22] The more recent documents of the World Council of Churches Faith and Order Commission, on Church and on Baptism[23], together with the outstanding achievement of the Joint Declaration on the Doctrine of Justification between the Roman Catholic and Lutheran Churches[24] not only indicate the doctrinal closeness of many Christians living in separate congregations, but also raises the question as to what else would need to happen to better enable more practical and visible expressions of Christian Unity. After many years of service on ecumenical dialogues, I think it is here that we need to turn a self-conscious attention to ecclesial practices, as well as to doctrine, as themselves bearers of faith, culture, and understanding. In

---

21. Watkins, "Practising Ecclesiology."

22. An accessible indication of this can be found in Kasper, *Harvesting the Fruits*.

23. *The Church: Towards a Common Vision*; *One Baptism: Towards Mutual Recognition*.

24. Available at: http://www.vatican.va/roman_curia/pontifical_councils/chrstuni/documents/rc_pc_chrstuni_doc_31101999_cath-luth-joint-declaration_en.html

the end it may well be the alienating effects of different practices, and the inability to read them across denominations, that prove the most difficult obstacle to Christians working, worshipping, and missioning to the world together.

Here Sundmark's historical study is especially helpful. The narration of both pre-Reformation and Reformation practices is done in such a way as to demonstrate the ambiguity of what is being experienced, theologically, in these different practices. The pre-Reformation procession of the sacrament to the sick, which gathered people from the homes and made Christ's presence among them a vivid reality in the ordinary streets and tasks of their daily living, clearly offered one kind of possible reading of the sacred and the everyday. However, it is also clear that the Reformed practice, while different on a number of counts, could not simply be seen as giving a contradictory account of this same question. The understanding that Christ is already present in people's homes and places of work, in ways not dependent on priest-led rituals, is no less affirming of the sacredness of the everyday. What becomes crucial in these readings of different practices is a sense of them as truly participative in their communication of meaning. They are not "objects" to be externally observed and analysed, but can only properly be understood in terms of those participating in them.

In passing I would mention here that this observation opens up a difficulty with using historical practices in a practical ecclesiology—that of being unable to check out how we "read" or understand a practice with those actually involved in it. In fact, this is all too often a difficulty with contemporary empirical research into church, where researchers fail to fully take account of faith practices as participative, and end up treating the church as if it were simply another sociological object. My own practice and development of theological action research focusses in a particular way on both ecclesiological research as participatory and the importance of ongoing conversation with the practitioners themselves, who co-own and co-shape the research and its interpretations. That being said, Sundmark's study speaks into ecumenical ecclesiology today precisely at the point of practice as a participatory bearer of meaning. Fundamentally it is only in sharing in the practices of "the other," in habituating ourselves to one another's ways of being church, that the fulness of meaning will become clear. What is required for ecumenical progress is not just a growth in doctrinal agreement, but convergence in the ways of practising and embodying our doctrinal convictions and instincts. The challenge of ecumenism demonstrates the correctness of these authors' intuition that—to use Ideström's account of Afdal's understanding of theory—ecclesiology is best understood as an "expressive theory," "formed by means of an interpretative and dialogical approach [which is] empirically informed."[25] This is the real church we need to work with for the advancement of Christian unity and our mission in and for the world.

THE VOCATION AND FORMATION OF THE PRACTICAL ECCLESIOLOGIST

In a 2013 research report into the use of action research in practical theology, Elaine Graham raises interesting questions about the ways in which—surprisingly—action research as a social science practice is often more aware of questions of the self-reflexivity and positionality of the researcher than those working in practical theology.[26] Reflecting on the points Graham makes has led me to think more carefully abut the kind of formation that is needed for researchers embarking on practical theological methods of exploring church and developing ecclesiological thinking and practice. The sense that these processes draw on the very *person* of the researcher—an idea well-recognised in action research as such—both resonates with a traditional understanding of theology of "faith seeking understanding," and highlights the extent to which traditional academic training will fall short of what is demanded of the ecclesiological researcher. As the research studies described in this section of the present volume make clear, the practical ecclesiological researcher is implicated at the deepest personal levels of faith, interpretation (prejudice and pretences), and intellect. It is to our authors' credit that they have resisted the academic temptation to keep themselves "off the page."

In fact these studies present us not only with the challenges of particularity and normativity in relation to the object of the empirical research; they also confront us, in different ways in each case, with the particularity of the researcher himself. This is, Graham would argue (and I would in principle agree), a necessary step in practical theological approaches, which can clarify that the radical particularity of our strange discipline lies not only in the objects of our study, but in the very person of the researcher herself. To work in the careful discernment of the real living text of Christian communities is, at best, to participate in a practice of *spirituality*.[27]

---

25. See Idström in this volume, 137.

26. Graham, "Is Practical Theology."

27. I am indebted here, especially, to the work of David Coghlan, a Jesuit priest and action researcher, who has demonstrated stimulating correspondences between the processes and demand of action research and Ignatian spirituality. See Coghlan, "Seeking God."

By way of a conclusion to this chapter, and so as to open up possibly new areas of conversation for this practical ecclesiological project, I simply want to draw out the implicit spirituality that is at work in these studies. In doing this I am, of course, interpreting what I see here in the light of my own practice. In this interpretation, I am especially informed by the task of trying to enable others through training in theological action research to be better shaped and skilled for the complexities of the journey ahead of them—an intellectual, personal and faith journey, vividly described, for example, by Jonas Ideström in the present volume. I would begin to describe this underlying spirituality in terms of three characteristics: an attentiveness in humility before multiple voices in conversation; an eschatologically formed expectation regarding outcome; and, above all, a pneumatological understanding of the reading of incarnational realities of faith.

Dealing with a plurality of detailed and particular realities makes demands of the practical ecclesiological researcher in terms of our attentiveness. This attentiveness is not just a matter of paying attention and noting things—though this is involved. Rather, it is, I suggest an attentiveness of a *kenotic* quality, which names the position of the researcher so as to de-power it in an act of self-emptying before what is other in the practices explored. Such an attitude of kenosis and de-powering reaches beyond the reading of data and into a certain kind of proper agnosticism as to what will result from our careful accounts of practices. As soon as we have a fixed idea of what we hope to "get out of" the research—those clear outcomes so often required by funding bodies in the academic world!—we run the risk of shaping the practices to our own desires and needs, rather than allowing them to direct our gaze on their own terms. There is an *eschatological* attitude, an openness to an unknown but promised "outcome" which necessarily characterises the radical commitment to particularity as theologically authoritative.

At the heart of such a spirituality of kenosis and eschatology is a pervasive and personally appropriated *pneumatology*—a lived sense of the presence and activity of the Holy Spirit not only in the ecclesial practices being studied, but also in the very practice of practical ecclesiological research itself. Practical ecclesiology is nothing other than a participation in, and, simultaneously, a discernment of, the work of the Spirit in the church and world. The question that must be asked is: if this is the case, what is required for the training and sustaining of authentic practical ecclesiology? For sure, such formation will need to go beyond the modern traditions of the academy and its disciplines; it is likely, I propose, to return us to the longer theological tradition of our faith—a tradition of faith seeking understanding, of discernment of divine presence, and of a refusal to allow our lived realities of ecclesial faith to be boxed into any one discipline or theory. Then, perhaps, the complexity and difficulty of practices as such will be recognised for the christological and pneumatological—which is to say *Trinitarian*—mystery that it is.

PART THREE

Embedded Ecclesiology under Construction

The authors in Part Three are working with different aspects of church practice: liturgical renewal, biblical motives, feminism, gendering, church architecture, and church floor plans. The common thread is liturgy, and their doctorial theses are based on data from liturgical books, liturgical rooms, and liturgical practices.

With the dialectic reading we are proposing for the partition of this book, this third part can be read as the *synthesis*, because the authors are presenting an approach in the ecclesiological studies that creatively combines dogmatics and empirical data. The "given" theological texts of the liturgy (the thesis of Part One) are here consciously connected to the empirical data (the antithesis of Part Two). The outcome of this interface can be seen as the synthesis, and thus, a starting point for a further dialectic process.

In the previous chapters the authors have developed theories of an embedded ecclesiology in ecclesial practices and ecclesial spaces, and the reader has been presented with concepts such as *implicit* ecclesiology and *operative* ecclesiology. In Part Three the authors analyze ecclesiology *embedded* in liturgical texts (chapter 10) and in church floor plans (chapter 11). In the final chapter (chapter 12), Ninna Edgardh reflects over gendered aspects of ecclesial practices and thus of gender as embedded in ecclesiology.

The context for Part Three is the Lutheran Church of Sweden. Although professor Brodd describes the research field as an "ecumenical endeavour" (p. 27–28), and observes that the members of the research seminar are a "diverse group of people from different ecclesial traditions," most of the doctoral theses have been related to the Church of Sweden. This is reflected in this book too. It is natural for historical reason, but it is a challenge in the postsecular Swedish society, as well as in relation to the ecumenical identity of the Church.

While starting in a present practice within the Church of Sweden the following chapters still exemplify the ecumenical character of the seminar. Karin Oljelund reflects on the ecclesiology in the Lutheran Sunday Service in a conversation with the help of the Orthodox liturgical theologian Alexander Schmemann and the Catholic liturgical theologian Aidan Kavanagh. Gunnar Weman analyzes church floor plans also from Church buildings built before the Reformation.

Feminist studies of ecclesiology have ecumenical roots, and Ninna Edgardh's feminist analyses have contributed to a broadening of the scholarly scope of the research seminar. Thus, also the gender perspectives can also be an eye-opener for a deeper equmenical endeavor in the ecclesiological studies.

Finally, professor Teresa Berger reflects on these chapters in Part Three in conversation with a novel she inadvertent read—the memoir of Catalina de Erauso, the "lieutenant nun." Berger concludes her "accidental" reflections with this sentence, which covers well the themes in the following chapter:

> The fact that liturgical subjects always come situated and particularized will lead one to ask, for example, how gendered identity shapes liturgical meaning-making; how material realities, including our bodies, interpret liturgical practices; and how liturgy might be a contested terrain, the site of multiple and conflicting claims.

10

Ecclesiology in Liturgical Texts

In Search of a Method

KARIN OLJELUND

EDITORS' INTRODUCTION

The Church of Sweden is the largest Lutheran church body in the world; with 6.5 million members it represents about 70 procent of the Swedish population. In 1986, the current service handbook was approved.

Karin Oljelund's doctorial thesis (2009) examines the effect this and the former handbook have had on the actual parish practice, especially how the participants in the liturgy perceive what "church" is. The thesis and the following chapter take the starting point in two biblical images of church: Body of Christ and People of God. Which of those is the most common in the liturgy? What are the possible ecclesiological impacts of these images?

In this chapter Oljelund reflects on the methodological questions she faced when she was studying the ecclesiology embedded in the Church of Sweden Sunday liturgy. Both her research and Weman's do not examine the experiences the worshipers have but instead focus on the factors that have an impact on the experiences, what Oljelund defines as Primary Ecclesiology.

Oljelunds reflections also show an awareness of factors, which also the researcher has in the pre-understanding of the study object.

> For Edgardh gender is such a pre-understanding (chapter 13), present before the experience of the liturgy (Primary liturgy).
>
> **Karin Oljelund** (born 1944) is a minister in Church of Sweden since 1978. Beside parish work, she has worked for the Lutheran World Federation with its local organization in Tanzania (1989–1992), and she has also lived in Kinshasa, Rome and Brussels. Oljelund has a PhilCand-degree, in which she mainly focused on classical archeology in Rome.
>
> Her doctorical thesis is presented in the article "Method in Liturgical Ecclesiology: An Attempt to Understand the Formation of Primary Ecclesiology" in *The Meaning of Christian Liturgy: Recent Developments in the Church of Sweden*, (2012). Forthcoming is an article on a Swedish theologian and journalist, Anne-Marie Thunberg.

INTRODUCTION

When it is time for the Gospel to be read, a small procession comes down the aisle, the cross, two candle bearers, a minister with the Gospel Book, and the reader. The assembly stands up and turns towards the Gospel. It is the first Sunday of Advent. The text from Matthew tells us how Jesus rides into Jerusalem on a donkey and how people receive him as a king. When the reader ends with the words from Matthew: "The crowds that went ahead of him and those that followed shouted," the whole assembly joins in, singing the anthem for the king of Israel, the Messiah: "Hosanna to the Son of David! Blessed is he who comes in the name of the Lord! Hosanna in the highest!"[1] During the song the procession goes up towards the altar, the Gospel—Christ in the Word—surrounded by candles and cross, churchwardens, deacons, and priests move up towards the holiest, towards the chancel and the altar.

This is, to me, a very clear picture of how the People of God greet the Son of God, who is carried towards the temple of Jerusalem. The mass follows the Service of the Word, and the assembly joins their voices with the priest when he breaks the bread: "The bread which we break is a sharing in the Body of Christ. Though we are many, we are one body, for we all share in one bread."[2] The church defines itself as the Body of Christ.

---

1. The text from Matt 21:1–9 is the Gospel text of the First Sunday of Advent.

2. The official translation of parts of *The Swedish Service Book, Part I*, (Den svenska kyrkohandboken I) in which translations are available in English, German, and French

The scene could take place in any Church of Sweden church.[3] Last year on First Sunday of Advent I experienced it in the Cathedral of Gothenburg. But the Hosanna is sung in every church that day, and the words accompanying the breaking of the bread are spoken in every mass.

Those two pictures are conceptions of how the Church[4] is regarded: as the Body of Christ and as the People of God. Both are firmly grounded in the Bible texts,[5] and both are constantly used in most church services. Over time the one or the other has been accented more or less in talk about Church. There is a clearly seen increased talk about the People of God around and after the time of the Second Vatican Council, not only in the Roman Church, but also in most churches. Although the Vatican Council is often mentioned as the inspiration for many of the "liturgical" churches to start rearranging their liturgies, the growing emphasis on the image of the People of God started before the council, as can be seen for example in the Faith and Order meeting in Lund 1952.[6]

My doctoral thesis, *The Body of Christ and the People of God*, is a study of the ecclesiology expressed in the Church of Sweden Sunday service.[7] What is explicitly said about the Church, what is implicit in the words we use, and what is implicit in the way we act in the service? My starting point when working on my thesis was the two biblical images of the Church: Body of Christ and People of God

In this chapter I will share some methodological questions that I met when starting to work on that thesis and in the work that followed. I begin with the theoretical questions and problems, mentioning some of the problems I found trying to do liturgical ecclesiology, my search for a method that suited both my goal and my material, and follow up with some notes on how the method I developed functions. For an idea of how I apply this method

---

of a selection of the Order of Service for High Mass and the Order of Service for baptism, wedding and funeral.

3. For an introduction to Church of Sweden, see Bexell, "Church life," 1–23.

4. In this essay I will capitalize "Church" when I refer to the one and only Church, the Church which exists in and above all denominations and also when it is used as a name, as in Church of Sweden.

5. Some biblical sources are for Body of Christ: 1 Cor 12:12–15; 1 Cor 10:16–17; Rom 12:4–8; Eph 1:22–23; 4:15; Col 1:18; 2:17–20. For People of God see Genesis and Exodus in the Old Testament, and Matt 28:19 in the New Testament. For texts about the old and new Covenant, see 1 Cor 11:25 and Luke 22:20.

6. Eckerdal, *Vägen in i kyrkan*, 12.

7. Oljelund, *Kristi kropp*. My doctoral thesis found its room within the project *The Meaning of Christian Liturgy*, which was financed by Riksdagens jubileumsfond (The Swedish Foundation for Humanities and Social Sciences). The four students and two professors in the project have reported on their work in English, see Bexell, *Meaning*.

on liturgical texts please look at my thesis or, for those who do not read Swedish, at my article "Method in Liturgical Ecclesiology" in *The Meaning of Christian Liturgy*.[8]

MATERIAL FOR MY STUDY

The material that I find for my study is of two main characters, two different types of *texts*. The first kind of *text* belongs in two different Missals of the Church of Sweden, that of 1942 and that of 1986 (the later one is still in use as I write this, but work on a new Missal is ongoing).[9] That text consists of the proclamations, prayers, Bible texts, and songs proscribed in the manuals. I worked only with the ordinary texts, leaving out the varying, such as Bible readings and collects.

The second kind of *text*, the advice or prescriptions for the praxis of the service, is partly also found in these Missals—who is doing what in the service, and where from in the church building, turning this way or that, kneeling or standing or sitting. I also found that second *text* in two different surveys as to how the services were actually conducted. The first questionnaire stems from 1965,[10] when it was sent to all parish priests in Church of Sweden, and almost all of them answered questions about what prayers and songs they would use when given a choice as well as how often mass was celebrated, how they were robed, and whether anyone else but the priest was sometimes the reader of texts.

The second questionnaire,[11] from 1997–1998, was addressed to a number of parishes and advised to be answered by a worship-responsible group of people, such as priests, organists and churchwardens. More questions in this survey considered whether there was any visible lay participation and also the church space. Such questions were concerned with from where the gospel was read and by whom, from where did the priest preach and was he/she celebrating mass turned towards or from the congregation? The very questions stated in each survey mirror expected changes in the worship.

---

8. Oljelund, "Method," 91–113.

9. *Den svenska kyrkohandboken* (1942 and 1986).

10. This survey has not been published. It consists of two diskettes. A paper transcript is available from the author: "Svenska kyrkans liturgiska nämnds undersökning 1965: Liturgiska bruk vid högmässa inom Svenska kyrkan".

11. Axner, *Utvärdering*.

INITIAL QUESTIONS AND METHOD

When I started to write my study, one of my questions regarding the worship of the Church of Sweden was: Is it true that the People of God image became more important to worship and ecclesiology during the sixties, or even before that, from the 1952 meeting in Lund of the Faith and Order Committee?[12] And whether or not that happened, what impact does the accentuation within the liturgy of one or the other image have on our conception of Church?

Underlying that last question you will find the basic theory that, like theology, ecclesiology is intimately tied to liturgy. Our image of God is formed when we talk, sing, pray and experience God in prayer, worship and mass, and our image of Church is formed when we, *as* Church, pray, worship, and meet in the Liturgy.

There is a quite a library to sort through should one want to study Liturgical Theology.[13] I will not enter into a description of it in this article, but only state that the same way of thinking applies to both theology and to ecclesiology. If our theology, our understanding of God, starts in the collective meeting of worship in the church, so does also our ecclesiology, our understanding of what Church is. Maybe even more so, since our view of Church must be extremely limited if it has not been experienced in meeting *as* Church. God can, after all, also be experienced outside the liturgy, in solitary prayers, in morning prayers at school, or suddenly on the road to Damascus. One can certainly have an idea of what the church is without having ever been to church, but that will be more of a theory than a real knowledge experienced from partaking, and more of a knowledge of structures.

METHODOLOGICAL QUESTIONS IN DOING LITURGICAL ECCLESIOLOGY

The problems of studying liturgical ecclesiology remain the same as with studying liturgical theology. Liturgical theology has been described by many, but nowhere have I been able to find a method to examine the theology or ecclesiology born in the liturgy. Thus far, then, liturgical theology remains a secret knowledge among those that experience it. There is no theory about how one can research it, no method described in the literature. If theology is something that happens both only in the liturgy and as an exclusively collective experience (as it is described by Schmeeman and

---

12. As witnessed by Eckerdal, see Eckerdal, *Vägen*, 12.

13. Schmemann, *Liturgy;* Kavanagh, *On Liturgical;* Irwin, *Context;* Fagerberg, *What is;* Lathrop, *Holy People.*

Kavanagh), how then can one examine it? Is it at all possible? How could one find a method for examining a collective experience that is constantly deepening, as described by those authors?

Problem Number One: How Does One Study an Experience?

Liturgical theology is based on the idea that theology is God experienced. The meeting with God takes place in the liturgy, and that experience *is* primary theology. Secondary theology is the systematization of theology. It is what I do now—university or school theology, the description of theology. The same applies to liturgical ecclesiology. Primary ecclesiology is what I am looking for, secondary ecclesiology what I am doing.

The problem I face is: how does one study primary ecclesiology if that is ecclesiology born out of the experience of liturgy? Will the primary ecclesiology not turn into secondary the moment one starts studying it, discussing it, and rationalizing it?

Problem Number Two:
How Does One Study a Collective Experience?

The writers about liturgical theology stress the collectiveness of liturgy and of the experience of liturgy, God, and Church. In contrast, the tradition of liturgy and theology in the Church of Sweden has been individualistic and hierarchical. This might have been changing during the later part of the twentieth century, which is one of the questions I ask in my study, but whether it has or has not, the question remains: how does one study a *collective* experience? That could possibly be done in a sociological study, and preferably over time, since liturgical theology is described as deepening and changing the God-experience of the assembly.

That kind of study would include interviewing people about services they had taken part of, and it would have to be carried out over time, starting as of today and being repeated at later intervals. But what I am interested in is what has happened up to today. In doing that I have to work with material that is accessible now. Also, a sociological study is something different from a study of ecclesiology. Would it at all be possible to study the *collective* experience?

Problem Number Three: Where in the Ongoing Collective
Experience Could One Find the Primary Ecclesiology?

When Kavanagh describes the process of experiencing liturgical theology, he uses quite drastic terms. The assembly is regularly being brought to the brink of chaos, resulting in deep change in the very lives of those that participate in the liturgy, and that change will affect their next liturgical act. The primary theology is not a result of an assembly's first liturgical experience, but that experience will affect their next liturgical act. The process is described as "collision, chaos and a certain violence."[14] The adjustment to change between the liturgies is theology, *theologia prima*.[15]

Some of the writers commenting on or writing liturgical theology describe the process in which the theology of the assembly is born as dialectic. Kavanagh sees the assembly as it enters the liturgy as the thesis, "the assembly's changed condition as it comes away from its liturgical encounter with God" as its antithesis, and "the assembly's adjustment in faith and works to that encounter" as its synthesis.[16] Irwin uses a dialectic terminology when discussing secondary theology, describing a dialectic relation between text and context: "*Context is text*," and "*text shapes context*." Irwin considers *context* as everything that contributes to the liturgy, and includes not only liturgical texts, room, music, gestures, prayers, and symbols, but also a comparison of how the executed liturgy compares with the written agenda, and studies of how the liturgy is adequately formed in its cultural and theological context. All of this constitutes the liturgical *text*, which is studied as liturgical theology. *Context is text*. This will, in a second step, form the church's theology, life, and spirituality, i.e. *text shapes context*.[17] Although Irwin here is mainly discussing secondary theology while Kavanagh explicitly describes primary theology, they both use a dialectic terminology.

Whether liturgical theology, and with it liturgical ecclesiology, is understood as dialectic, a linear, or a circular process, my question remains: where in this process is the primary theology/ecclesiology to be found?

Problem Number Four: Pre-Understanding

Another problem that I recognize is the concept of pre-understanding. It seems evident to me that no one, with the exception of a newborn, can come to church without a pre-understanding of what God is or of what Church is. Some, but not all, participants of that First of Advent service would have understood the connection between the assembly as the People of God and the people of Israel that surrounded Jesus when he rode into Jerusalem, as evident in the procession and the Hosanna-singing. Others probably understood the singing of Hosanna as a sign of the start of the Christmas-season.

---

14. Kavanagh, *On Liturgical*, 74
15. Ibid., 73–74.
16. Ibid., 76.
17. Irwin, *Context*, 54–55.

In either case there is some sort of pre-understanding. There is no such thing as a primary ecclesiology without pre-understanding. Even a person from a different religion altogether would carry with her some conception of God—or the absence of a god.

So, what is primary and what is secondary, if there is already a pre-understanding before the experience?

LITURGICAL ECCLESIOLOGY AS A HERMENEUTICAL CIRCLE

I consider it reasonable to understand pre-understanding as a complement to liturgical theology/ecclesiology and to see the process between pre-understanding, experience, deepening understanding, and new experience as a circular process, a hermeneutical circle. In this circle there will be an ongoing process: from liturgy and pre-understanding to primary ecclesiology, on to written secondary ecclesiology, and again on to liturgy and primary ecclesiology. In this circle liturgy, primary, and secondary ecclesiology influence, change, and deepen each other. It will be a great problem to describe primary ecclesiology, since it is an ongoing process, whether collective or personal. My entry point into this circle is at the liturgical texts and what we know about liturgical praxis. In doing this I will not understand primary ecclesiology as such, but some of the conditions for the experience of primary ecclesiology in a church which uses these texts and this liturgy.

My answer to the problems indicated above is thus: my study is neither a way of *doing* liturgical ecclesiology, nor a study *of* liturgical ecclesiology, but is rather a study of *the preconditions* for the formation of a liturgical ecclesiology in the Church of Sweden Sunday service. These preconditions I find mostly in *texts*, i. e. the written texts of Missals that instruct on what should be spoken in a liturgy, but I also find them in instructions in the same Missals as to how the liturgy should be carried out. Answers to questions on how the liturgy is normally carried out, found in the above-mentioned surveys, also constitute *texts* that I study.

The problem of pre-understanding also applies to my reading of these *texts*, since I am indeed familiar with them, having listened to them, spoken them, and performed them during many years. I have, in not a few instances, been surprised when working with them; in trying to understand them from the criteria I used in my thesis-work, they have given me another understanding than the one I expected.[18]

---

18. Hans Engdahl has an interesting reasoning on close-reading and "fore-understanding" in his chapter of this book: "There is no innocent, objective reading of theological texts. Many factors influence such reading." Engdahl in this volume, 34.

IN SEARCH OF A METHOD FOR UNDERSTANDING THE TEXTS

Starting with the text of the Missals, I soon found that it was not enough to ask the ecclesiological questions only by arranging texts into "Body of Christ" or "People of God" categories. That task, looking for Body of Christ or People of God images of Church, was much more complicated than I had ever imagined. In prayers, confessions, and proclamations those images were often interwoven with each other and hard to disentangle. Analyzing the images as such also soon showed that they enclose different and sometimes contrary views on what it is to be the People of God or the Body of Christ. To simplify, the People of God image may imply a people harshly ruled by a distant monarch, or a people joined by a common goal, on its way towards heaven, stopping by the roadside to share a meal. And the Body of Christ is described by Paul as many members dependent on each other and therefore equally important but also, by the same Paul, as some members being more decent than others, some closer to the head than others.[19]

I had to find an instrument that was more efficient which I could use to analyze the different kinds of texts to find which view of the church was inherent in them. In my search I found an article by Avery Dulles that helped me.[20]

Dulles writes about communion ecclesiology "from above" or "from below," i.e., as "universalist" or "particularist." In the universalistic understanding of communion, the church/parish understands its *communio* first with God. The particularistic understanding of communio is as *communio* first with other Christians in the local church. The different perspectives that Dulles writes about could be used also in my study, although that is not a study of communion ecclesiology as such. If I used those distinctions I could find a way of cutting through the biblical images, which I had already discovered as inclusive of both perspectives. When in the People of God image the emphasis is on God the monarch, and in the Body of Christ image the emphasis is on Christ as the head of the church, the church is, as I understand it, interpreted as seen from above. The opposite also applies; the People of God on its way through deserts and waters and the different limbs of the Body of Christ working together, dependent on each other, are images of the church as seen from below.

In order to discover, in the *texts* that I set about to study, how the two biblical images were used, I had to find a number of signs that I could use to distinguish between the two perspectives of ecclesiology. Those *motifs*

---

19. See 1 Cor 12.
20. Dulles, "The Church," 125–39.

should be adaptable to both the biblical images, and they should be possible to use also when the biblical images were not explicitly pronounced in the texts. They should also be adaptable to the text of the praxis in the services, such as that can be read out of the answers to the surveys as well as from the instructions in the Missals.

There was no ready-made schedule for establishing these motifs, so in the end my method to find a few indications of this kind was to read the texts of the Missals. The motifs presented themselves in those readings, and I decided on three motifs for each perspective: under the universalistic perspective I put *distance, individuality,* and *inclusivity* and under the particularistic perspective *closeness,*[21] *community,*[22] and *exclusivity.* I will not here describe them explicitly as I did in my thesis.[23] I could have chosen other motifs, which would also have worked, and I could have chosen more motifs, but these worked well enough for me. When I started my close reading of the manuals, in my view they stood for two different views of Church, and I suspected that one was mainly to be found in the earlier and the other in the later Missal. In that respect I was not entirely correct.

Can my method be used for the study of other texts than Missals? The motifs that I chose for my study developed from a close reading of my specific text material. It is clearly possible that in studying another material, other motifs should be used, namely those that are inherent in that text. It is also possible that my two perspectives could be exchanged for other perspectives more applicable to another material. Although not all motifs were found in my study and the categories/perspectives of universalistic and particularistic were not always applicable, they still served to analyze the material. The very fact that certain motifs are missing in a text tells us something about that text. Other categories and motifs might well serve for other materials while using the same method.

LIMITATIONS OF THE MATERIAL

There is no doubt that although there are very many different images of the Church in the books of the Bible, the People of God and the Body of Christ are the two most frequently used. Paul S. Minear records ninety-six different images in the New Testament alone and subordinates twenty of

---

21. The Swedish word is "närhet," which could also be translated "intimacy."

22. Community, which I use to translate the Swedish "gemenskap," could have been translated differently, for example as "fellowship" or "communion." In order not to confuse the terminology, I opted against "communion."

23. See also Oljelund, "Method."

those under the People of God and eleven under the Body of Christ.[24] Those images are normally rather explicit in the Bible texts, but not always so in my material. In prayers, hymns, and worship they are sometimes hidden, although recognizable by verbs such as moving, walking, and eating for the People of God, and in bodily images such as bread, temple, or wine tree for the Body of Christ.

Searching for the two categories, Body of Christ and People of God, in the Missals' texts proved as a whole to be unproblematic. There are of course texts that fall outside of these images, but not many that are entirely free of them. In such cases it was still generally productive to apply the motifs for a universalistic and/or a particularistic perspective on the church.

The surveys were different. The motifs were possible to read out in the answers, and while studying the situations, the acts, and the setting in the church room,[25] but the images were not as easily readable. I found that I had to add another category to the discussion. That is *active participation*, which I define as participation, by other members of the congregation than the priests, and visible to the assembly of the church. I choose to discuss active participation, and whether it in a given situation is inclusive or exclusive, as a sign of distance or of closeness, of individuality or community.[26]

I did use material apart from the two main kinds of sources I have described. Beside background reading and literature from the time of birth of the Missals, I found the Church yearly statistics an interesting source. From that I could understand which of a number of allowed forms of service were used and when and, most importantly, how often the Sunday worship was celebrated as Mass, how often weekday masses were celebrated, how many people actually went to church, and how many received the communion over the years.

I am old enough to have experienced "going to church" many years before the introduction of the 1986 Missal. The 1942 book was still in use when I was ordained in 1978, but a few years later it was replaced by a test-version of the coming Missal. Of course I have used my own experience and

---

24. Minear, *Images*.

25. How the priest and the assembly act in the church room is certainly dependent on how that space is formed and made possible to use. Gunnar Weman's chapter in this book and his dissertation both deal with this aspect of liturgical theology; see Weman in this volume, chapter 11, and Weman, *Nutida*. Stina Fallberg Sundmark also deals with space and acts in her chapter when she researches the ecclesiology of the liturgy of the visitation to the sick. See Fallberg Sundmark in this volume, chapter 7.

26. Please note that I use *"active participation"* in a limited way that has been adapted to my material. Completely quiet worshippers can certainly be participating actively in both prayers and praise, but it may not be possible to be understood by others and may not visible or audible.

my knowledge of the two different versions. I know from experience that especially the later order of worship can be used in many different ways. It can be adapted to follow the older 1942 order almost literally, to form a worship that is closer to an ancient or classical form (as described by for example Gregory Dix[27] or Josef Jungmann[28]) or even to form a worship which is quite far from the universally celebrated Sunday mass, sometimes without any evident order.

LIMITATIONS OF MY METHOD AND SOME RESULTS

When analyzing the texts of the Missals, I started with a search for the biblical images. If I found any traces of Body of Christ or People of God I tried to establish the biblical source. There are usually one or several significant biblical passages used in those texts. I examined that text, its biblical place and its implications and the role that image plays in its place in the worship. After that I started to look for any motifs, universalistic or particularistic.

I was sometimes surprised to find how frequently those biblical images are used, often both of them and often side by side. And very often motifs from both views stand side by side in the same prayer. One exception stands out in all my material; I could not find any motif of exclusivity, either in the texts or in the surveys. When I discussed active participation in the service I looked out for a behavior that would signify exclusion, but I did not find it. I still discussed it, because as I see it, a newcomer in a tight assembly could easily feel excluded. Questions should be asked about what we really mean when speaking of participation.

When analyzing the behavior of priest and assembly according to prescriptions in Missals and in the surveys, looking for biblical images was not fruitful. Instead I looked into who is doing what and where in the church things were happening. Also, how often was the Sunday service celebrated as mass, and did people come forward to receive the gifts of bread and wine? Were the names of the dead announced, or were they prayed for? Was a lay member of the assembly leading the intercession from the ambo, praying for the world and for the parish, or was it the priest at the altar?

I found it both possible and quite fruitful to establish distance or closeness, inclusivity or exclusivity, and emphasis on the individual or on the community, also when analyzing the "behavior" of the ministers as well as members of the assembly. This does say a great deal about whether the assembly is (allowed to be) actively participating.

---

27. Dix, *The Shape*.
28. Jungmann, *The Mass*.

The Intercessions

I found biblical references in almost all proclamations, prayers, and hymns, with one great exception—the intercessional prayers, the assembly's prayers for the world, the church, and the parish. Although they often lack biblical references and images, the motifs of a universalistic or particularistic standpoint are evident. In fact there is a considerable difference between the 1942—1965 way of regarding church and world and that of 1986—1997.

In 1942 the priest would pray on behalf of the assembly, for the Swedish society, for the universal church, for the mission in foreign countries, and for missionaries and martyrs, but not much for the parish and the people living there. He would pray for peace in the world, for good homes and schools, for the work done, and for those that lead the country. He would also pray for the individual salvation of each person present, for forgiveness of sins, a serene death, and a blessed demise.

In 1997 the assembly could be represented by either a priest or a lay person, who would lead the prayers from the ambo and would pray for the world, for peace, for man's work to do good for those in need, and for justice and good leaders.

I found that the best description of the difference could be that according to the 1942 formula the congregation as the Swedish nation, the People of God, prayed *for the church* and for each member of the present assembly, while in the 1986 prayers it is the congregation as the local church, the People of God, that prays *for the world* and for everyone to responsibly act for the best of other people in need. In the first instance God is asked to help the world while in the second God is asked to help man to do something about it. Also, while both books talk about the "people," there are quite different perspectives in the first and second Missal. In 1942 there are still reminders of an old view, one from the seventeenth century, which regarded the nation as the People of God.

Motifs in the Surveys and in Missal Prescriptions

There are considerable differences between the prescriptions in the 1942 Missal and the advices in the 1986 book. The earlier book states mainly what the priest should do when he goes to the altar, when he turns towards the congregation or towards the altar, when he kneels, and when he should move to the pulpit or to the altar. The congregation is also advised as to when to stand up or sit down, when to kneel—kneeling is allowed at the confession and during the words of institution and the Lord's Prayer and prescribed at the altar when receiving the sacrament. The congregation answers the priest in some prayers and litanies but is not supposed to pray aloud the confession of sins or the Lord's Prayer. They may join the priest in saying the creed.

In the 1986 Missal lay members of the assembly, especially church wardens, are advised to take part of the planning of the service and to assist the priest in it, by reading the texts and leading the intercessions. They are advised to carry not only the collections but also the Eucharistic gifts to the altar. They can also be asked to assist with the distribution of the gifts. The readings and the sermon can be held from the ambo or from the pulpit and the intercessions from the ambo or from the altar. Only the Eucharist and the end of the service, with the Benedicamus and the Blessing, always take place at the altar. There are no prescriptions as to how the priest should turn, kneel, or stand, and the congregation is supposed to join in all prayers, some prayers being prayed alternatively between the reader, whether a priest or a lay person, and the congregation.

The surveys also pointed to considerable differences, the most important being that in 1965 most of the services held were celebrated without the Eucharist, while in 1997 most of the services were Eucharistic. In 1965 many priests would wear the black caftan even to the altar, while in 1997 most would wear an alb during the whole service, as well as during the sermon, and wear a chasuble at the altar.

Another significant difference is the way the baptized, the married, and the dead are announced. In 1965 this was done from the pulpit as an announcement followed by a prayer. Even the deaths of the members of the parish were announced, and the prayer was for those present and alive, for them to be prepared for death so as to achieve a blessed demise. In 1997 the baptized, the married, the dead, and the mourners are prayed for as members of the congregation and the assembly.

Images and Motifs in the Missals

In the first part of the High Mass, in both Missals, many of the images are taken from the Old Testament, resulting in the People of God as the common image. God the Father is sometimes pictured as embracing or enclosing. All those texts in the 1942 Missal belong to the universalistic group, the distance between God and man being apparent and the individual person presented as a sinner.

Although the 1986 Missal uses many of the same texts as the 1942 version, some of the added texts are particularistic, some universalistic, as are those that are the same in both books. In the 1986 images one will also find the closeness and community motifs.

The Eucharistic prayers are interwoven with both images, as well as some others. The motifs are often both universalistic and particularistic in the same prayer. The two images, the Body of Christ and the people of the covenant, are intrinsically present when the Eucharist is celebrated: "This is my body" and "This cup is the new covenant in my blood."

In both books I found some universalistic motifs, distance, and individuality, and in both books, but more significantly in the 1986 book, I found the particularistic motif of closeness and community. What stands out is that the motif exclusivity is never found in any text.

In the theological discussions and descriptions of the Church there has been an adjustment in the most common image used, from the Body of Christ in the 1940s to a more frequent use of the People of God in later decades. There is, however, no apparent connection between the use in literature and in worship. In the worship according to the 1942 Missal the People of God image is used frequently, while the Body of Christ image is mostly used in the prefaces and in the Words of Institution. Since the Eucharist was seldom celebrated—once a month or less—the People of God image is the most common in the worship. Since Mass has been celebrated more and more often after the 1960s, and since the Body of Christ image is the most frequent in the Eucharistic texts, the image of the Body of Christ has actually been used more and more often.

That fact is not the only result of my work with those Missals of 1942 and 1986. A result that stands out is that the distance between the congregation and the priest has shrunk, as a sign of how the distance between God and man has also diminished in the texts. The inner side of the biblical images has shifted. The People of God image today signifies a community that shares the responsibility for the world and for other people. Emphasis is on this life, not on the afterworld.

MATERIAL, METHOD, AND LIMITATIONS

I found the material for my study, my different kinds of *texts*, sufficient to work out interesting aspects of how the image of Church has shifted over time. The initial problem, i.e. to examine liturgical ecclesiology in its *Sitz im Leben*, remained a difficult, not to say an impossible, task. Given that I already understood that problem early in the process of my study, I will still say that it is possible to research, study, and understand the preconditions given in a certain liturgy so as to learn how Church might be understood in a worship service when this liturgy is used. So, and I find it important to point this out again, my study was not a study of liturgical ecclesiology as such or of primary ecclesiology as a collective experience and a process of "collision, chaos and a certain violence." It was a study only of the given liturgy in words and space and participation as a precondition for the possible understanding of Church by those worshipping.

The images of Church as the People of God and the Body of Christ were given depth by the motifs that I used. I am convinced that other motifs could also have been used with good results, as I am also sure that in another study, one looking into other churches' self-understanding or ecclesiology, other criteria or motifs could be used with accurate results.

11

Church Floor Plans as Ecclesiological Texts

GUNNAR WEMAN

EDITORS' INTRODUCTION

In this chapter church floor plans are interpreted as ecclesiological texts. Already in his doctorial thesis (2006), Gunnar Weman developed theory and methods for an ecclesiological reading of liturgical space. His main quest in the thesis, and in the following chapter, is to discover how various church buildings are shaping worshipers' imagination of God and of church.

Using church floor plans makes it possible for Weman also to compare the ecclesiology embedded in liturgical spaces in several historical periods and to present lines of ecclesiologcal development. He relates this analysis to the liturgical books in use. In this respect, there are similarities with Karin Oljelund's methods (chapter 10).

Weman establishes a text from a church floor plan. It is that text which is the empirical data used in the study. In the next step the established text is interpreted in light of the liturgy performed according to the possibilities the space provides. Weman assumes that ecclesiology is embedded in the liturgical space, as it has been constructed and how it can be used. Thus, the liturgical space is both a *sine qua non* for what ecclesiology the liturgy can express, and it shapes the worshipers' imagination of what church is.

> Together with Sven-Erik Brodd, Weman has published a book—*Kyrka i olika meningar* [Church in different respects]—with several examples of how different kinds of texts can be read ecclesiologically, e.g. in poems, novels, symbols, and essays. Like this chapter, Weman's and Brodd's approach shows that ecclesiology goes far beyond the church walls. Ecclesiology is a much greater dynamic study object than that.
>
> **Gunnar Weman** (born 1932), is an archbishop emeritus of Uppsala. In his retirement, Weman is working with liturgical issues concerning church buildings, church music, and hymnology. The title of his doctorial thesis is *Nutida gudstjänst och medeltida kyrkorum* (Contemporary worship and medieval churches). His latest book (2015) is a historical study of his father Henry Weman, organist and choir leader in the Cathedral of Uppsala 1927–1964.

INTRODUCTION

Let us imagine that a subcommittee in a parish is preparing for the renovation of their local church building, i. e. their place of worship. A file containing available drawings is collected from the parish archive. Perspective sketches and detailed drawings are laid aside in order for the group to focus on a number of floor plans (plan drawings) from different periods. What will the members of this group discover at their initial look?

First of all, they will probably focus on the walls that surround the actual space. As such, these denote an outward, non-changeable framework. It is inside this "limitation" that the group will work out its proposal for a renewed worship space in relation to the late twentieth century process of liturgical changes.

What else do they see in the floor plans? Well, presumably the altar, the altar rail, the baptismal font, the pulpit, probably an abundance of pews, and at the back a gallery where the main organ is located. At this stage, the floor plan is primarily a tool that enables them to find their orientation in this room.[1] Access to floor plans from different periods can provide a basis for comparative liturgical discussions about the way in which the actual parish church has been used for both services of worship and occasional liturgical offices during different periods in its history. Whenever one or more floor

---

1. References to the floor plan as an orientation tool are found throughout in Bonnier and Sjöström, *Kyrkornas hemligheter*.

plans begin to serve as more conscious theological materials for liturgical deliberations, theses drawings begin to be established as ecclesiological texts. It can be conversations and studies like this chapter about how the different places for the altar, the font, the pews etc. relate to one another, and how the congregation is interpreting its possibilities of celebrating the liturgy in its specific church building.

Such a study can, like other ecclesiological texts, disclose different ecclesiologies—maybe even some diametrically opposed ones—within one and the same church building. Each church building may have gained its particular shape against the background of both the existing, actual Church Service Book and locally worked-out liturgical customs and contemporary trends in church architecture style. Focusing on ecclesiological challenges, conversations within a parish group about an outline for a new floor plan could help the participants to pay closer attention to the character of their specific church building and to open their eyes to its possibilities and problems, i. e. challenges as well as hindrances.

There is an extensive debate about what space, place, and room are. It is not my intention to deliberately enter into that discussion. I have chosen, in a rather reductionist way, to focus on a basic structure in architecture: the floor plan. From the perspective of ecclesiology the floor plan is interestingly productive. There is also an ongoing discussion whether architecture could be understood as language or text, and if so, in what way. This is not the place to elaborate on that. If one presumes that different floor plans actually can be seen as texts, these texts can be read in different ways. One way is to read them as ecclesiological texts. Then ecclesiology is the means of interpretation; it offers necessary hermeneutical tools. Lastly, the result of an ecclesiological reading of the floor plans as ecclesiological texts might disclose various ecclesiologies, either inherent, as a result of the reading, or given by the limits or purpose of the floor plans.

It is important, however, that the floor plans are read in light of the liturgy performed according to the possibilities the space provides. The floor plans of churches are neither ideologically or theologically neutral, nor can they be separated from the intentional function of the buildings they are intended to constitute. The drawings establish themselves as ecclesiological texts at the moment a reader realizes that there is a connection between ecclesiology and the liturgical use of each of the specific liturgical rooms.

A Church of Sweden Context

By way of introduction, it should be noted that my discussion in this chapter about the ecclesiological character of the church interior takes the discussion in the Church of Sweden at the beginning of the twentyfirst century as its starting point. That implies an abundance of medieval church buildings in rural areas—which in one way of the other has to be reworked for present day liturgical intentions. It also means that a great part of theses church buildings, so to speak, are situated in the "wrong" place. Many people have left the countryside; the rural population continues to emigrate with increasing frequency to new, more densely populated centers.

All over Sweden there is also an obvious downward trend in the number of participants in services of worship among the parishioners. In order to create something positive in a (humanly speaking) difficult situation, there is a striving to structure the interior of the church as a holy place for fellowship and closeness, a goal based on experience gained within the worldwide liturgical renewal-movement.

During my thesis-work I made use of the available floor plans for the former Dominican church at Sigtuna, *Mariakyrkan*, as data material for a liturgically-orientated discussion about the structure of the actual worship space. It was obvious that a floor plan could say much more in a concentrated manner than few descriptive paragraphs on how a specific church building is planned to be used at the liturgical celebration.[2] A presentation, at a later stage, of the works of the church architect Jerk Alton (b. 1937) made it clear that his floor plans of various churches were far more than simply drawings of a number of local worship spaces. Through his way of marking the location of the altar, the font, the organ, the church choir within the church space, the arrangement of the pews in relation to the altar, and the pulpit as well as the extent of the non-furnished areas in the room used for the purpose of communication, it became obvious that these drawings contained a deliberate liturgical program. As such, they were liturgically well-founded texts, which could be used for the discussion of how an architect and members of a building committee could together contribute to the shaping of the life of worship within a specific parish church.[3]

It goes without saying that photographic images reflect details, colors, and the environment of the church.[4] To some extent, they give the viewer a general idea of the particular room and its most important items. Floor plans, on the other hand, give an overall perspective on the way in which the various parts within one and the same room relate to one another, and thus

---

2. Weman, *Nutida gudstjänst*, 40, 56, 213, 220, 223, 238–39.

3. Weman and Harlin, *Jerk Alton*, 75–78, 81–87, 91–93, 95, 100–103, 104, 110, 115.

4. Bexell and Weman, *Kyrkorummet*, 140–44. See also Bonnier and Sjöström.

can constitute a text for a discussion of the relationship between the specific room, the actual liturgy, and the worshipping community.[5]

Floor Plans from Two Medieval Church Buildings

The following presentation and analysis is focused on two completely different churches and how they are being used. Both of them can be more or less clearly traced back to the Middle Ages: *the church of Västra Ryd* in the parish of Kungsängen (Västra Ryd is located in the Diocese of Uppsala) and *the church of Västra Vingåker* in the parish of Västra Vingåker (located in the Diocese of Strängnäs.) I start by viewing an early twentieth century floor plan as an ecclesiological text for each of these two churches. These drawings establish themselves as ecclesiological texts at the very moment when a spectator—as reader—realizes that there is a connection between ecclesiology and the liturgical use of each of these specific church rooms.

These churches—like all other church buildings—have of course been erected for the primary purpose of serving the life of worshipping people within a certain geographical area (a parish within the system of a people's church).[6] The presumption that a church is not primarily characterized by some historical or artistic facts, but that it is essentially a room built and arranged for worship, lays the foundation for a coherent analysis of what it stands for.

It could therefore be claimed that a floor plan expresses a kind of materialized theology. It is the bearer of ecclesiological content. What the viewer can see in the floor plans from different periods of a church's life are different models of what has characterized and still characterizes the specific liturgical process of renewal (and change), which the parish has adopted as its own. These various adaptations are not mutually exclusive but provide different openings for the interpretation of the building as the space for worship, related to the use of the actual Church Service Book. Even though the concepts of "church" and "worship" are not explicitly mentioned in a floor plan of a church interior, they are nevertheless present in such a plan and thus constitute the tools for the analysis itself.

Against the backdrop of a short introduction to the relationship of the process of liturgical renewal to the church interior in general as well as to the structure of the two church buildings mentioned above, before, and after their renovations carried out during the early part of the twentyfirst century, I will undertake a comparative study of the relevant floor plans as ecclesiological texts. My intention is now to make use of the floor plans of the two

---

5. *Kyrkorummet*, 169–73. See also Weman, *Nutida gudstjänst*, 140–74.
6. Rappe, "Det liturgiska rummet," 176.

church buildings mentioned above and read the plans before and after the renovation as a text—and not just as an architectonical piece of work.

In sum, the purpose of this chapter is to clarify the way in which an ecclesiological reading of a floor plan can say something very specific about the worship of a parish, its self-understanding as a Christian community, and its fundamental view of how the sacraments are being celebrated. The ecclesiology becomes the key to the interpretation of these rooms as spaces for worship—and in that process the floor plans are established as a liturgical text.

A GENERAL LITURGICAL AND HISTORICAL BACKGROUND

Compared to its fundamental liturgical concept, each medieval worship space in Sweden has more or less thoroughly been altered over time. The Reformation showed comparative tolerance towards both the forms of worship of the church and the worship spaces. Major alterations in the room began primarily with the seventeenth century Lutheran orthodoxy, when the pulpit came to occupy a dominant place in the front part of the nave—with the result that the even more dominant pews filled up virtually every available space. The pews were directed towards the pulpit, a clear indication of where in the room the central point of worship was to be found: i.e., in the preaching with its teaching intention. The fundamental character of the room was thus changed, and the changes may be programmatically described by the phrase "From Worship Room to Teaching Hall." This altered room emphasized the proclamation of the Word at the cost of the Eucharistic celebration, and the change had ecclesiological reasons and results.[7]

With the eighteenth century Enlightenment and the emerging nineteenth century Pietism, a few more very specific alterations took place in Swedish churches. Medieval reredoses and statues of the saints were gradually lifted out of their previous liturgical contexts and were hung instead on the church walls or stowed away in the bell-towers of the parishes. New altar ornaments in accordance with the tastes of the times—in the form of more or less graphic images of Christ's sacrifice—were put in their place.

Liturgically inspired forces for change can of course also be observed, although to a lesser extent, during the first half of the twentieth century. These were based on the 1942 Church of Sweden Service Book (with its predecessor, the 1894 Church Service Book). These movements for change, however, became more pronounced in connection with the 1986 Church Service Book (and with its successor, the 2013 liturgical experiments in

---

7. Bergman, "Predikan." See also Bergman and Brodd, *Mångtydigt rum*.

preparation for yet another Church Service Book, preliminarily slated for a 2017 release).[8] With regard to the church interior, this liturgical, ecclesiological process of change can be summarized by the phrase "Altar and Pulpit in Collaboration."

When we use ecclesiology as a means of interpretation in the study of the general disposition and the furnishing of a church interior, it is easier to perceive how these two relate to one another in a state of tension. To look at and to interpret a floor plan from the point of view of worship (which such a drawing provides) counteracts the fragmentary perception of a number of individual items that have been arbitrarily placed around in that room. Such a reading can also underline the problems that might exist there, for example in the distance between the worship-leader and the celebrating community, or in furnishings that counteract the liturgical thread of the service, etc.

The Church of Västra Ryd—a Local Introduction

The church of Västra Ryd became a kind of district church in the parish of Kungsängen as this mother church of the parish was renovated in 2004–2010 under the leadership of the architect and dr. Lotta Gustafsson, (b. 1958).[9] The church has a number of medieval statues and other furnishings, including a triumphal crucifix hanging between the choir (quire) and the nave. Of the medieval murals, only a few fragments are still existant today.

The oldest part of this church building is the middle part of the nave, which is believed to be part of a small Romanesque church building from the early half of the thirteenth century.[10] During the fifteenth century, the church was extended towards the East and the sacristy was added at the same time towards the North-East. In the mid-eighteenth century the church was expanded with a new choir. In 1868 a burial chamber for the Rålamb family (from the farm of Granhammar) was erected to the East of the choir, using biblical and theological argument in every sense. The large organ gallery in the Western portion of the church provides a roof over the back pews; altogether the pews fill up that and every other possible space of the building. Surprisingly, given their locations, three gravestones have been inserted into the front part of the central aisle.

The altar with its reredos (an altarpiece) was erected against the East wall of the church. The altar rails clearly divide the altar zone (with the priest) from the congregational part of the room. As a reminder that the sacrament of baptism creates community, the font is placed in the choir,

---

8. Bexell, "Church Life," 1–23. See also Byström and Norrgård, *Mer än ord*.
9. Gustafsson, *Medeltidskyrkan*.
10. Tuulse, "Västra Ryds kyrka."

in front of the pews. The pulpit is located on the North wall of the nave in close proximity to the sacristy. The three poles for the administration of the means of grace are thus denoted in the traditional liturgical furnishings of the choir: the altar (the Sacrament of Holy Communion), the baptismal font (the Sacrament of Baptism), and the pulpit (the Word of God).

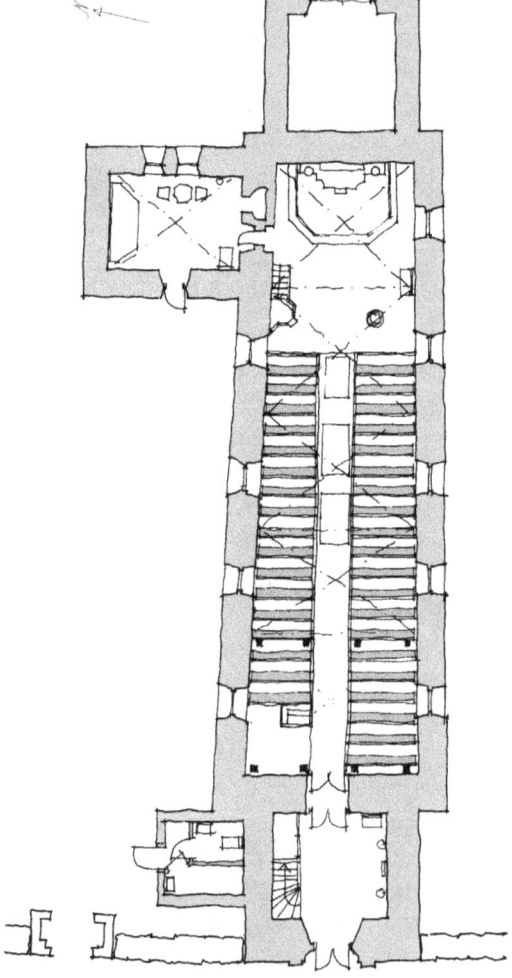

Figure 10. The Church of Västra Ryd at the end of the nineteenth century and throughout the twentieth century.

The tower (from the 1760s) is found at a short wall at the West End of the nave with the main entrance into the worship area. North of the tower a storage room can be seen, which up until the beginning of the twentieth century functioned as a mortuary chapel.

The Church of Västra Vingåker—a Local Introduction

This church is one of the largest rural church buildings in Sweden. Its current shape originates from the latter part of the eighteenth century—although it has a shell from the end of the thirteenth century.[11] Including the double galleries in the two transepts, this church would have housed some 3,000 people in its heyday. There were three entrances: in the West through the tower and through each of the transepts. The medieval sacristy had been pulled down in favor of a new and larger sacristy to the East of the choir. At the West end of the church, a large organ gallery had also been erected. The medieval wooden statues and the burial memorials were mostly lost during this major period of alteration, but the medieval baptismal font was kept in use.

The damage caused by a bolt of lightning in the mid-1880s allowed the parish council to remove the extensive galleries in the transepts during the following restoration. That gave a more obvious appearance to the interior cross-shape of the church, while at the same time the new pew arrangements gave the church the liturgical character of being a large central church. The reredos, an altarpiece from the end of the seventeenth century, was placed against the East wall in a Romanesque-shaped niche.

After intense preparations in the parish, the latest renovation took place in 2011–2012 with the architect Jerk Alton as contributor of ideas and as artistic leader.

In every essential aspect, the floor plan for the Church of Västra Vingåker gives the same ecclesiological image as that for the Church of Västra Ryd. The large number of pews—placed within the rectangular squares of the floor plan—shows with overwhelming clarity that, in accordance with the thinking at that time, even this church was primarily a room for preaching. It was, liturgically speaking, a worthy room for solemnity. The worship-place and the liturgy were congenial with the worship ideals of its time and could thus be perceived as supporting one another towards this goal. The large organ gallery at the West end was the place for the organist and the church-choir. The priest entered into the church from the sacristy, located behind the East wall of the church building. Those who visibly and audibly led the worship of the congregation—here and elsewhere during this period—were first and foremost the priest and the church musician. The worshippers were primarily participants in their listening, praying, and singing.

---

11. "Västra Vingåkers kyrka." *Sörmlands kyrkor nr 3.*

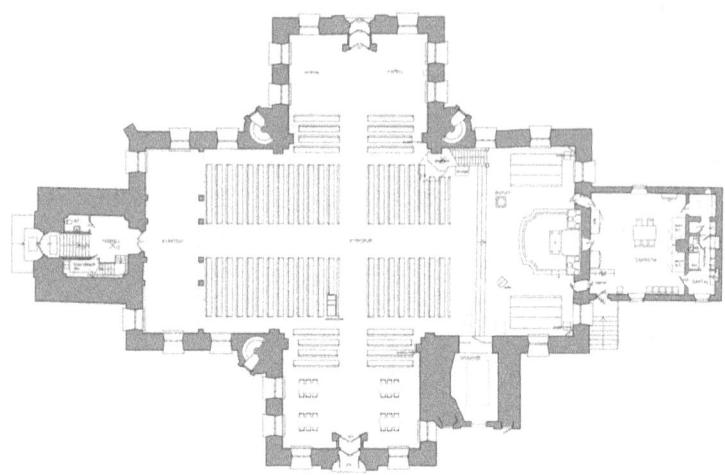

Figure 11. The Church of Västra Vingåer in the early nineteenth century and at the beginning of the twentieth century.

AN ECCLESIOLOGICAL READING OF THE TWENTIETH CENTURY FLOOR PLANS

In ecclesiological terms, the floor plans presented above show two church buildings, which in every essential aspect correspond to the orders of worship that liturgically and spatially characterized the application of current orders of worship up until the emergence of the 1942 Church of Sweden Service Book.

The Church Service Books from 1894, 1917, and to some extent also the Book from 1942 did not, as such, ask for any liturgically motivated alterations in the choir of the church building. Those orders of service prescribed a service that was in every liturgical part constructed in the same way for the cathedral in the diocesan city as well as for the large or small church buildings at the countryside. The liturgical centers of worship—located at the altar in the choir (and when required at the baptismal font), the pulpit in the nave, and the organ in the West end gallery— did not pose specific liturgically-founded demands for changes voiced by the parishes for the contemporary national and regional antiquarians to consider. Simply put, it was primarily aesthetic and historical concerns, besides regular maintenance, that guided the renovation processes that aimed to improve the conditions of the church buildings during this period.

From a pastoral point of view, it was possible, right up until the mid-twentieth century, to speak of the ministry of the pew as the vocation of active parish members. The floor plans thus reflect the basic ecclesiology that divided the clerical teaching estate of the church from its listening estate. At the same time it could be said that these worship spaces also functioned to create a sense of belonging. With their walls and their space, these buildings encompassed the worshipping congregation. With their furnishings, lighting, and colorings they provided the outward character for the event that the liturgy as such constituted, performed from its contemporary prerequisites. For the regular worshippers, these buildings created a kind of familiarity and sense of home in the meeting of heaven and earth. With regard to their content, they could be described and locally experienced as something of an *axis mundi*.

The ecclesiological study of the floor plan of a church thus clarifies the way in which a congregation celebrates its worship; as such, the study does not result in a historical abstraction. From an epistemological point of view it could be said that this approach finds the material for the study in a specific place, i.e. in a church building. From a pastoral and theological point of view, it contributes in helping the parishioners to understand the "inner" material asset that they possess in their local church building in addition to helping them become aware of the challenges that the on-going processes of liturgical renewal has presented to their place of worship.

The Liturgical Renewal Efforts from an Ecclesiological Perspective

For the Church of Sweden, the liturgical process of a more catholic (worldwide) renewal made its first impact with the publication of the 1942 Church Service Book. With its desire to develop the worship of the Swedish parishes further on that basis, the emerging high church movement acted as something of an internal revivalist movement. Through its emphasis on liturgy, pastoral care, and the sacraments, it sought to vitalize the worship life in the Church of Sweden.[12]

With reference to the firmly regulated framework of the orders of service, the renewal process initially focused on the worship area with its extensive pew furnishings and exalted pulpits.[13] If more (visibly) active forms of fellowship were to be established, it was thought that a reduction of the number of pews in the nave would be important—at least at the front towards the choir and at the back, towards the porch. As an expression for the common celebration of worship by the people of God, the church should be

---
12. Byström and Norrgård, *Mer än ord*, 30–34.
13. See for example Adell, *Guds rika hus*, 141–45.

seen as a wholeness in which the altar and the priest, as well as the organ and the church musician, should come spatially closer to the worshippers in order that something of a liturgical "we" might be established. It was also important to seek to arrange for some kind of a smaller chapel within the larger room for parishioners to use for services of prayer, intercession, and for weekday Mass, as well as for private prayer.

With both the liturgical experimentation in the 1970s and the following reception-process of the 1986 Church Service Book, it became obvious that every kind of renewal of the worship areas in the Church of Sweden necessarily ought to take the current forms of worship as a starting-point.[14] If the liturgy and the church building were not reasonably coherent, the room as such could become a force that was counterproductive to that which the new liturgical order sought to present. Committee members (together with the church musician and the parish priest) should return to the floor plans and discover where the critical points were to be seen in the worship-site. Without such a process it might be difficult to adapt the inner church building discussed above with the general intentions behind the 1986 Service Book.

The two parishes we are following in this chapter obviously sought, on the basis of their cultural and historical heritage, to find structural form within their church buildings that could open up and liberate rather than internally isolate and cement the current state. It is not difficult to note that towards the end of the twentieth century, it was generally tight between the pews and scarce between the worshippers.[15] The challenge was, so to speak, to make the churches "usable" from the perspective of a more catholic liturgical intention and at the same time to show appropriate respect for the historical uniqueness of these two rooms. From a more general perspective it could also be claimed that they should be part of the public space, while at the same time the experience of the holiness of these rooms and their different character ought not be dissolved into triviality.[16]

Although the two church buildings discussed here are very different in regard to their dimensions and their designs, we will see below how, from an ecclesiological point of view, the renovation processes in the twentyfirst century were expressed in the floor plans. It is important to bear in mind how the respective parishes planned for the future use of their church buildings. It was thought that the church of Västra Ryd should be a complementary smaller room for theme-services and occasional offices within the

---

14. Eckerdal, "Gudstjänstrummet," 107–10.
15. Bäckersten, "Salskyrkan," 273.
16. Granberg, *Stora kyrkor*, 49–52; See also Senn, "Protestantism," 160–64.

CHURCH FLOOR PLANS AS ECCLESIOLOGICAL TEXTS 185

framework of the church of Kungsängen, since it is the main church of that parish. The church building of Västra Vingåker was in every respect the center of that parish and should be used for both larger and smaller services all through the year.

AN ECCLESIOLOGICAL READING OF THE FLOOR PLAN FROM THE PERSPECTIVE OF LOCAL APPLICATIONS OF A "NEW" LITURGY

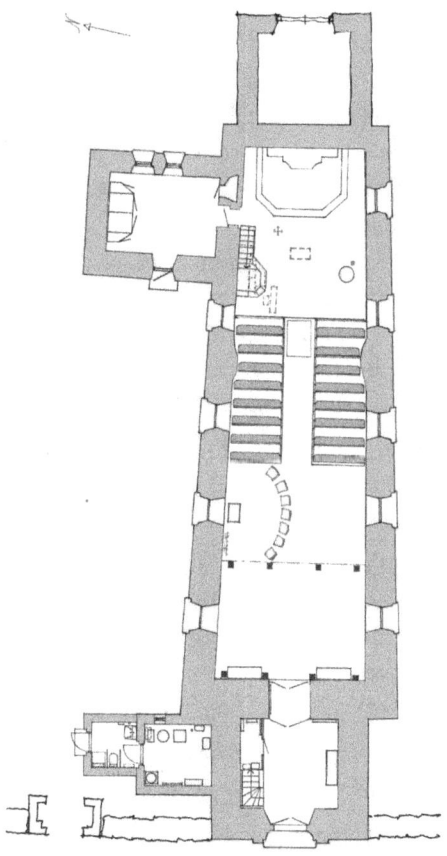

Figure 12. The church of Västra Ryd after the renovation from 2004–2010.

If we compare this floor plan of the current layout of the church of Västra Ryd with the layout in Figure 1, we see that the altar with its reredos and the pulpit were left intact without alteration as something of a mental reminder of the former church interior with its specific structure.

One alteration has, however, taken place in the altar zone: the altar rail has been removed, but the exalted podium with its two steps has been kept so that it is possible to use hassocks on the lower step for kneeling to receive communion.

The obviously new and challenging change that has been achieved in the church building of Västra Ryd is the openness and the possibilities of variations created by Lotta Gustafsson, the architect responsible for the renovations. The plan emphatically shows that this in turn was made possible by a considerable reduction of the previous number of pews. This new openness and mobility thus becomes, in our context, an ecclesiological concept for analysis that is employed to grasp "the liturgical result" of this renovation process.

The flexible structure of this room can be a reminder to the worshippers that they here have "no lasting city" and "the city that is to come" (Heb 13:14). They will thus be reminded in one way or another that they are a pilgrim people within their own church. As we seek to read the current floor plan, we find the following:

- In the middle of the North wall of the nave, in close proximity to one of the medieval statues of the Virgin Mary and her child Jesus, there is a movable altar-table with a semicircle of chairs designed as a place for weekday Mass. The lighting arrangement is placed in connection with this demarcated space for devotion.

- The same altar-table can be placed in the choir with the lectern, processional cross, electrical piano, and Easter candle at the font in order to demarcate the space for a larger theme-Mass.

- The chairs placed in a semicircle around the baptismal font create an almost defined room in which baptism can be celebrated in case the baptism is not included in the ordinary Sunday celebration in the church of Kungsängen.

- The open space in the nave without any pews creates the pre-requisites for theme-days, retreats, confirmation classes, and conversations. Furniture and other items can then be arranged as needed.

- The church in its full length can also be used for concerts (with choir and orchestra up in the choir) as well as for marriage services and funerals. On such occasions the open space can be complemented by using folding chairs (which otherwise are kept in special cupboards in the porch).

- From a functional point of view it is finally worth noting that, through this latest renovation, the building—and the bell tower in particular—has become a space for technology and appliances, and the parish has also gained permission to erect a necessary bathroom with an entrance from the churchyard (it was too expensive to open up an entrance through the tower wall).

Altogether, an ecclesiological reading of this floor plan shows that, following the completed renovation, this parish has gained something of a sanctified workshop for planning its worship life as well as a holy place for its ordinary worship. For encounters with the Holy One, a dedicated staff group, driven by the elementary aspects of the liturgy, can create varied forms for adoration, closeness, and community.

The mobility within this church is not an end in itself. Psychologically, it could counteract individual's sense of security that comes with familiarity, but it also provides a challenge in a way that has to do with the basic experience of the Christian faith.

All things considered, the example of the rearranged church interior of Västra Ryd points to a realistic alternative for numerous church buildings that are located within the same parish and have structures that are more or less liturgically comparable to one another and might therefore (maybe in a non-articulated manner) be perceived as "superfluous," thus running the risk of becoming less-used (or in other terms, of becoming "under-used").

Through its floor plan, the church of Västra Ryd expresses not only stability within the church walls—with the traditional arrangement of the choir and the unaltered location of the altar, the pulpit, the baptismal font and the front pews in the nave—but also mobility at the West end of the room. The tension between firmness and mobility thus challenges the worshippers, including the worship leader and the church musician, to interpret and explain the language of faith through the different forms of worship that might be developed here.

The renovation of the church building of Västra Vingåker took its starting-point in the worship life of that parish and the form of worship that the local church council wished to develop (as was also the case in the Church of Västra Ryd). The decisive difference between these two church interiors was that here in Västra Vingåker, besides various theme-services, the Sunday Eucharist should be celebrated every week, something that also is reflected in the detailed floor plan of how this room in its totality should serve the worship as well as support various diaconal functions. An ecclesiological analysis of this room would rely on the ordinary worship, based on the orders of service in the 1986 Church of Sweden Service Book, and the social, diaconal intention of this parish.

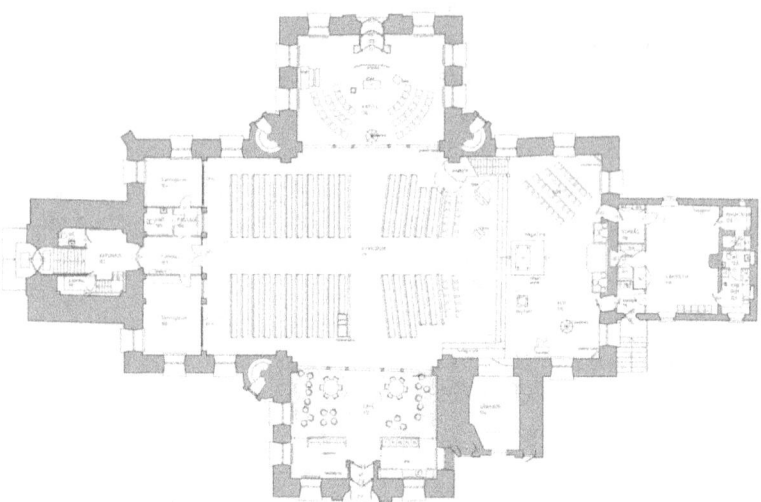

Figure 13. The church of Västra Vingåker after the renovation of 2011–2012.

Together with their architect, Jerk Alton, the parish committee created the pre-conditions for a pastorally-directed life of worship in this large room while taking into account the desire for a radical reduction in the number of pews. The floor plan shows that here too, the altar, the reredos, and the pulpit have been left untouched in their places; however, the altar rail has been removed as a visible sign that the "main altar" of this worship space is the new altar-table that has been placed in front of the choir steps. There is no altar rail because there is a desire to administer the gifts of Communion to the communicants standing in a semi-circle.

In order to visually clarify that this part of the church building is the middle point, a large ring of light is dispensed above the altar zone with its matching lectern. This lighting helps to create a clear focus for the liturgical events. Altered spatial and visible pre-conditions have resulted in an organically coherent hub for the worship of this parish.

The new altar-table is standing on a small podium, which can be wheeled aside on the occasions when a larger free space is required at the front of the church. The rest of the choir contains a well-proportioned area for the medieval baptismal font as well as for the choir organ and the church choir. A grand piano is placed below the choir steps (for use with the songs of praise in the Hymnal).

The pews in the central aisle are divided into two parts. The back pews are intended for major solemnities, while the two front parts have been placed at an angle towards the altar in order to spatially emphasize the fellowship among the worshippers gathered around the Word of God and the Sacraments. This arrangement of the front pews could be said to reduce the superfluous capacity of available space in that very large room. This arrangement of the furniture is also a challenging application of the relationship between the Lord of the Church and his people, expressed in the parable of the vine and the branches (John 15:1–10), the body and its members (Rom 12:4–5), and the bread and the community (1 Cor 10:16b–17). The disposition of the room expresses the difference between the perception that the people of God attend church and that these people in the church *are* the church, the new temple, built by living stones (1 Pet 2:4–5).

Under the large organ gallery at the West end, two meeting-rooms with glass-walls that look out into the worship site have been added. One of these rooms is primarily intended to function as a sacristy in connection with the Sunday services. The entrance procession at High Mass can naturally start from here and open the Sunday worship as well as act as a reminder of the common calling of the people of God to walk towards the East and the Light of the resurrection.

Through the removal of the pews from both the transepts, the church room has shifted its character. Having been a sort of central church in a previous period, it became a church with a marked central axis. At the same time, it now offers a Eucharistic room at the front part where the worshippers, including the choir, can gather around the new free-standing altar. The parish also has the possibility to arrange for a chapel with some 30 seats, the Chapel of St. Mary, in the Northern transept. In the Southern transept a generously receptive "church square," a kind of internal church green pastures, was developed with a bookstall, a café, and opportunities for conversations "on the hoof."

An ecclesiological reading of the floor plan for the church of Västra Vingåker provides a coherent image of an inner church building, thought-through in its detail, in which both regular worshippers and more occasional visitors gather during weekdays as well as on holy days. With reference to the front part of the church with its main altar, the Lady Chapel in the Northern transept, and the social functions in the Southern transept, we here encounter a fundamental ecclesiological view that, after the latest renovation, presents this room as a space for both worship and fellowship. The structure makes it obvious that this room wants to challenge its visitors to conversations about the meaning of walking as a pilgrim-people towards the Light of Christ in the East as well as being a member, together with the other worshippers, in the one and only body of Christ, the Church of Christ. At the same time the disposition of the room points very specifically to the alterations that have taken place, primarily for reasons of changing population patterns, with regard to individual people's participation in worship. In the church of Västra Vingåker the architect and the building-committee have thus created several different rooms within the one church: for the weekday Mass, for High Mass on lesser Sundays, for the major festivals of the liturgical year, and for church concerts.

AN ECCLESIOLOGICAL READING IN THE MIDST OF LITURGICAL REVIVAL: A SUMMARY

When I return to my thesis and my main question concerning the relation between the worship and the church buildings it is obvious that this was—and is—the basic issue when representatives from the Church of Sweden parishes and the antiquarian authorities meet for discussions concerning the maintenance of these buildings. Unless there is a liturgical celebration in front of the triune God, these buildings sooner or later lose their aim and are threatened to change their character, becoming more like museums with interesting inventories, paintings, etc. The church buildings are exponents of that cultural heritage which primarily has its basis in locally-celebrated worship.[17] In the floor plans we have a tool of understanding their liturgical character; they are—as has been my argument in this chapter—texts to be read and interpreted as liturgical documents.[18]

Just one rather late example out of these floor plans: when the out-drawn debate concerning the church pews during the latter part of the twentieth century reached some kind of a *modus vivendi*, it was easy to see what a strong effect these pews had possessed (and still possess). As soon as a reduction of the number of pews became possible to carry out, the room could become quite different and thus allow for different ways to celebrate the liturgy and express another ecclesiological understanding of the worship space—but even so, it of course remained the same building as before. Even in other church traditions, the pews are becoming, in one way or another, less dominant.[19]

With new free spaces in the choir, the floor plans can demarcate new places for the altar-table, the lectern, the choir organ (and the choral singers). Given that the disposition of the choir can be different, it will also become possible, from an ecclesiological point of view, to give the space for worship a clearer and more coherent interpretation. The baptismal font, which

---

17. Weman, *Nutida gudstjänst*, 307.
18. See above, footnotes 2 and 3.
19. Yates, *Liturgical Space*, 27.

earlier had been located in front of the worshippers in order to remind them of the meaning of baptism as integration into the parish community, is no longer exhibited as a solitary item; it is now naturally integrated into the basic liturgical and sacramental character of the room.

The more it becomes possible to consider different floor plans for one and the same church building in detail, the more obvious it becomes that there is no "ecclesiologically innocent" church interior. Disposition and structure show, through their enforced or deliberately chosen solutions, which ecclesiology lies behind the floor plans and thus implies the way in which a parish celebrates its worship. An inductive analysis of the relationship between the church interior and the celebration of worship from a number of floor plans can thus reveal the operative ecclesiology in that specific parish—and the analysis may therefore, negatively or positively, serve as the decisive factor in any process of renewal. The intention is of course that the shape should correspond to the purpose, i.e. that, as far as it is physically possible, the view of the room should be attuned to the form and structure of the Mass.

From an overall point of view, it could be said that a church interior that has some kind of an anteroom, a nave, and a choir is in the best sense the architectural expression of the parish idea. In such a room the worshipping congregation can express itself as a community. Against the background of the process of liturgical renewal during the second half of the twentieth century, we have seen in the floor plans studied here that the worship space has reclaimed its basic idea as *one* room rather than the several-rooms-idea that had been developed over time. The altar has moved away from the East wall and the worshipers have come closer to the front part of the church (or have formed a semi-circle in the newly established "small church" or place for devotion). In order to facilitate an experience of fellowship (*koinonia*) among the worshipers, it has been important that the liturgical gathering could find its form in an organic way around the altar/altar-table, as well as around the lectern/pulpit and the baptismal font. On the basis of the floor plans for the two churches that we have studied, it is worth noting that, when the structure of the church interior is altered in order to correspond better to a catholic, biblically-deeper view of the character of worship with various actively-contributing participants (or groups), the issue of the functionality of the room easily comes to the fore. In order to avoid the risk that important categories of holiness and exultation are lost, it is essential not only to preserve but also, if possible, to develop the beauty, the sense of space, and the liturgical clarity of the room. As far as possible, both material and immaterial factors must therefore be given the opportunity to collaborate with one another in order that the worship space might speak to both thoughts and feelings.

We have seen different structural solutions worked out in response to the local circumstances of each respective parish church, which has been renovated on the basis of the same liturgically characterized basic attitude. The task for the architect and the members of the building-committee has been to achieve a well-working balance between the church building as the exponent of a historically determined cultural heritage and as the holy place for the meeting of that congregation with the Holy Triune God, the God of heaven and earth.

The church of Västra Ryd has been given the character of a district church within a larger parish and as a result has a limited number of services. The church of Västra Vingåker is the main church of that parish and has a varied number of services on both Sundays and weekdays in the same room. These two worship spaces show different floor plans due to their functions within the respective local situation—and in that they ought to be of interest for other parishes and church communities who seek to consider their own issues with regard to their church interior and their worship for the future.

12

(De)gendering Ecclesiology

Reflections on the Church as a Gendered Body

NINNA EDGARDH

EDITORS' INTRODUCTION

Ninna Edgardh introduced feminist studies to the research seminar in Ecclesiology in Uppsala through her doctoral thesis *Feminism and Liturgy—An Ecclesiological Study* (2001).

In this chapter she argues that social constructions of gender interrelate with churches' self-understanding of their existence and mission, both in theory and practice. (De)-gendering, as referred to in the title, is defined as a continuous process of questioning gendered structures that are sometimes obvious and explicit and sometimes hidden.

Feminist approaches to ecclesiology are confronted with several interrelated obstacles according to the author. The obstacles discussed are gendered symbolic language, the male gendering of the theoretical field of study, and hegemonic ecclesiological claims, legitimized by divine authority.

With the help of examples from her own extensive studies of liturgy and Christian social practice (*diakonia*), the author shows how a gendered approach to ecclesiology may accumulate new and critical knowledge. The main conclusion is that cracks, tensions, and disharmonies in theologies of the church reveal surprising ecclesiological aspects of (de)-gendering, visible only with a mindful attention to both gender and theology.

All the authors in Part Three disclose ecclesiological aspects, but from different practices: Weman in liturgical space, Oljelund in liturgical texts, and Edgardh in gendered practices of both liturgy and *diakonia*. The researchers are in search of lived, concrete ecclesiology. The results may open our eyes to aspects of ecclesiology as lived church practice, insights which may in turn give impulses to change.

Ninna Edgardh (born 1955), professor in ecclesiology, especially social and diaconal studies, Uppsala University, and priest in the Church of Sweden. Her research is focused on both ecclesiology and social change, with particular attention to gender. This is reflected for example in *Welfare and Religion in 21st Century Europe: Volume 2. Welfare and Religion in 21st century Europe: Gendered, Religious and Social Change* (2011).

WORKING WITH "THE MALE AS GOD"

One day, while perusing my Facebook feed I find an update by a man who has realized that most of the books he reads, most of the films he sees, and most of the music to which he listens are all created by men. Now he has decided that over the next year, he will consciously choose books written by women, films directed by women, and music composed and performed by women. He wishes to see how this will change how he perceives the world around him. After reading his update, I cannot stop thinking about it. I find a Twitter campaign, #readwomen2014, promoting a year of only reading books written by women. Enthused, I imagine what that would look like for me, but I quickly realize that, for me, such a year is impossible. Professionally, I am caught in a world of texts written almost exclusively by men.

Part of my working week is spent serving as a priest in the Church of Sweden and the other part as a professor of ecclesiology at Uppsala University. In both of these contexts I am bound to traditions where "the male is God," as Mary Daly has so poignantly formulated it.[1] Preaching and celebrating liturgy without referring to texts written by and about men—even just for a year—would be unthinkable, as would excluding male authors from the curriculum in theology. Exclusion of women's voices is, however,

---

1. Daly, *Beyond God*, 19.

neither impossible nor uncommon, though it is politically incorrect in a country known as one of the most egalitarian in the world.[2]

I do not write this as a complaint from a victim. I have chosen both my jobs fully cognizant of their heritage. I see both positions as vocations that stimulate and challenge me, even in their gendered biases. What I want to do in this article is instead to give some examples of how I have been approaching the gendered worlds of both church and academy in my ecclesiological research.

Doing research has in fact been a way for me of making sense of the gendered situation I work and live in, allowing me to discuss it, as if it was not ultimately decisive for my everyday life and my very sense of being. Research helps me explore those small cracks in reality where, as Leonard Cohen says, "the light gets in."[3]

(DE)GENDERING

Gender is part of how we perceive reality. It is a basic part of human culture. We are born into a gendered sea of social life, and the water in which we swim limits our perception of reality. To research on gender is to question the quality of the water. It is to ask if the type of water where I swim is the only possible or the most sustainable water for human beings. It is to question normality.

From this statement it should already be clear that I do not see research as simply describing and analyzing "how things are." Nobody can claim to recount exactly "what really happened," either in history or in the contemporary world. Research is always made from a perspective, revealed in the questions posed and the theoretical and methodological tools employed. Interestingly, in this attitude towards reality the New Testament is good company, as it provides us with four versions of the same story in order to tell the Gospel.[4] To abstain from claims of telling absolute truths does not imply, however, that there is no difference between research and telling a good story. What makes my research credible is the extent to which I can make an argument that is possible for others to follow and test. The questioning of seemingly self-evident gendered orders in church and society belongs to my motivation for research.[5] In that way there is an obvious normativity in my

---

2. Sweden was ranked as number four in the *Global Gender Gap Report 2013*.
3. Cohen, "Anthem."
4. Lathrop, *Four Gospels*.
5. For the role of normalization in our perception of gender, see Edgardh, "A Gendered Perspective," 83–88.

research. But it doesn't mean that I have any more specific agendas for how such systems are to be changed or what the ultimate system would look like.

Gendering Church

In my research I study how churches understand and express their task and mission, in relation to changing gender relations in contemporary society. Now the crucial term "gender" is sometimes misunderstood to mean "women," or even "woman" in a generic sense. This has to do with the fact that social inequalities, negatively affecting many women, have been a major driving force behind the growing academic field of gender studies, as well as behind more activist and political feminist movements, both of which highlight gender inequalities in society. The situation of women in church and society was a major topic for the first generations of gender researchers in theology. Gender became visible when women began to question the normality of the given situation. To equalize gender with women (or even "woman") is thus to obscure what is at stake. A more adequate definition of gender has to include men and the relations between women and men. But even that is not enough.

As the feminist historian Joan Scott shows, for example, staying within the binary categories of women and men is to continuously rebuild the cage that locks you in. In one of her books Scott takes her starting point in the struggle for women's rights in France, referring to the dilemma these early feminists were faced with: Are demands for equal rights for women to be grounded in their likeness with men or in their difference from men? Both positions had obvious disadvantages from their relating to men as the norm. But as long as these two alternatives were seen as the only options, women were caught and confronted only with paradoxes.[6]

The option that Scott argues for coincides with the turn feminism took from the 1990s and onwards, redirecting the interest from the comparison between two binary categories of women and men towards the deconstruction of these categories and a new focus on differences within them:

> The only alternative, it seems to me, is to refuse to oppose equality to difference and insist continually on differences—differences as the condition of individual and collective identities, differences as the constant challenge to the fixing of those identities, history as the repeated illustration of the play of differences, differences as the very meaning of equality itself.[7]

---

6. Scott, *Only Paradoxes*, x.

7. Scott, "Deconstructing Equality," 145.

As theories on gender have developed from the 1990s and onwards, it has become clear that the categories we call "women" and "men" are constructions undergoing continuous change, while still being very stable at some levels. Doing research on gender thus includes studying both how "women" and "men" are produced as binary categories and how this construction is related to the social organization of inequalities.[8]

Following theories of intersectionality, gender studies also includes researching the intersectional construction of gender and other structuring factors such as race, class, ethnicity, sexuality, and even religion. A woman is never only a woman but has multiple identities, all of which contribute to her social position and freedom to act.[9]

Degendering as a strategy

(De)gendering, as referred to in the title of this chapter, may be defined as a continuous process of questioning gendered structures that are sometimes obvious and explicit and sometimes hidden. This is done with the normative aim of enabling a freer approach wherein gendered structures do not decide to the same extent the quality of the water in which we swim and where it might be possible—or just interesting—to crawl in hitherto unknown directions, where the water may provide other and possibly better potentials for swimming:

> [D]egendering attacks the structure and process of gender—the division of people into two social statuses and the social construction of what we call opposites. In methodological terms, degendering is a counterfactual heuristic, posing the challenge of *what if?* I ask, What if we did not divide people by gender?[10]

Doing this in relation to the church implies exploring—and questioning—how specific understandings and embodiments of church interact with the construction of gender, as well as with class, ethnicity, and sexual preferences.

Degendering may sound confusingly like ignoring gender. But as the feminist theorist Judith Lorber observes, ignoring gender

> [. . .] allows gendered processes and practices to proceed unhindered. To deliberately degender, you have to attend to those

---

8. Wharton, *Sociology of Gender*, 217.

9. For an introduction to theories on intersectionality see for example the thematic issue of *The European Journal of Women's Studies*, 2006:13.

10. Lorber, *Breaking*, 7.

processes and practices in order not to do them. You have to do gender to degender.[11]

There is a double edge in the process Lorber describes. Hidden structures need to be made visible and seemingly gender neutral realities revealed as gendered. There is however an obvious risk that this process reinforces the gendered structures rather than challenging them. Thus the need for degendering; that is for questioning, neutralizing, queering, or in other ways exploring "cracks" that may reveal new horizons.

CHURCHES AS GENDERED BODIES

As a researcher of ecclesiology, my specific interest is how the social constructions of gender relate to how churches understand their own existence and mission in the world, both in theory and practice. The binary categories of "women" and "men" are also produced and organized in patterns of inequality in church contexts. Likewise such patterns are continuously broken and disrupted in these contexts. This means that churches, like any other organizations, are suitable for sociological gender studies. However, churches also have traits that require a theological approach. From a feminist perspective, studies of church practices need to be complemented by studies of how these practices relate to the churches' own ideas of its task and mission.

I want to suggest three interrelated aspects of ecclesiology, which are quite easily observed, but which together constitute major obstacles for feminist ecclesiology. These aspects are the role of gendered symbolic language; the male gendering of the theoretical field of study; and hegemonic ecclesiological claims, legitimized by divine authority.

Gendered symbolic language

Anyone approaching the Christian church as a gendered body is bound to observe that the church is regularly called "she," implicating a person of female gender. An equally simple observation is that God is regularly talked about in male terms. This gendered symbolic structure is what Sallie McFague calls metaphoric language turned into a model: a metaphor with staying power.[12] The Christian God is called Father, Son, and Holy Spirit—three in one, but male gendered. "He" is seen as having revealed "himself" in the historic man Jesus from Nazareth. "He" is almighty. "He" is good. "He" knows everything and has created everything. In fact "His" divine ex-

---

11. Ibid., 27.
12. McFague, *Models of God*, 31–40.

istence, earthly incarnation, and calling to discipleship, is understood as the very reason behind the existence of all Christian churches. "He" acts in the world through "his" church and "she" is supposed to listen and obey "his" will, as "he" is also to "her" as the head is to the body. They have a hierarchical relation. In this way a highly gendered symbolic language is tied to the very being of the Christian church as it has hitherto appeared.

A gendered field of study

A second observation is that while many church members, and many active such members, are women, most authors writing about the church are men. Women have not primarily expressed their ecclesial belonging in writing and lecturing, mostly because until the very last century they have not had the possibility to be ordained ministers, and in some churches they still do not have this option. As a consequence theological academic training historically has not been easily available for women.

This means that the church as a "she" is largely reduced to a symbol, with a lopsided relation to real women in the Christian tradition. The male dominance of the whole area of theological reading and writing is striking and a real problem for the researcher who wants to approach ecclesiological issues. Natalie Watson observes in her hitherto unique *Introduction to Feminist Ecclesiology* (2002) that mainstream ecclesiological literature does not include any major works written by women and thus, "writing formal ecclesiology from a feminist perspective, I am entering a conversation to which I have not been invited."[13]

Hegemonic claims, legitimized by divine authority

The third observation I want to reflect upon has to do with the "theandric character" of ecclesial identity that Sven-Erik Brodd refers to in the introductory chapter.[14] This character implies that the theologian approaching ecclesiology has to deal with strong explanatory claims from the object of study. I am thinking of claims like the world being created and sustained by God, the church being a case of ongoing incarnation, or the ministry of the priest being instituted by God. Academic theologians handle such claims differently, but it is not uncommon in theological writings to see these claims adopted as implicit premises for the discussion. In this type of argument *the essence* or *the nature* of *the Church* is presupposed, quite like how the nature of women has been discussed historically.

---

13. Watson, *Introducing Feminist Ecclesiology*, 5.
14. Brodd in this volume, 18.

Confessional writers have, moreover, regularly identified their own preferably Roman Catholic or Orthodox tradition with *the Church* and thus limited their discussion to that specific church tradition in a hegemonic way.

The central role of the idea of the incarnated God, the infinite taking shape in the finite, and the symbolic role gender have been given in this understanding may together explain some of the complexity of feminist approaches to ecclesiology. What is particular in a feminist study of the church, in contrast to the study of other social bodies, is that the power that is questioned is legitimated by claims on divine authority and that these claims are expressed in a highly gendered language.

FEMINIST ECCLESIOLOGY

From the 1960s and onwards Christian traditions have been criticized by feminist theologians from many different points of view. However, it seems that many feminist scholars have tended to regard church and feminism as a contradiction in terms rather than as an important field of study. In a preface to *Introduction to Feminist Ecclesiology*, Mary Grey observes that "it takes great courage to write about ecclesiology from a feminist standpoint [. . .] indeed many feminist theologians have shied away from the task, viewing it as inconsistent with feminist integrity."[15] Admittedly, there are exceptions. Some titles among the major early works of feminist theologians focused on the theological understanding of the church. I am thinking, for example, of Letty Russell's *Church in the Round* (1993) and Rosemary Radford Reuther's *WomenChurch* (1996).[16] As a sub current Western feminist ecclesiology has definitely had a role in the development of ecclesiology during the recent decades.[17] However, comparably little of the large amount of feminist theological writing produced in a Western context over the last decades has been dedicated to the church as such.

It is worth observing though, that the same decades have seen a growing body of ecclesiological reflection produced by female writers from Africa, Latin America, and Asia, sometimes using the feminist label and sometimes consciously avoiding it because of its associations to Western feminist heritage. Contributions by authors such as Sarojini Nadar, Isabel Apawo Phiri, Elsa Tamez, Yong Ting Jin, and Meehyun Chung highlight gendered aspects

---

15. Grey, *Introducing Feminist*, vii.

16. Russell, *Church in the Round*; Ruether, *Women-Church*.

17. Veli-Matti Kärkkäinen includes a chapter on "The Feminist Church" under the sub-heading "Contextual Ecclesiologies" in Karkkäinen, *Introduction to Ecclesiology*, 2002, 184–93. Bryan P. Stone includes a few Western feminist scholars in his nearly all male reader in ecclesiology, see Stone, *Reader in Ecclesiology*, 2012.

that have to do with the shift of Christian gravity, from Europe towards what today is often labeled the Global South, which has taken place during the last decades.[18] Whereas about two-thirds of the world's Christians lived in Europe a hundred years ago, today European Christians account only for about a quarter of all Christians.[19] Throughout the decade spanning from 1988 to 1998, proclaimed as a decade for *Churches in Solidarity with Women* by the World Council of Churches, important gender aspects of this challenge towards traditional Western ecclesial authority were highlighted.[20]

Many Western feminist theologians have instead chosen the option I initially stated as impossible for me and opted out of the church. Mary Daly, author of the groundbreaking works *The Church and the Second Sex* (1968) and *Beyond God the Father* (1973), was a Roman Catholic who eventually chose to leave the church. Her academic position at Boston College was called into question when she refused male students in some of her classes.[21] In her later writing she developed a post-Christian experimental feminist philosophy, of her own special brand, which envisioned a world where the root metaphors would not be male but female. Other feminists have, rather than envisioning such a future, projected their dreams backwards, trying to reconstruct a pre-Christian era of the Goddess, with the implicit message that it could happen again.[22]

Many women, especially in the Global North, have followed the Post-Christian feminists out of the church and today seek their spiritual nourishment elsewhere. And yet, women are church and have always been church. Natalie Watson's conclusion is that "Thinking about the church in theological terms has been a central part of being church throughout its history. It is time for women to participate in it on their own terms."[23]

This position has guided my own research. I have sought for sources documenting women "being church" in ways that have challenged gendered biases and symbolisms dominating the major Christian traditions. In doing so it has been obvious that the relation between the feminist movement and the churches is an ambiguous one.

---

18. Nadar and Phiri, *On Being Church*; Nadar, "On being the Pentecostal Church;" Tamez, "An Ecclesial Community;" Ting Jin, "On Being Church;" Chung, "Korean Feminist Ecclesiology;" Chung, *Breaking Silence*.

19. *Global Christianity*.

20. Ecclesiological reflection in the wake of the decade was documented in a special issue of *The Ecumenical Review*, vol 53/1, January 2001.

21. Daly, *Church and*; Daly, *Beyond God*. For her own version of her academic story, see Daly, *Amazon Grace*.

22. See for example Baring and Cashford, *The Myth of the Goddess*.

23. Watson, *Introducing Feminist*, 6.

The feminist scholar of liturgical history, Teresa Berger, has shown that the issues at stake have to do with the positions of the "separated sisters" of the church and the asymmetrical gender divisions as a source of disunity and fragmentation within the church itself.[24] As a result of the enforced separation, feminist theologians often have defined themselves as on the margin, struggling to hold together loyalty and critique. Elisabeth Schüssler Fiorenza has suggested the metaphor of "resident aliens" to characterize this position.[25] "Defecting in place" and "dissident daughters" are other wordings used to characterize feminist ecclesiological ambiguity.[26]

Liturgy as a Site of Struggle

My dissertation (2001) focused on the feminist liturgical movement as it had so far been enacted in Swedish churches.[27] The last decades of the twentieth century saw a range of new forms of worship emerging, and women across the world shaped worship services in ways that they themselves found liberating.[28] "The feminist liturgical movement" was a label used by a number of scholars in Europe and the US who were trying to summarize what was going on when women tried to shape Christian liturgy in ways that questioned patterns of women's subordination in church and society.[29] In my analysis of expressions of this movement in Sweden I used theoretical tools from liturgical theology as developed ecumenically and in the US during the same period, in order to see how feminist worship related to ecumenically recognized liturgical patterns. With the help of feminist theory I analyzed the attitudes towards gender constructions expressed in my material. My main approach, however, was ecclesiological. My aim was to analyze how new patterns of worship, created within a Christian framework, challenged the gendered ecclesiological framework of the church settings where they took place.

Feminist liturgies are by definition created in order to be both within and outside of, simultaneously belonging to and leaving the church traditions from which they are born. The position may well be described as "on the margin." It is however important to note that this marginal position is

---

24. Berger, "Liturgical Renewal," 71.

25. Fiorenza, *But She Said*, 185.

26. Winter, *Defecting in Place*; Berger, *Dissident Daughters*.

27. Edgardh, *Feminism och liturgi* (diss. in Swedish). Shorter versions in English in Edgardh, "Lady Wisdom;" Edgardh, "Mrs Murphy's Arising;" Edgardh, "Theology of Gathering."

28. Berger, *Dissident Daughters*.

29. Procter-Smith, *In Her Own Rite*.

not purely negative. Poststructuralist theorists like Rebecca Chopp argue instead that it is exactly this marginal position that makes room for something new to be born.[30]

To summarize I found the feminist liturgical movement, as it had been expressed in Swedish churches in the 1990s, to be a creative example of women trying to reconstruct the relation between church and gender; though not always successful, from either a feminist or from a liturgical perspective, it still comprised an effort to give women a more explicit ecclesiological voice.

Christian Social Practice

While my initial research on feminist liturgies was focused on activities on the margins of the major church traditions, my later research has focused on the much more traditional field of Christian social practice or *diakonia*, as this service is often named by churches themselves. My interest in these studies is the obviously highly gendered role of the church in this field.

The opportunity was given to me thanks to a research grant for research collaboration on the role of the historic churches in various types of welfare systems in Europe in the beginning of the twentyfirst century. In the project *Welfare and Religion in a European Perspective* we were able to document a field of church activity marked by a distinctly gendered division of labor.[31]

Diaconal work is still dominated by women all over Europe, especially on the ground level. The contributions of the churches as social actors are appreciated by both authorities and the European populations and often seem to serve as a legitimizing factor for the presence of the churches in the public sphere. This is reason enough to document and analyze the presence and influence of gender in these church-related practices. However, there is a dilemma built into the role of the churches as social caregivers. The increasing expectations on the churches in the social field might well be interpreted as a result of secularisation and loss of authority for the churches, pressing them to accept a devalued female gendered role rather than losing even more ground. Alas, few feminist researchers have been engaged in the study of diaconal work, perhaps because it involves women who voluntarily serve others, often with neither payment nor substantial influence on decision-making. Much of feminist analysis has been "religion blind" in that it has not been aware of the transformative potentials of Christian theology.[32]

---

30. Chopp, *Power to Speak*.
31. Bäckström et al., *Welfare and Religion*, vol. 1 and vol. 2.
32. Edgardh, "Gendered Perspective," 96–104. The concept "religion blind" has

This is regrettable. Surprising potentials of change and transformation may be contained in the role of the churches in the social field if that role is combined with a gendered consciousness. To the extent that the churches manage to promote theologically-grounded values of care and solidarity, which are downplayed in society at large, while simultaneously promoting a higher status for women and for values associated with female gender, they might well play an important transformative role in society at large.[33] Christian social practice, in acting both as voices for the suppressed and as contrast examples of how care and solidarity may be enacted in search for social cohesion and wellbeing, could hence become a sign of so-called prophetic *diakonia*.

THE ACADEMIC STUDY OF ECCLESIOLOGY

Sven-Erik Brodd admits in the introductory chapter that he hesitated to accept me as a doctoral student, twenty years ago, as the seminar had no experience of feminist studies and would therefore not constitute a supportive milieu for a new doctoral student with an interest in such a perspective.[34] I appreciate the self-critical reflection and do think it is essential for feminist studies in ecclesiology to be supported by a benevolent atmosphere, with at least a basic orientation in gender theory. On the other hand, the lack of such a milieu made me look outside the framework of the seminar and put me into contact with research partners from other areas, partners who have highly enriched my studies. The researchers from all over Europe and beyond, engaged in the project *Welfare and Religion* referred to above, have taught me a great deal about religious change in late modern societies. I have found other stimulating conversation partners in feminist theologians and liturgical scholars from all over the world, whom I have met at conferences. A third example would be gender theorists, for example at the Centre for Gender Studies at Uppsala University, who have helped me to sharpen my tools for gendered analyses.

That said, I would like to express my gratitude towards the persistent interest in ecclesiology in the seminar I have been part of in Uppsala, especially with its unique double focus on empirical studies and systematic theological theories and methods. In the modern Swedish academic context empirical studies of multitudes of confessional church bodies are conducted both by Church historians and by sociologists in religion. However,

---

been used in the Swedish context to describe the exclusion of religious motives from historic research on women's emancipation. See, Hammar, *Emancipation och religion*.

33. Edgardh, *Social agent*.
34. Brodd in this volume, 23–24.

systematic theological theories and methods are seldom applied in these areas of study. Systematic theological studies of ecclesiology, on the other hand, are not regularly anchored in empirical material, even if such studies have become more frequent. For feminist studies in ecclesiology aiming at challenging the three-fold gendered hegemony discussed above, the combination is indispensable. The non-confessional, but still distinctly theological character of the ecclesiology seminar in Uppsala has been an important prerequisite for my own work of problematizing the understanding of what it may mean to be a Christian church from the perspective of gender. This volume shows that ecclesiology may be enriched by, but never reduced to, empirical and ethnographical methods. That is true also for studies from a feminist perspective.[35]

GENDERED WATERS REVISITED

We swim in gendered waters. Church waters are full of gendered currents and reefs that feminist theologians have started to map. Much of the critique has concentrated on language. That is no coincidence, as gendered symbolic language is so pervasive in Christian theology and is closely related to a gendered order of male dominance.

Feminists have differed in their attitude towards the problem. One strategy has been to try to escape the gendered waters by de-gendering our language for God.[36] Another strategy has been to re-gender, that is to add feminine pronouns and female names to Christian God-language. The basic principle behind that strategy is that these words are equally adequate (and non-adequate) designations for God as male gendered words.[37] Feminist theologian Sallie McFague talks about a double strategy of first disorienting and then reorienting gendered language for God and the world—disorienting by introducing alternative models and reorienting in underlining the metaphorical character of any theological language.[38]

Still, whereas "inclusive language" was a hot issue in the 1990s, causing endless debates, some of the energy seems to have been lost in recent years. A positive interpretation would be that feminist theologians have succeeded. At least in some churches that is true to a certain extent. My own Church of Sweden would be a case in point. However, as shown by

---

35. For an introduction to ethnographic and empirical methods in ecclesiology, see Ideström in this volume, chapter 8.

36. Probably the most influential author representing this strategy is the Lutheran theologian Gail Ramshaw. See for example Ramshaw, *God beyond*.

37. One of the most influential books in this genre is Johnson, *She Who Is*.

38. McFague, *Models of God*, 182.

Swedish colleagues both the Church of Sweden hymnal from 1986 and the order for Sunday High mass from the same year, is markedly dichotomous and value discriminatory to women's disadvantage.[39] Recent revisions of worship manuals have been guided by principles seeking a consciously liberating language for worship, which also applies in regards to the use of gender.[40] Looking closer at the actual revisions, however, not much seems to have changed with regard to the basic gendered symbols, irrespective of principles and guidelines.[41]

That these structures remain should not be a surprise. Qualities of water do change, and that is an acute problem in our time, at least with regard to temperature. But they change subtly and slowly and never by political decision alone. Quite the contrary, politics trying to save our climate from over-heating seems to result in endless discussions, without much effect, and I would argue that the same goes for the gendered quality of church waters. They do change, and hopefully the changes will be for the better. But they do not change because of theological decisions alone, and they do not change quickly.

The most important feminist contribution with regard to the use of gendered Christian symbolic language is probably the revelation of the inadequacy of its use. Feminist theologians remind us that there always has to be both a yes and a no in a language trying to reach beyond this world to express divine mystery.[42] Symbolic language aims at speaking the unspeakable. In doing so it both connects to, and breaks with, ordinary language.[43] Sometimes, when language fails, while still trying, glimpses of a wider reality shine through. A major feminist critique concerns that this "yes and no" character of symbolic language has been lost. Gendered symbolic language has been reified in what the Catholic theologian Elizabeth Johnson calls an "ecclesiastical desire to make simple positive and authoritative statements about the divine."[44] She argues that the problem is not primarily the

---

39. Lejdhamre, *Psalm—kön*; Eriksson, *Meaning of Gender*.

40. *Teologiska grundprinciper* [Basic Theological Principles].

41. Lejdhamre, "Genusperspektiv."

42. McFague, *Models of God*, 33; Ramshaw, *God beyond*, 108; Johnson, *She Who Is*, 115.

43. Both analogy and metaphor are used in this type of language. Analogy primarily invites us to see the similarities between human conditions and the divine, while metaphor works by surprising us in connecting things that have no immediate likeness. Analogical speech has roots in medieval Thomistic theology, whereas feminist theologians today rather have been inspired by theories on language as metaphorical. Cf. Johnson, *She who is*, 116 and Ramshaw, *God beyond*, 94–95.

44. Johnson, *She Who Is*, 116.

male gendering of the Christian language for God; "Rather, the problem consists in the fact that these male terms are used exclusively, literally, and patriarchally."[45]

Gendered waters do not change as a result of political decision alone. But they do change in the communities using the waters. They change in churches. That is one reason for feminist theologians to overcome their instinctive reluctance towards ecclesiology. Gendered symbolic language will probably change in the long run, at least in its patriarchal, literal, and exclusive usage, as the community of women and men experience a need for more adequate ways of talking about God and the world. Gendered ecclesial relations will change too, as they change in society at large. Churches are no isolated spheres, as waters blend and mix. Gender is produced and it produces. It is reproduced, but it is also broken. But this all needs conscious and qualified gendered reflection.

It is hard to dismantle the house of patriarchy with gendered tools produced in that very house.[46] The field of ecclesiology is full of gendered tools that have been used, and are still used today, in order to uphold binary gendered divisions of labor and status, often at the cost of women, but also of homo-, bi-, and transsexual people, who do not fit into the established order of the house. However, as shown by Teresa Berger, among others, church history is full of surprises for a person shaped by the twentieth century's ideas on normality with regard to gender and sexuality.[47] The ecclesiological potential of these cracks, tensions, and disharmonies in theologies of the church largely remain to be explored. Feminist ecclesiology has a task of its own in providing churches with tools for understanding and expressing their own mission and thus helping them become more of what they understand themselves to be: spaces for transcendence and transformation, possibly also with regard to gender, race, and class. Ecclesiology might have been a house primarily designed by white Western male architects. Still, the house is full of cracks and hidden doors, through which light may shine from the future.

---

45. Ibid., 33.

46. Here I rely on the well-known image provided by the black, lesbian, feminist poet Audre Lourde, that "The master's tools cannot dismantle the master's house." See Lourde, *Sister Outsider*, 112.

47. Berger, *Gender Differences*.

13

Reflections on the Church at Worship and the "Lieutenant Nun"

TERESA BERGER

> **Teresa Berger** (born 1956) holds doctorates in both liturgical studies and constructive theology. She is professor of Liturgical Studies and Thomas E. Golden Jr. Professor of Catholic Theology at Yale University. Before coming to Yale in 2007, she was a professor at Duke University's Divinity School. Berger has written extensively on liturgy and women's lives, for example *Gender Differences and the Making of Liturgical History* (2011). She focuses her research at the intersections of liturgical studies and Catholic theology with gender theory, specifically gender history. Berger is a member of the American Academy of Religion, Societas Liturgica, and the European Society of Women in Theological Research, among others.

While reading the essays in Part Three of *Ecclesiology in the Trenches*, I was also perusing a newly-published volume in the field of gender studies. Titled *Critical Terms for the Study of Gender*, the book opens with the extraordinary story of Catalina de Erauso, known as the "lieutenant nun."[1] Born to a wealthy Basque family toward

---

1. Erauso, *Lieutenant*. Thus the English translation of the title of her memoir: *La*

the end of the sixteenth century, Catalina fled the convent in which she was raised, turned her female clothing into men's clothes, and crossed the Atlantic to make her life as a soldier in colonial Peru and Chile. Twenty years later, she revealed her secret to a saintly bishop and re-donned a veil. She had remained a *virgo intacta* and returned to Europe with much fanfare. Yet Catalina departed again for colonial Latin America, where she lived out her life as the merchant Antonio de Erauso.

Several elements of the story of the "lieutenant nun" connected with my reading of the essays in *Ecclesiology in the Trenches*. Not least was the militaristic world evoked in both titles: A "lieutenant nun" must certainly live in "ecclesiological trenches," although I am unsure that in the Swedish cultural imagination the "trenches" evoke warfare as much as they do in English, especially with the recent centenary of the opening salvos of World War I with its infamous "trench warfare" looming large in the media. In reading these texts together, I began to wonder whether one might imagine the church as a "lieutenant nun," cross-dressing, gender-shifting, skilled in battle, and cherishing virginity, all in one. Certainly the traditional image of the church as *ecclesia militans* bears connections to both femininity and military prowess.

Catalina's story, it must be noted, has nothing to say about ecclesial practices. Rather, the authors take Catalina's life to illustrate "the fluidities of gender."[2] The ecclesial subject-position of this Roman Catholic Basque-Peruvian would-be-nun-turned-soldier is simply occluded. Why is Catalina's religious journey so marginal to scholars, even under the logic of postmodernity with its supposed "implosion of the secular" (to borrow Graham Ward's phrase)? This marginalization is telling especially because Catalina's memoir itself is full of pointers to her liturgical and devotional practices. Not only is Catalina about to take religious vows when she changes course and gender, but she also describes herself as attending various masses, reciting the rosary, and invoking St. Joseph. At some point, faced with a group of priests who want to hear her deathbed confession, she identifies as a "self-professed Lutheran."[3] Yet when she reveals the secret of her gender identity to a saintly bishop, it is in the context of a long confession, after which she receives absolution and communion. Returning to Europe, Catalina makes her way to Rome during the year of great Jubilee and is received in audience by Pope Urban VIII. The Pope grants her leave to live her life in men's cloth-

---

Historia de la Monja Alférez. The sub-title is the choice of the editors of the 1996 English edition, *Memoir of a Basque Transvestite in the New World*.

2. Stimpson, *Critical*, 1–19; here p. 1.

3. Erauso, *Lieutenant*, 42.

ing. On the feast of St. Peter, Catalina attends mass at St. Peter's Basilica. A life does not get much more Catholic and liturgical than that, one might think.

Why then the occlusion of Catalina's ecclesial-liturgical journey in the scholarly reception history of her memoir? One can take this occlusion as an example of the scholarly unease with ecclesial realities and faith claims, both past and present. It is regrettable but not entirely surprising that the essay on "religion" in *Critical Terms for the Study of Gender* is one of the weaker essays in this volume,[4] written by a literary scholar rather than by a historian of religious life or a theologian. One way of responding to this, from the theologians' side, is to strengthen theological work with cognate disciplines. Through such work, theological concerns speak within broader scholarly discourses and can hope to be not only understood but also validated there.

In the Swedish context, from what I can tell from my own stay at the Ecclesiology Seminar at Uppsala University in 2001 as well as from the essays in *Ecclesiology in the Trenches*, this has meant attention to empirical research, social theory, and sociological inquiry into ecclesial life. In my North American context of research and teaching, such enriching (and credibility-granting) cross-disciplinary work is certainly also being performed. I am thinking here, for example, of Mary McClintock Fulkerson's theological-ecclesiological work, done in conversation with, successively, feminist and discourse theory, critical race theory and disability studies, ethnography, and postmodern place theory. In her book *Places of Redemption*, McClintock Fulkerson offers a theological reading not only of liturgical practices but also of practices that often are occluded in ecclesiological reflection, e.g. home-making practices, including maintenance/janitorial labor.[5] Interwoven with this cross-disciplinary scholarship are two other foci that have emerged in North American theological work, which also have relevance for ecclesiological investigations, namely the study of ecclesial *practices* (rather than texts),[6] and the pursuit of "lived theology"[7] (rather than of dogmatic statements).

The broadening of the theological repertoire of tools is no doubt important both for ecclesiology and also for liturgical studies. I myself, for example, begin a seminar on liturgical theology by asking students to read

---

4. Schwartz, "Religion," 428–48.

5. McClintock Fulkerson, *Places*, esp. chapter 5. See also McClintock Fulkerson, "Theological Reflection," 23–42.

6. Volf and Bass, *Practicing*, 228–42.

7. See, for example, the project on "Lived Theology" online at: http://livedtheology.org/ (last accessed August 14, 2014).

together chapters from *Primary Sources of Liturgical Theology*[8] with Mark Chaves's chapter on "Worship," from his sociological study *Congregations in America*.[9] The point is to acknowledge from the outset that ecclesial practices invite both theological reflection as well as sociological, anthropological, ethnographic, and gender-attentive scholarly inquiry (to name just a few possibilities). At the same time, as a theologian I have to remind myself again and again that my work is not done when I have attended to practices of worship through the lens of, say, the sociology of religion or gender theory. A memorable passage from C.S. Lewis helps to remind me of the theological task embedded within my work as a scholar of liturgy (rather than, simply, a scholar of ritual). In a famous passage in his *Screwtape Letters*, C.S. Lewis put the following words in the mouth of the senior devil named Screwtape, who advises a junior devil, Wormwood, on how to tempt a recent convert (his "patient") away from his new-found Christian faith:

> One of our great allies at present is the Church itself. Do not misunderstand me. I do not mean the Church as we see her spread out through all time and space and rooted in eternity, terrible as an army with banners. That, I confess, is a spectacle which makes our boldest tempters uneasy. But fortunately it is quite invisible to these humans. All your patient sees is the half-finished, sham Gothic erection on the new building estate. When he goes inside, he sees the local grocer with rather an oily expression on his face bustling up to offer him one shiny little book containing a liturgy which neither of them understands, and one shabby little book containing corrupt texts of a number of religious lyrics, mostly bad, and in very small print. When he gets to his pew and looks round him he sees just that selection of his neighbors whom he has hitherto avoided. [...] Make his mind flit to and fro between an expression like "the body of Christ" and the actual faces in the next pew.[10]

Lewis's description of "the Church as we [i.e., devils!] see her spread out through all time and space and rooted in eternity, terrible as an army with banners" evokes the image of the Church as *ecclesia militans*. In relation to the essays in *Ecclesiology in the Trenches*, the description also helps to identify the basic tension underlying all ecclesiological investigations, namely between "the Church [. . .] spread out through all time and space and rooted in eternity" and "the actual faces in the next pew." One way to

---

8. Vogel, *Primary*.
9. Chaves, *Congregations*, 127–80.
10. Lewis, *Screwtape*, 12–13. The book was first published in 1942.

read the essays in cluster three of *Ecclesiology in the Trenches* is to see them attend to different features of this basic tension highlighted in C.S. Lewis's text, especially with regard to actual liturgical practices, i.e. the "faces in the pews." What the three essays focus on are practices mentioned in Lewis's text as facets of what is visible of the church. They are also facets that easily prevent one from seeing the Church as "spread out through all time and space and rooted in eternity, terrible as an army with banners."

In her essay, Karin Oljelund ponders the ecclesiology of liturgical texts, or what C.S. Lewis described as "one shiny little book containing a liturgy which neither of them understands, and one shabby little book containing corrupt texts of a number of religious lyrics, mostly bad, and in very small print." In the second essay, Gunnar Weman attends to the ecclesiology embedded in architectural floor plans of church buildings. This element of liturgical life hides behind Lewis's dismissive description of a "half-finished, sham Gothic erection on the new building estate" (granted that in the Swedish Lutheran context the church building would in all likelihood be a medieval one). Finally, Ninna Edgardh's essay wrestles with something that is clearly present in Lewis's text but—as so very often—remains unnamed: gender differences.

In what follows, I attend to these essays in turn, beginning with the last.

THE CHURCH AT WORSHIP AND THE PRACTICE OF GENDER

Having long appreciated Ninna Edgardh and her work, I found her "reflections on the church as a gendered body" congruent with my own thinking. For both of us, gender is a crucial analytical tool in liturgical studies, ecclesiological investigations, and the daily lived life of faith. Equally important, ecclesial practices matter and they matter deeply to both of us. When I edited a collection of feminist liturgies in global context some years ago, it was Ninna Edgardh's essay on the *Sofia-mässor* in Stockholm that came closest to my own vision of feminist liturgical practices.[11] I appreciated especially that the *Sofia-mässor* did not leave ecclesial space behind for the sake of a separate feminist enclave but rather claimed ecclesial space for themselves.

Thinking about both of our research and writing now, I suspect that my own work on gender and liturgical practices in the last decade or so has moved in a slightly different direction from Ninna Edgardh's. Not that this constitutes a problem; it is simply part of the rich diversity of voices on gender and church life today. Yet the slightly divergent paths are worth

---

11. Edgardh, *Lady Wisdom*, 159–74.

pondering. This divergence could simply be related to the fact that Edgardh is now ordained and works part-time as a parish priest, while my own work remains squarely within an academic context. Such life choices matter, especially in how we think about the church. I suspect, however, that the difference between Ninna Edgardh's and my own thinking lies elsewhere. At root, this difference has to do with what we emphasize in our shared concern with gender differences and with where the center of our work lies: in my case, in historical inquiry, in Ninna Edgardh's case, in contemporary ecclesial life. Moreover, I have become somewhat hesitant with claims about "women"—even when these were clearly the focus of my own earlier writings. In my most recent monograph, I have moved beyond my own work on "women's ways of worship" and instead analyze gender differences in the broadest possible sense.[12] For the early centuries of Christian liturgy, for example, I highlight the complex position of "eunuchs," and for later centuries, the emergence of a specific "priestly masculinity."

I also see very different temporalities of struggle around gender differences in the churches today. Consider the following: Some of the women-specific gains in liturgical language by now have been overtaken by newer gender-specific concerns. An example is the addition of "sisters" to the traditional "brothers." This hard-won linguistic change has been supplanted in some North American faith communities by a liturgical language that does not reproduce the traditional gender binary but instead signals openness to all genders. New rituals are emerging, e.g., the annual Transgender Day of Remembrance on November 20. On the other side of the ecclesial spectrum, there has been a growing insistence among some conservative Protestant and evangelical groups that Christian ministry needs to regain a "masculine" feel, and that the preponderance of "girly" worship songs is a problem. Gender also plays out in very different ways among the more than two billion Christians worldwide—all of whom live in startlingly different cultural and ecclesial temporalities. For example, while the Old Catholic Church in North America ordained its first openly transgender priest in 2014, some Christian communities in parts of Africa continue to struggle against female genital cutting. Granted, the recognition is growing overall that gender matters in Christian assemblies gathered for worship, and that worshippers come to church—whether in Africa or Europe, Oceania or Latin America—already shaped by (and performing, tweaking, and contesting) broader cultural gender codes. Yet the temporalities of struggle with regard to gender in the global church are anything but the same.

---

12. Berger, *Gender Differences*.

What I myself would like to know is what an ecclesiology looks like that takes gender seriously as a practice of possibilities, beyond stable binary categories. What if the "lieutenant nun" is not supremely odd? I have argued elsewhere that our ecclesial-sacramental tradition is quite gender-ambiguous, and that it is so in its traditional expression, not in some marginal space.[13] Here are some pointers to that reality: in its Head, the Body of Christ might be considered male—yet Christ "was male but born of no male matter."[14] In most ecclesial assemblies, the presider is male, yet priestly masculinity is defined around a sexual abstinence that renders the priest, liturgically at least, hyper-generative. The presider also stands *in persona ecclesiae*, a male body standing in for an ecclesial Virgin Bride, who is at the same time *casta meretrix* (the "chaste whore") and *mater ecclesia* (Mother Church), pregnant with life, giving birth, and nursing. And there is Mary, the Mother of God, who is both the daughter of the Father as well as the mother and sometimes the bride of the Son.

My question, in the face of such gender-bending, is this: What if we rendered visible our ecclesial and liturgical tradition as a distinctly gender-fluid space? A space with a powerful stream of natality running through it; a space where God the Father can give birth and might have breasts; where Jesus' eucharistic body certainly is "no longer Christ as simply and biologically male;"[15] and where Jesus's gift of himself in the Eucharist can be understood as nursing. This is a space where Jesus's body on the cross is in labor, torn open, bleeding, groaning, and in the midst of all the violence to the maternal body, giving new life; where monks can understand themselves as receptive, submissive brides, or as pregnant women, careful not to abort but to bring to full term the new life that grows within them; where the Spirit can be glimpsed as a mother, giving new life in baptism (as in the early Syriac tradition), or as a male lover, who inseminates the baptismal womb of the font (in many Western sources); where Mary is venerated as a priest, the *virgo sacerdos*, the first to offer us the body and blood of Christ. And what if, rather than claiming all these Christian gender instabilities to be "queer," we simply acknowledged them for what they (also) are: deeply and wonderfully traditional? I suspect that Ninna Edgardh and I have much to talk about and much work left to do here.

---

13. Berger, "Spying," 28–41.
14. Stuart, "Exploding," 228–36; here 234.
15. Ward, "Bodies," 163–81; here 168.

THE CHURCH AT WORSHIP AND ITS AUTHORIZING LITURGICAL TEXTS

Karin Oljelund's essay displays a different way of doing ecclesiology. This approach singles out for analysis not various gender codes as they shape liturgical life but rather liturgical texts, namely official books of worship and questionnaires about worship life. The specific focus is on two prominent biblical images for the church: the body of Christ, and the people of God. In her essay, the author ponders methodological issues involved in her quest for a liturgical ecclesiology. I appreciate the thoughtful elaboration of what it means to pursue "a study of the preconditions for the formation of a liturgical ecclesiology." My response focuses on some methodological concerns of my own that emerge in conversation with Karin Oljelund's reflections.

First, I write in a North American context where worship life is not always governed by authorized texts (except by the most important liturgical book, namely the Bible). Pentecostal and evangelical churches, for example, routinely worship without an official service book. This leads me to ask what it means to focus one's analysis on written texts? When we study liturgical texts, we study a score—can we ever really hear the music playing through the score? And this is only the first problem. The scholarly troubles with interpreting Christian worship go deeper. This has become clear, for example, with the emerging use of ethnographic methods in liturgical studies. Clearly, valuable insights are gained through this methodology of studying people at worship. Theologically, however, what is crucial in Christian worship, namely the life-giving presence of the Holy Trinity, cannot be rendered visible and intelligible under the knowledge protocols of contemporary academia, ethnography included. In a roundabout way, this points to the power of Christian liturgy: At its heart is a presence that cannot be rendered intelligible under a microscope. Divine Presence reveals itself to other ways of knowing than our contemporary research methods prize, namely ways of self-emptying, un-knowing, humility, and adoration. At best, one can argue, with the subaltern theorist Dipesh Chakrabarty, that modern cultures of scholarship can make gods and faith interesting topics of study.[16] Since these forms of scholarship are predicated on a secular, disenchanted universe, however, they cannot but do violence to "the times of gods" and the people who co-inhabit these times with the gods. Despite the occasional scholarly recognition that many people inhabit a world permeated by the Divine, the vast majority of intellectual production nowadays assumes a universe emptied of Divine Presence. Over and against such productions, theologians search for "the beyond in the midst of life" (Dietrich

---

16. Chakrabarty, "Time of history," 35–59.

Bonhoeffer). At the same time, this search has to be rendered intelligible in the context theologians inhabit, namely not only the church but also the scholarly community and the wider world. This is a true challenge. I share Karin Oljelund's sense that what is termed "liturgical theology" often seems like an esoteric exercise, a *disciplina arcani,* and that this does not serve scholars of liturgy well. My predecessor here at Yale, Aidan Kavanagh, on the other hand, reveled in this understanding of liturgical theology in his well-known book of the same name:

> *Liturgical Theology* [. . .] appears to be part equivocation and part rumor. It is equivocation in that nearly anything theologians write on liturgy is often called liturgical theology, [. . .] But the very existence of the equivocation contributes to the rumor that there may indeed be something somewhere which is properly *liturgical* theology, although its face is known only in silhouette, its method is elusive, its practitioners nameless, and its results problematic."[17]

In the face of such liturgical rumors, Karin Oljelund grounds her quest for a liturgical ecclesiology in actual, established texts that govern a worshipping community's liturgy. This is a welcome move. I attempted something similar years ago when I used the hymns of Charles Wesley to think through the relationship between doxology and theology.[18] At the same time, there is so much more than authorizing liturgical texts when it comes to primary ecclesiology. What about sacred music? Liturgical art and architecture? Popular devotions? Sacred silence? And what about the worshippers for whom authorizing texts are not accessible, e.g., the unborn child, the elderly woman with dementia, or the neuro-diverse teenager? What about their primary ecclesiology? Surely the Triune God who gathers God's people is as present in their lives as in those who worship with the help of liturgical books?

THE CHURCH AT WORSHIP AND ITS ARCHITECTURAL FLOOR PLANS

With the essay by Gunnar Weman, we enter yet another basic element of liturgical life. If Ninna Edgardh's essay reflects on the always-gendered bodies of worshippers and Karin Oljelund analyzes liturgical texts that govern the celebration, Gunnar Weman takes the materiality of the church building as the starting point of his investigation. More particularly, he reads

---

17. Kavanagh, *On liturgical,* IX–X.
18. Berger, "Liturgical."

architectural floor plans of churches as ecclesiological texts. I find this perspective intriguing, although (or maybe especially because?) I have no training in reading such floor plans. As a worshipper "in the pews" for well over half a century now, I know well the importance of sacred space and its renovations for liturgical celebration. Gunnar Weman's point that ultimately the architectural floor plan of a church has its telos in the gathered community at worship is well-taken.

The Anglican bishop and theologian J. A. T. Robinson is quoted as having said, rather pessimistically, "the building will always win." (I imagine this conviction emerged during his time as a Church of England bishop in the 1960s). Gunnar Weman takes a different and less pessimistic approach to ecclesial architecture and its renovations. He invites us to read architectural floor plans as far more than simply drawings of a worship space. Rather, he suggests that these floor plans represent a kind of "materialized theology" and can be read as ecclesiological texts. He exemplifies his approach by analyzing the floor plans of two Swedish Lutheran churches that have recently undergone substantial change. Both church buildings can be traced back to medieval times, as I understand most church buildings in Sweden can—a rich heritage but not an easy one to incorporate into the twenty-first century. Living in the United States as I do, where this part of the Christian liturgical tradition is simply absent, I think of medieval church buildings as a rich heritage, but I am sure that those who have to care for these buildings in the twenty-first century also struggle with them.

Two issues in Weman's essay invite further reflection. The first issue has to do with the gap that always exists between "liturgical texts" (of whatever kind) and actual liturgical celebrations. This gap troubles, for example, historians of liturgy as they try to discern, from within ancient texts, the actual shape of a liturgical celebration. This gap, as I have already mentioned, also underlies the liturgical ecclesiology of Karin Oljelund, since it remains uncertain whether what the liturgical texts have to say about the church is received as such in the minds of the worshippers. The gap, finally, is present also in the reading of architectural floor plans as ecclesiological texts.

This first issue is closely related to the second one. In Gunnar Weman's essay, the way to read architectural floor plans—their meaning, one might say—appears to be clear, and stable. For example, the flexible structure of the liturgical space after the renovation "can be a reminder to the worshippers that [. . .] they are a pilgrim people within their own church." That is one possibility. But of course worshippers may also make meaning with such a flexible structure in quite different ways. An older worshipper may find it disorienting, a neuro-diverse teenager threatening. Who decides which meaning is the ecclesially and/or ecclesiologically appropriate one? Weman acknowledges this problem in his essay, yet where precisely the interpretive authority over architectural floor plans lies deserves further conversation.

In recent years, scholars attentive to contemporary social and literary theories have insisted that the process of meaning-making, rather than being unified and given with a text or rite, is better understood as a plurality of meaning-makings. The meaning of liturgy, then, comes to be seen as always actively negotiated (and "produced") by those present. There is thus no simple way to identify the site of liturgical meaning, since there is never a single meaning in any liturgy that can be said to be definitive. The particularities of liturgical subjects, rather than being secondary factors that qualify as "con-text" to that which is supposedly primary, namely the liturgical "text," are co-constitutive in the making of liturgical meaning. Moreover, not only are there "as many interpretations, or 'meanings,' for any liturgical act as there are people attending,"[19] there are, in fact, *more* meanings than there are people attending, since, rather than being a unified self, most people are better understood as sites of multiple and contesting meanings.

Liturgical meaning-making also does not stop when people file out of the sanctuary. Much liturgical meaning-making happens outside of the specific time-frame of the liturgy itself, as people ponder, find solace in, resist, and subvert liturgical celebrations and their powers in lived life. If liturgical subjects come to be seen as co-constitutive of the production of liturgical meaning, one will have to take situated knowledges and subjectivities into account when theorizing the meaning of a liturgy. The fact that liturgical subjects always come situated and particularized will lead one to ask, for example, how gendered identity shapes liturgical meaning-making; how material realities, including our bodies, interpret liturgical practices; and how liturgy might be a contested terrain, the site of multiple and conflicting claims. Renovations of sacred space and architectural floor plans obviously are not immune from these particularities. What do they mean for an ecclesiological reading of the church building and its transformations over time?

CONCLUSION

In conclusion, I return to where I began, namely my reading of the essays in Part Three of *Ecclesiology in the Trenches* together with the memoir of Catalina de Erauso, the "lieutenant nun." The coincidence of reading these two very different texts together suggested something about inadvertent, "accidental" conversation partners to me. In hindsight, such inadvertent conversation partners seem to be an important part of the church's journey through time, and therefore also of the theologian's task. Ultimately, God's

---

19. Stringer, "Text," 365–79; here 378.

own presence may be revealed in such inadvertent, "accidental" conversations, as those on the road to Emmaus (Luke 24)—then and now—know.

Bibliography

Titles translated within brackets.

Adell, Arthur. *I Guds rika hus.* Stockholm: Svenska Kyrkans Diakonistyrelses Bokförlag, 1954 [Within the Rich House of God].
Adolfsson, Lars. "Mother of Jesus, Mother of Me. An ecclesiological Study on the Marian Sermons of Thomas Merton." Master's thesis, Uppsala University. Uppsala, 2010
Adorno, Theodor. "The Actuality of Philosophy." *Telos* 31 (March 1977) 120–33. (Originally a lecture in German in the Philosophical Faculty at the University of Frankfurt, 1931.)
Afdal, Geir. *Researching Religious Education as Social Practice.* Münster: Waxmann, 2010.
Ahlbäck, Lennart. *Socialdemokratisk kyrkosyn: En studie i Socialdemokraternas kyrkopolitiska riktlinjer 1979–1996,* Lund: Arcus, 2002 [Social Democratic Ecclesiology: A Study in the Outlines of Church Politics of the Social Democratic Party 1979–1996].
Ahlberg, Bo. *Laurentius Petris nattvardsuppfattning.* Lund: Gleerups, 1964 [Laurentius Petri's Concept of the Lord's Supper].
Almond, Gabriel, et al. "Politics, Ethnicity, and Fundamentalism." In *Fundamentalisms Comprehended,* edited by Martin Marty and Scott Appleby, 483–515. Chicago: University Chicago Press, 1995.
Alvesson, Mats, and Kaj Sköldberg. *Tolkning och reflektion: Vetenskapsfilosofi och kvalitativ metod.* Lund: Studentlitteratur, 1994 [*Reflexive Methodology: New Vistas for Qualitative Research.* Second edition. London: SAGE, 2009].
Andrén, Åke. "Kyrko- och samfundsvetenskap." In *Religionsvetenskap: En introduktion,* edited by Annagreta Dyring, 71–75. Uppsala: Teologiska institutionen vid Uppsala universitet, 1975 [Studies in Churches and Denominations].
———. "Kyrkovetenskap ur ett Uppsalaperspektiv. En vetenskapshistorisk introduktion." In *Kyrkovetenskapliga forskningslinjer: En vetenskapsteoretisk introduktion,* edited by Oloph Bexell, 11–36. Lund: Studentlitteratur, 1995 [Studies of the Church from an Uppsala Perspective: A Historical Introduction].
———. "Practical Theology." In *Uppsala University 500 years.* 1, Faculty of theology at Uppsala University, edited by Helmer Ringgren, 112 (105–18). Uppsala: Uppsala universitet, 1976.

Aulén, Gustaf. *Till belysning af den lutherska kyrkoidén, dess historia och dess värde.* Uppsala: Almqvist & Wiksell, 1912 [An Elucidation of the Lutheran Idea of the Church, Its History and Value].

Avis, Paul. "Anglican Ecclesiology." In *The Routledge Companion to the Christian Church,* edited by Gerard Mannion and Lewis S. Mudge, 202–16. New York: Routledge, 2008.

Avril, Joseph. "La pastorale des malades et des mourants aux XIIe et XIIIe siècles." In *Death in the Middle Ages,* edited by Herman Braet and Werner Verbeke, 88–106. Leuven: Leuven University Press, 1983 [The pastoral care of the sick and dying in the twelfth and thirteenth centuries].

Axner, Torbjörn. *Utvärdering av 1986 års kyrkohandbok.* Uppsala: Svenska kyrkans centralstyrelse, 1998 [An Evaluation of The Swedish Service Book, issued in 1986].

Bäckersten, Björn. "Salskyrkans utmaning. Att bygga om och bygga in." In *Kyrkorummet—kulturarv och gudstjänst: En samtalsbok om ett förändringsskede,* edited by Peter Bexell and Gunnar Weman, 271–82. Skellefteå: Artos, 2008 [The Challenge of the Wide and Long Church Building: The Question of Rebuilding and Renewal].

Bäckström, Anders, et al., editors. *Welfare and Religion in 21st Century Europe: Volume 1. Configuring the Connections.* Farnham: Ashgate, 2010.

———. *Welfare and Religion in 21st Century Europe: Volume 2. Gendered, Religious and Social Change.* Farnham: Ashgate 2011

Bakke, Tore, and Tor Hernes. *Autopoietic Organization Theory: Drawing on Niklas Luhmann's Social System Perspective.* Oslo: Abstrakt forlag AS, 2003.

Baring, Anne, and Jules Cashford. *The Myth of the Goddess: Evolution of an Image.* London: Penguin Books, 1991.

Barruffo, Antonio. *Sui problemi del metodo in ecclesiologia.* Cinisello Balsamo: San Paolo, 2003 [The problem of method in ecclesiology].

Barth, Karl. *Church Dogmatics.* Vol. 1. Edinburgh: T. & T. Clark, 1956.

———. *Practicing Our Faith: A Way of Life for a Searching People.* San Fransisco: Jossey-Bass, 2010 (1997).

Berger, Teresa, editor. *Dissident Daughters: Feminist Liturgies in Global Context.* Louisville: Westminster John Knox, 2001.

———. *Gender Differences and the Making of Liturgical Tradition: Lifting a Veil on Liturgy's Past.* Burlington: Ashgate, 2011.

———. "Liturgical Renewal, Separated Sisters and Christian Unity." In *Liturgical Renewal as a Way to Christian Unity,* edited by James F. Puglisi, 71–86. Collegeville, MN: Pueblo, 2005.

———. "Spying in the Promised Land: Sacramental Sights, Through Women's Eyes." In *Proceedings of the Catholic Theological Society of America* 67 (2012) 28–41.

———. *Theology in Hymns?: A Study of the Relationship of Doxology and Theology according to A Collection of Hymns for the Use of the People called Methodist* (1780). Nashville: Kingswood, 1995.

Bergman, Carl-Göran, and Sven-Erik Brodd, editors. *Ett mångtydigt rum.* Skellefteå: Norma, 2001 [A Manifold Room].

———. "Predikan och kyrkorummet." In *Predikohistoriska perspektiv: Studier tillägnade Åke Andrén,* edited by Alf Härdelin, 96–132. Älvsjö: Verbum/Skeab, 1982 [The Sermon and the Church Room].

Bexell, Oloph. "Church life and Worship in a Lutheran Church: The Example of the Church of Sweden—A Historical Introduction." In *The Meaning of Christian Liturgy*, edited by Oloph Bexell, 1-23. Grand Rapids: Eerdmans, 2012.

———. "Kyrkan som forskningsobjekt—om kyrkovetenskapens uppgift." *Kyrkohistorisk Årsskrift* 101 (2001) 100-104 [The Church as a Research Object. Regarding the Task of Ecclesiology].

———. "Om kyrkans praxis och dess teologi." In *Kyrkovetenskapliga forskningslinjer: En vetenskapsteoretisk översikt*, edited by Oloph Bexell, 155-67. Lund: Studentlitteratur, 1995 [On the Church's Praxis and Its Theology].

Bexell, Oloph, editor. *Meaning of Christian Liturgy: Recent Developments in the Church of Sweden*. Grand Rapids: Eerdmanns, 2012.

Bexell, Peter, and Gunnar Weman, editors. *Kyrkorummet—kulturarv och gudstjänst: En samtalsbok om ett förändringsskede*. Skellefteå: Artos & Norma, 2008 [The Inner Church Building—Cultural Heritage and Worship: A Conversation about a Period of Change].

Biko, Steve. *I Write What I Like*. Edited by Aelred Stubbs. Northlands: Picador Africa, 2007 (1978).

Blückert, Kjell. *The Church as Nation: A Study in Ecclsiology and Nationhood*. Frankfurt: Peter Lang, 2000.

———. "Kyrkan som... Att studera ecklesiologi från olika horisonter." In *Kyrkovetenskap som forskningsdisciplin*, edited by Sven-Åke Selander, 47-60. Stockholm: Kungliga Vitterhets historie- och antikvitetsakademin, 2001 [The Church as... on Studying Ecclesiology from Various Horizons].

Boethius, Anicius Manlius Severinus. *The Consolation of Philosophy*. Auckland, New Zealand: Floating, 2009.

Boeve, Lieven. *God Interrupts History: Theology in a time of upheaval*. London: Bloomsbury Academic, 2007.

Bohman, James. "Two Versions of the Linguistic Turn: Habermas and Poststructuralism." In *Habermas and the Unfinished Project of Modernity: Critical Essays on The Philosophical Discourse of Modernity*, edited by Passerin d'Entr Ves et al., 197-220. Cambridge: Polity, 1996.

Bonnier, Ann Catherine, and Ingrid Sjöström. *Kyrkornas hemligheter*. Stockholm: Medströms, 2013 [The Secrets of the Church Buildings].

Bratt, James D., editor. *Abraham Kuyper: A Centennial Reader*. Grand Rapids: Eerdmans, 1998.

Bretherton, Luke. "Coming to Judgment: Methodological Reflections on the Relationship between Ecclesiology, Ethnography and Political Theory." *Modern Theology* 28 (2012) 167-96.

Brodd, Sven-Erik. "Åke Andrén och den teologiska fakulteten." In *Åke Andrén: Ett mångsidigt professorsliv*, edited by Sven Arne Flodell and Vivi-Ann Grönqvist, 42-74. Stockholm: Stiftelsen Sverige och kristen tro, 2008 [Åke Andrén and the Faculty of Theology].

———. "The Church as Sacrament in the Writings of Yngve Brilioth. Texts and Contexts." In *Glaube—Freiheit—Diktatur: Festschrift fur Gerhard Besier*, edited by K. Stokłosa and A. Strübind, 301-20. Göttingen: Vandenhoek Ruprecht, 2008.

———. "Church, Organisation and Church Organisation. Some reflections on an ecclesiological dilemma." *Swedisch Missiological Themes* 93 (2005) 245-63.

———. *Diakonatet: Från ecklesiologi till pastoral praxis*. Uppsala: Svenska kyrkans forskningsråd, 1992 [The Diaconate: From Ecclesiology to Pastoral Praxis].

———. "A Diaconate Emerging from Ecclesiology: Towards a Constructive Theology on the Office of a Deacon." *Internationale Kirchliche Zeitschrift* 59 (2005) 266–88.

———. "Diaconia through Church History. Five Ecclesiological Models." In *The Theology of Diaconia*, edited by Sven-Erik Brodd et al., 5–26. Uppsala: Diakonistiftelsen Samariterhemmet, 1999 (2005).

———. "Ecclesiological Research and Natural and Human Sciences: Some Observations of an Unconventional Phenomenon." *International Journal for the Study of the Christian Church* 9 (2009) 312–32.

———. "Ecclesiology." In *Encyclopedia of Sciences and Religions*, edited by Anne L. C. Runehov and Lluis Oviedo, 655–60. Heidelberg: Springer Reference, 2013.

———. "Ecclesiology and Church Music. Towards a Possible Relationship." *International Journal for the Study of the Christian Church* 6 (2006) 126–43.

———. "Ecklesiologi och ecklesialitet: Kyrkovetenskap ur dagens uppsalaperspektiv." In *Kyrkovetenskapliga forskningslinjer. En vetenskapsteoretisk översikt*, edited by Oloph Bexell, 100–119. Lund: Studentlitteratur, 1996 [Ecclesiology and Ecclesiality—The Study of the Church from a Contemporary Uppsala Perspective].

———. "Einige Bemerkungen zur Ekklesiologie Melanchthons in schwedischer Reformationsforschung." In *Philipp Melanchthon und seine Rezeption in Skandinavien*, edited by Birgit Stoltz, 147–50. Stockholm: Kungliga Vitterhets historie- och antikvitetsakademien, 1998 [Some Comments on Melanchthon's Ecclesiology in Reformation Research in Sweden].

———. "Electronic Church and Webb Community: Some Marginal Notes to an Ecclesiological Problem." In *Kirko—Taide—Viestintä: Markku Heikkilän juhlakirja*, edited by Sari Dhima, 253–66. Helsinki: Suomen kirkkohistoriallinen seura, 2005.

———. "El esquema trinitario en el bautismo y la eucaristía. Una conversación eclesiológica con Martín Lutero (1483–1546) desde la perspectiva del siglo xxi." In *Yo te bautizo en el nombre del Padre, y del Hijo y del Espíritu Santo. Ecumenismo y diaálogo interreligioso. Con ocasión del 525 aniversario del nacimiento de Martín Lutero*, edited by Vincente Dominigo Canet Vayá, 113–23. Madrid: Fecha publicación, 2008 [The Trinitarian Pattern in Baptism and Eucharist. An Ecclesiological conversation with Martin Luther (1483–1546) in a Twentyfirst century perspective.]

———. "En gemensam förståelse av den gudomliga uppenbarelsen: Principiella perspektiv på de ekumeniska dialogerna." In *För att världen skall tro: Texter om ekumenik och kyrkans enhet*, edited by Markus Hagberg, 117–32. Skellefteå: Artos, 2007 [A Common Understanding of the Divine Revelation: Fundamental Perspectives on Ecumenical Dialogues].

———. *Evangelisk katolicitet: Ett studium av innehåll och function under 1800- och 1900-talen*. Lund: LiberGleerup, 1982 [Evangelical Catholicity: A Study of Content and Function during the Nineteenth and Twentieth Centuries].

———. "A Female Face of the Church: Sisterhoods from an Ecclesiological Perspective." In *Nuns and Sisters in the Nordic Countries after the Reformation: A Female Counter-Culture in Modern Society*, edited by Yvonne Maria Werner, 355–84. Uppsala: Swedish Institute of Mission Research, 2004.

———. "The Hidden Agenda. Implicit Achievements of the Dialogues between Roman-Catholic and Lutheran-Melanchthonian Traditions." In *Catholic-Lutheran Relations Three Deacades after Vatican II: Conference at the International bridgettine center* (Farfa Sabina, 12–15 March 1995*)*, edited by Peder Nørgaard-Højen, 67–71. Rome: Libreria Editrice Vaticana, 1997.

———. "Kirche als Kultursystem? Jahreszyklische und lebenszyklische Teilnahme an kirchlichen Angebote als ekklesiologisches Problem." In *Die Religiöse Dimension (in) der Gesellschaft und die Aufgabe der Theologischen Fakultäten: Internationale Fachkonferenz der Theologischen Fakultät Rostock vom 28. bis 31. Mai 1996*, edited by Anna-Katharina Szagun, 113–16. Rostock: Universität Theologie Fakultät, 1997 [Church as Cultural System? Ecclesial Participation in Age and Life Cycles as an Ecclesiological Problem].

———. "Kyrkan som kommunikativ gemenskap. Om ecklesiologi och kyrkomusik." In *Teologica practica et musica sacra: Festskrift till Karl Johan Hansson*, edited by Gustav Björkstrand et al., 121–39. Åbo: Åbo akademi, 2003 [The Church as Communicating Community: On Ecclesiology and Church Music].

———. "Kyrkosyn och gudstjänst. Om ecklesiologiskt studium av liturgi," In *Forskning om gudstjänst*, edited by Hedvid Brander Jonsson, 83–99. Uppsala: Svenska kyrkans forskningsrå 2000 [Ecclesiology and Worship. On Ecclesiological Studies of Liturgy].

———. "Kyrkosyn och kyrkohistoria. Ett studium av ecklesiologin i Carl Olbers syn på kyrkohistoria." In *Kyrkoliv i 1800-talets Sverige: Festskrift till Oloph Bexell*, edited by Stina Fallberg Sundmark and Göran Lundstedt, 95–122. Skellefteå 2007 [Nineteenth Century Ecclesiology and Historiography: The Swedish Theologian Carl Olbers' View of the Relationship between Church History and the Understanding of the Church].

———. "Kyrkovetenskap: Något om utvecklingen av praktisk teologi i Sverige." *Halvårsskrift for Praktisk Teologi* 1 (1995) 16–23 [Ecclesiology: Some remarks about the development of Practical theology in Sweden].

———. "Liturgy Crossing Frontiers: Interplay and Confrontation of Ecclesiological Patterns in Liturgical Change During the Twentieth Century." In *The Meaning of Christian Liturgy: Recent Developments in the Church of Sweden*, edited by Oloph Bexell, 24–52. Grand Rapids: Eerdmans, 2012.

———. "Papal Ministry in a Communication Ecclesiology. A Search for Some Possible Themes." In *How Can the Petrine Ministry be a Service to the Unity of the Universal Church?*, edited by James Puglisi, 155–68. Grand Rapids: Eerdmans, 2010.

———. "Stewardship and Ecclesiology." In *Stewardship— Our Accountability to God: Documentation from the LWF/DMD International Consultation on Stewardship in Bolawayo*, Zimbabwe, 8–12 November 1993, 19–29. Geneva: Lutheran World Federation, 1994.

———. "Stewardship Ecclesiology: The Church as sacrament to the World." *International Journal for the Study of the Christian Church* 2 (2002) 70–82.

———. "Theological Focus: Ecclesiological Elements in Understanding 'Church' in the HIV and AIDS Pandemic." In *A Theology of HIV and AIDS on Africa's East Coast: A Collection of Essays by Master Students from Four African Academic Institutions*, edited by Edwina Ward and Gary Leonard, xvi–xxxix. Uppsala: Swedish Institute of Misson Research, 2008.

———. "Theology/religious studies." In *The Future of Theology in Europe: Report on the Consultation of the Theological Faculties in Europe, Graz, 4–7 July 2002*, edited by Viorel Ionita and Gerhard Larcher and Grigorios Larentzakis, 66–77. Geneva: Uppsala Universitet, 2003.

———. "Themes in Operative Ecclesiology." *International Journal for the Study of the Christian Church* 6:2 (2006) 124–25.

———. "Upptäcker av dolda uppfattningar—om operativa ecklesiologier." In *Religion och Existens. Årsskrift för Teologiska Föreningen i Uppsala 2007*, 7–19. Uppsala: Uppsala Teologiska föreningen i Uppsala, 2007 [Discoveries of Hidden Conceptions—on Operative Ecclesiologies].

———. "Vad är praktisk teologi? Ett försök till diskussionsöversikt 1964–1974." In *Meddelande till Svenska Prästförbundet 1974*, 230–40. Stockholm: Svenska prästförbundet, 1974 [What is Practical Theology? An Attempt to Make a Survey of the Discussion 1964–1974]."

———. "Die Zukunft der Theologie." *Ökumenisches Forum. Grazer Jahrbuch für konkrete Ökumene* 25 (2002) 263–74.

Brodd, Sven-Erik, and Gunnar Weman. *Kyrka i olika meningar: Kortklippta texter med ecklesiologiska kommentarer*. Skellefteå: Artos, 2012 [Church in Different Meanings: Brief Texts with Ecclesiological Commentaries].

Browning, Don S. *A Fundamental Practical Theolog: Descriptive and Strategic Proposals*. Minneapolis: Fortress, 1991.

Brunner, Emil. *The Divine Imperative: A Study in Christian Ethics*. London, 1964 (1937).

———. *Justice and the Social Order*. Cambridge: Lutterworth, 1945.

Byström, Jan and Leif Norrgård. *Mer än ord: Liturgisk teologi och praxis*. Stockholm: Verbum, 1996 [More than Words: Liturgical Theology and Practice].

Cameron, Helen, et al, editors. *Talking About God in Practice: Theological Action Research and Practical Theology*. London: SCM, 2010.

Cavanaugh, William T. *Migrations of the Holy: God, State, and the Political Meaning of the Church*. Grand Rapids: Eerdmans, 2011.

———. *Theopolitical Imagination: Discovering the Liturgy as a Political Act in an Age of Global Consumerism*. New York: T. & T. Clark, 2002.

———. *Torture and Eucharist: Theology, Politics and the Body of Christ*. Malden: Blackwell, 1998.

Chakrabarty, Dipesh. "The Time of History and the Times of Gods." In *The Politics of Culture in the Shadow of Capital*, edited by Lisa Lowe and David Lloyd, 35–59. Durham: Duke University Press, 1997.

Chaves, Mark. *Congregations in America*. Cambridge: Harvard University Press, 2004.

Chodorow, Stanley. *Christian Political Theory and Church Politics in the Mid-Twelfth Century: The Ecclesiology of Gratian's Decretum*. Berkeley: University of California Press, 1972.

Chopp, Rebecca S. *The Power to Speak: Feminism, Language, God*. New York: Crossroad, 1989.

Chung, Mee-Hyun. "Korean Feminist Ecclesiology: A Wholistic Approach." *Madang Journal*, 5 (2007) http://madangjournal.com/bbs/view.php?id=issues&page=3&sn1=&divpage=1&sn=off&ss=on&sc=on&select_arrange=subject&desc=desc&no=33.

Chung, Mee-Hyun, editor. *Breaking Silence: Theology from Asian Women*. Delhi: ISPCK/EATWOT, 2006.

The Church: Towards a Common Vision. WCC Faith and Order Paper 214. Geneva: WCC Publications, 2013.
Cilliers, Paul. *Complexity and Postmodernism: Understanding Complex Systems*. London: Routledge, 1998.
Coghlan, David. "Seeking God in all things. Ignatian spirituality as action research." *The Way* 43/1 (2004) 97–108.
Cohen, Leonard. "Anthem." *The Future*. Columbia, 1992 (CD).
Collins, John. *Diakonia: Re-interpreting the Ancient Sources*. New York: Oxford University Press, 2011 (1990).
———. *Diakonia Studies: Critical Issues in Ministry*. Oxford: Oxford University Press, 2014.
Comte, Auguste. *Social Statics and Social Dynamics: The Theory of Ordered and the Theory of Progress*. Albuquerque: American Classical College Press, 1983.
Congar, Yves. *L'ecclésiologie du haut moyen âge: De Saint Grégoire le Grand à la désunion entre Byzance et Rome*. Paris: Cerf, 1968 [The Ecclesiology of the High Medieval Ages: From Saint Gregory the Great to the Split between Byzantium and Rome].
Dahms, Harry F. *The Vitality of Critical Theory*. Bingley, West Yorkshire: Emerald Group, 2011.
Dalferth, Ingolf. "Representing God's Presence." *International Journal of Systematic Theology* 3:3 (2001) 237–56.
Daly, Mary. *Amazon Grace: Re-Calling the Courage to Sin Big*. New York: Palgrave Macmillan, 2006.
———. *Beyond God the Father: Towards a Philosophy of Women's Liberation*. London: The Women's Press, 1973.
———. *The Church and the Second Sex*. New York: Harper & Row, 1968.
de Certeau, Michel, *The Practices of Everyday Life*. Berkley: University of California Press, 1984.
de Gruchy, John and Steve de Gruchy. *The Church Struggle in South Africa*, 25th Anniversary Edition. London: SCM, 2004.
de Lubac, Henri. *Corpus mysticum: L'Eucharistie et l'Église au Moyen Age: Étude historique*. Théologie 3. Paris: Aubier, 1944 [*Corpus Mysticum: The Eucharist and the Church in the Middle Ages*. Notre Dame: University of Notre Dame Press, 2006].
Den svenska kyrkohandboken. Antagen för Svenska kyrkan av 1986 års kyrkomöte. Stockholm: Verbum, 2003 [The Swedish Service Book, issued 1986].
Den svenska kyrkohandboken. Stadfäst av Konungen år 1942. Stockholm: Verbum, 1973 [The Swedish Service Book, issued 1942].
Derrida, Jacques. *Of Grammatology*. Baltimore: The Johns Hopkins University Press, 1976.
Dews, Peter, editor. *Habermas: A Critical Reader*. Malden: Blackwell, 1999.
Dianich, Severino. *Ecclesiologia: Questioni di metodo e una proposta*. Prospettive teologiche 14. Cinisello Balsamo/Milano: Paoline, 1993 [Ecclesiology: Methodological Questions and a Proposal].
Dittrich, Achim. *Mater Ecclesiae: Geschichte und Bedeutung eines umstrittenen Marientitels*. Würzburg: Echter, 2009 [Mater Ecclesiae: History and Meaning of a disputed Title to the Virgin Mary].
Dix, Gregory. *The Shape of the Liturgy*. London: A & C Black, 1986 (1945).

Döring, Heinrich. *Grundriss der Ekklesiologie: Zentrale Aspekte des katolichen Selbstverständnisses und ihre ökumenische Relevanz.* Darmstad: Wissenschaftliche Buchgesellschaft, 1986 [Fundamental Features of Ecclesiology: Essential Aspects in the Catholic Self-understanding and its Ecumenical Relevance].

Duffy, Eamon. *The Stripping of the Altars: Traditional Religion in England c.1400–c.1580,* New Haven, CT: Yale, 1992.

Dulles, Avery. "The Church as Communion." In *New Perspectives on Historical Theology: Essays in Memory of John Meyendorff,* edited by Bradley Nassif, 125–39. Grand Rapids: Eerdmans, 1996.

———. "A Half Century of Ecclesiology." *Theological Studies* 50 (1989) 419–42.

———. *Models of the Church.* New York: Doubleday, 2002 (1978).

Dykstra, Craig. "Reconceiving Practice." In *Virtues and Practices in the Christian Tradition: Christian Ethics after MacIntyre,* edited by Nancey Murphy et al., 161–82. Harrisburg: Trinity, 1997.

Dykstra, Craig and Dorothy C. Bass. *For Life Abundant: Practical Theology, Theological Education, and Christian Ministry.* Grand Rapids: Eerdmans, 2008.

Ecclesiology and Ethics: Ecumenical Ethical Engagement. Moral formation and the Nature of the Church. Edited by Thomas F. Best et al. Geneva: World Council of Churches, 1997.

Eckerdal, Lars. "Gudstjänstrummet." In *Den nya gudstjänstordningen för Svenska kyrkan. Kommentarer,* edited by Lars Eckerdal, 107–12. Stockholm: Verbum, 1976 [The Worship Room].

———. *Vägen in i kyrkan. Dop, konfirmation, kommunion—aktuella liturgiska utvecklingslinjer.* Stockholm: Liber, 1981 [The Way into the Church. Baptism, Confirmation, Communion—Recent Liturgical Trajectories].

Edgardh Beckman, Ninna. *Feminism och liturgi—en ecklesiologisk studie.* Stockholm: Verbum, 2001 [Feminism and Liturgy—an Ecclesiological Study].

———. "Lady Wisdom as Hostess for the Lord's Supper." In *Dissident Daughters: Feminist Liturgies in Global Context,* edited by Teresa Berger, 159–74. Louisville: Westminster John Knox, 2001.

———. "Mrs Murphy's Arising from the Pew: Ecclesiological Implications." *Ecumenical Review* 53:1 (January 2001) 5–13.

———. "The Theology of Gathering and Sending: a Challenge from Feminist Liturgy." *International Journal for the Study of the Christian Church* 6:2 (2006) 144–65.

Edgardh, Ninna. "A Gendered Perspective on Welfare and Religion in Europe." In *Welfare and Religion in 21st Century Europe: Volume 2. Welfare and Religion in 21st century Europe: Gendered, Religious and Social Change,* edited by Anders Bäckström et al., 61–106. Farnham: Ashgate, 2011.

———. "Social Agent—a Queer Role for the Church." In *For the Sake of the World: Swedish Ecclesiology in Dialogue with William T. Cavanaugh,* edited by Jonas Ideström, 65–85. Eugene, OR: Pickwick, 2010.

Eisenstadt, S. N. "Frameworks of the Great Revolutions: Culture, Social Structure, History, and Human Agency." *International Social Science Journal* 133 (August 1992) 385–401

Engdahl, Hans. *Theology in Conflict. Readings in Afrikaner Theology: The Theologies of F.J.M. Potgieter and B.J. Marais.* Frankfurt: Peter Lang, 2006.

———. "Theology as Politics in Afrikaner Nationalism and Black Consciousness. A Close Reading of F. J. M. Potgieter and Steve Biko." *Journal of Theology for Southern Africa* 144 (Nov 2012) 4–25.
Eoyang, Glenda. *Voices from the Field: An Introduction to Human Systems Dynamics*. Circle Pines, MN: Human Systems Dynamics Institute Press, 2003.
Erauso, Catalina de. *Lieutenant Nun: Memoir of a Basque Transvestite in the New World*. Boston: Beacon, 1996.
Eriksson, Anne-Louise. *The Meaning of Gender in Theology: Problems and Possibilities*. Stockholm: Almqvist & Wiksell, 1995.
The European Journal of Women's Studies. August 1, 2006, vol 13.
Eynikel, Erik. "Western European Theological Challenges and Prospects." *Theologia Catholica Latina* 52 (2007) 47–55.
Fagerberg, David W. *Theologia Prima: What is Liturgical Theology?* 2nd ed. Chicago: The Liturgical Press, 2004.
———. *What is Liturgical Theology?: A Study in Methodology*. Collegeville: Liturgical, 1992.
Fahlgren, Sune. "Från blandad kör till lovsångsteam. Historiska och teologiska perspektiv påfrikyrkliga sånggrupper." In *Med skilda tungors ljud: Körsång och gudstjänstspråk*, edited by Stephan Borgehammar, 23–76. Skellefteå: Artos, 2013. [From Mixed Choir to Worship Teams. Historical and Theological Perspectives on Song Groups in the Swedish Free Churches].
———. "Preacher and Preachership as Fundamental Expressions of being Church." *International Journal for the Study of the Christian Church* 6 (2006) 181–200.
———. *Predikantskap och församling: Sex fallstudier av en ecklesial baspraktik inom svensk frikyrklighet fram till 1960-talet*. Uppsala: Uppsala universitet, 2006 [Preachership and Church. Six Case Studies of an Ecclesial Fundamental Practice within the Free Church Traditions in Sweden].
———. "Rum för möten med Jesus och för församlingsgemenskap i frikyrklig tradition." In *Heliga rum i dagens Sverige*, edited by Sven-Åke Selander and Stina Fallberg Sundmark, 50–79. Skellefteå: Artos, 2008 [Free Church Sanctuaries].
———. "The Loss of Theological Visions. Free Church Ecclesiologies in Sweden from nineteenth Century till present." In *Between the State and the Eucharist: Free Church Theology in Conversation with William T. Cavanaugh*, edited by Joel Halldorf and Fredrik Wenell, 55–67. Eugene, OR: Pickwick, 2014.
Fahlgren, Sune, and Odd Arne Joö. "Baptismens spiritualitet—speglad i dess gudstjänstliv." In *Samfund i förändring: Baptistisk identitet i Norden under ett och ett halvt sekel*, edited by David Lagergren, 104–135. Stockholm: Teologiska högskolan Stockholm, 1997 [Baptist Spirituality Reflected in Baptist Worship].
"Fakultetsprogram." In *UHÄ-rapport* 24 (1986) 14 [Faculty Program].
Fallberg Sundmark, Stina. "Bilden av dödsberedelsen. Några liturgiska och teologiska perspektiv." In *Memento Mori: Døden i middelalderens billedverden*, edited by L. Liepe and K. B. Aavitsland, 9–24. Oslo: Novus, 2011 [Preparing for Death: Some Liturgical and Theological Perspectives].
———. "Om konsten att dö på rätt sätt. Liturgi och teologi i den svenska utgåvan av Jean Gersons Ars moriendi (tryckt 1514)." In *Jean Gersons Ars moriendi. Om konsten att dö*, edited by M. Hagberg, 35–67. Skara: Skara stiftshistoriska sällskap, 2009 [On the Art of Dying. Liturgy and Theology in the Swedish Edition of Jean Gerson's Ars Moriendi (printed in 1514)].

―――. *Sjukbesök och dödsberedelse: Sockenbudet i svensk medeltida och reformatorisk tradition*. Skellefteå: Artos, 2008 [The Visitation of the Sick in Swedish Medieval and Reformation Traditions].

―――. "The Rosary and the Wounds of Christ. Devotional Images in Relation to Late Medieval Liturgy and Piety." In *Images and Objects in Ritual Practicies in Medieval and Early Modern Northern and Central Europe,* edited by K. Kodres and A. Mänd, 53–67. Cambridge: Cambridge Scholars, 2013.

―――. *Teologi för praktiskt bruk: Frälsningshistoriska perspektiv på* Summula av Laurentius av Vaksala: Artos, 2014 [A Theology for Practical Use in Medieval Sweden: The History of Salvation as Understood in the Summula of Laurentius of Vaksala].

Felbecker, Sabine. *Die Prozession: Historische und systematische Unter-suchungen zu einer liturgischen Ausdruckshandlung.* Altenberge: Oros, 1995 [The Procession: Historical and Systematical Theological Investigation of a Liturgical Expression].

Fiddes, Paul. "Ecclesiology and Ethnography: Two Disciplines, Two Worlds?" In *Perspectives on Ecclesiology and Ethnography,* edited by Pete Ward, 13–35. Grand Rapids: Eerdmans, 2012.

Flanagan, Brian, *Communion, Diversity, and Salvation: The Contribution of Jean-Marie Tillard to Systematic Ecclesiology.* London: T. & T. Clark, 2011.

Flanagin, David Zachariah. "Extra ecclesiam salus non est―sed quae ecclesia? Ecclesiology and Authority in the Later Middle Ages." In *A Companion to the Great Western Schism (1378–1417),* edited by Joëlle Rollo-Koster and Thomas M. Izbicki, 333–74. Companions to the Christian Tradition 17. Leiden: Brill, 2009.

Flanigan, C. Clifford. "The Moving Subject: Medieval Liturgical Processions in Semiotic and Cultural Perspective." In *Moving Subjects: Processional Perfor-mance in the Middle Ages and the Renaissance,* edited by K. Ashley and W. Hüsken, 35–51. Amsterdam: Rodopi, 2001.

Gadamer, Hans-Georg. *Truth and Method.* 2nd edition. London: Continuum 2004 (1975).

Geertz, Clifford. "Thick Description: Toward an Interpretive Theory of Culture." In *The Interpretation of Cultures: Selected Essays,* edited by Clifford Geertz, 3–30. New York: Basic, 1973.

"Global Christianity. A Report on the Size and Distribution of the World's Christian Population." http://www.pewforum.org/Christian/Global-Christianity-exec.aspx.

The Global Gender Gap Report 2013. http://www.weforum.org/issues/global-gender-gap.

Graham, Elaine. "Is Practical Theology a form of 'Action Research'?" *International Journal of Practical Theology,* 17 (2013) 148–78.

Granberg, Gunnar, editor. *Stora kyrkor och små församlingar. Nytänkande med idéer om framtiden.* Karlstad: Votum förlag, 2011 [Huge Church Buildings and Small Congregations: New Thoughts towards the Future].

Grey, Mary. "Editors' Preface." In *Introducing Feminist Ecclesiology,* edited by Natalie K. Watson. London: Sheffield Academic, 2002.

Gustafsson, Lotta. *Medeltidskyrkan i Uppland: Restaurering och rumslig förnyelse under 1900-talet.* Skellefteå: Artos, 2013 [Medieval Churches in Uppland. Renovation and Renewal during the 20th Century].

Habermas, Jürgen. "Communicative Freedom and Negative Theology. Questions for Michael Theunissen." In *The Liberating Power of Symbols. Philosophical Essays*, edited by Peter Dews, 66–72. Cambridge: MIT Press, 2001.

———. *Knowledge and Human Interests*. Translated by Jeremy J. Shapiro. 1971. Boston: Beacon, 2002.

———. *On the Logic of Social Sciences*. Cambridge: MIT Press, 1988.

———. *The Theory of Communicative Action*. Vol. 1: *Reason and Rationalization of the Society*. Translated by Thomas McCarthy. 1981. Boston: Beacon, 1984.

———. *The Theory of Communicative Action*. Vol. 2: *Lifeworld and System: A Critique of Functionalist Reason*. Translated by Thomas McCarthy. 1985. Boston: Beacon, 1989.

Haight, Roger, D. *Christian Community in History: Comparative Ecclesiology*. Volume 2. New York: Continuum, 2005.

———. "Historical Ecclesiology. An Essay on Method in the Study of the Church." *Science et Esprit* 39 (1987) 27–46, 345–74.

———. "Systematic Ecclesiology." *Science et Esprit* 45 (1993) 253–80.

Hall, Christine. *"Pancosmic Church—Specific Românesc: Ecclesiological Themes in Nichifor Crainic's Writings between 1922 and 1944*, Uppsala: Uppsala University, 2008.

———. "Research on the diaconate: a retrospective view of promise and challenge." *International Journal for the Study of the Christian Church* 13 (2013) 258–69.

———. "Spriritual tradition and ecclesiology in the Romanian Orthodox historical and political context." *International Journal for the Study of the Christian Church* 11 (2011) 152–72.

Hallesby Norheim, Bård E. *Practicing Baptism: Christian Practices and the Presence of Christ*. Eugene, OR: Pickwick, 2014.

Hammar, Inger. *Emancipation och religion: Den svenska kvinnorörelsens pionjärer i debatt om kvinnans kallelse ca 1860–1900*. Stockholm: Carlsson, 1999 [Emancipation and Religion: The Pioneers of the Swedish Women's Movement Debating Woman's Calling].

Härdelin, Alf. *Världen som yta och fönster: Spiritualitet i medeltidens Sverige*. Stockholm: Runica et Mediævalia, 2005 [The World as Surface and Window. Spirituality in Medieval Sweden].

———. "Spiritualitet—ny deldisciplin eller kyrkovetenskapligt totalperspectiv?" *Svensk Teologisk Kvartalskrift* 62 (1986) 160–66 [Spirituality—a New Part of the Discipline or an Overall Ecclesiological Perspective?].

Harnack, Adolf von. *Das Wesen des Christentums: sechzehn Vorlesungen vor Studierenden aller Fakultäten im Wintersemester 1899/1900 an der Universität Berlin*. Leipzig: Hinrich, 1920 [*What is Christianity? Sixteen Lectures Delivered in the University of Berlin during the Winter-term 1899–1900*. Ulan, 2012].

Hawksley. Theodora L. *What is Ecclesiology about?: The Provenance and Prospects of Recent Concrete Approaches to Ecclesiology*. Edinburgh: University of Edingburgh School of Divinity, 2012.

———. "Metaphor and Method in Concrete Ecclesiologies." *Scottish Journal of Theology* 66 (2013) 431–47.

Healy, Nicholas, M. *Church, World and the Christian Life: Practical-Prophetic Ecclesiology*. Cambridge: Cambridge University Press, 2000.

———. "Ecclesiology, Ethnography, and God." In *Perspectives on Ecclesiology and Ethnography*, edited by Pete Ward, 182–99. Grand Rapids: Eerdmans, 2012.

———. "Practices and the New Ecclesiology." *International Journal of Systematic Theology* 5:3 (2003) 287–308.

———. "Some Observations on Ecclesiological Method." *Toronto Journal of Theology* 12 (1996) 47–63.

Heberlein, Magnus. "Var står vi och hur går vi vidare?" In *Kyrkovetenskap som forskningsdisciplin. Ämneskonferens i Vitterhetsakademien, 12–13 november 1998*, edited by Sven-Åke Selander, 95–104. Stockholm: Kungliga Vitterhets historie- och antikvitetsakademin, 2001 [Where Do We Stand and How Do We Continue?].

Hegel, Georg W. F. *Phänomenologie des Geistes*. Germany: Norderstedt, 2009 (1807) [*The Phenomenology of Spirit*. Oxford: Oxford University Press, 1977].

Hegstad, Harald. "A Minority within the Majority. On the Relation between the Church as Folk Church and as a Community of Believers," *Studia theologica* 53 (1999) 119–31.

———. "Normativity and Empirical Data in Practical Theology." In *Difficult Normativity: Normative Dimensions in Research on Religion and Theology*, edited by Jan-Olav Henriksen, 77–93. Frankfurt: Peter Lang, 2011.

———. *The Real Church: An Ecclesiology of the Visible*. Eugene, OR: Pickwick, 2013.

Heith-Stade, David. "Marriage as the Arena of Salvation. An Ecclesiological Study of the Marital Regulation in the Canons of the Council of Trullo." Master's thesis, Uppsala University, 2011.

Hermans, Theo. "Cross-cultural translation studies as thick translation." *Bulletin of SOAS* 66:3 (2003) 380–89.

Hietamäki, Minna. "Is Comparative Ecclesiology Enough for the Oikumene? Remarks on the Adequacy of Haight's Comparative Ecclesiology in the Light of Recent Lutheran-Roman Catholoc Dialogues." In *Comparative Ecclesiology: Critical Investigations. Ecclesiological Investigations*, edited by Gerard Mannion. London: T. & T. Clark, 2008

Hjälm, Michael. *Liberation of the Ecclesia: The Unfinished Project of Liturgical Theology*, Södertälje: Anastasis Media, 2011.

Houlden, Leslie. "Is the Bible Still there?" Editorial in *Theology*, vol. 89 (March 1986) 87–89.

Ideström, Jonas. "In Dialogue with the Gospel: Reflections on a Method for Practical-Prophetic Ecclesiology." *Ecclesial Practices. Journal of Ecclesiology* 1 (2013) 72–91.

———. *Lokal kyrklig identitet: En studie av implicit ecklesiologi med exemplet Svenska kyrkan i Flemingsberg*. Skellefteå: Artos, 2009 [Local Church Identity: A Study of Implicit ecclesiology with the Example of The Church of Sweden in Flemingsberg].

Irwin, Kevin W. *Context and Text: Method in Liturgical Theology*. Collegeville, MN: Liturgical, 1994.

Iserloh, Eerwin. *Kirche—Ereignis und Institution: Reformationsgeschichtliche Studien und Texten*. Supplementsband 3. Munster, Westfalen: Axhendorff, 1985 [Church: Event and Institution: Studies and Texts in Reformation History].

Iversen, Hans Raun. "Ekklesiologi og ekklesialitet: Om empiriske kirkestudiers teologiske nødvendighed." *Dansk Teologisk Tidskrift* 60 (1997) 125–36 [Ecclesiology and Ecclesiality: On the Theological Necessity of Empirical Studies of the Church].

———. "Purpose, Background and Methodological Issues." In *Rites of Ordination and Commitment in the Churches of the Nordic Countries: Theology and Terminology*, edited by Hans Raun Iversen, 15–33. Copenhagen: Museum Tusculanum Press, 2006.

———. "'Theological and Liturgical Considerations behind this Research of Rites for Ordination and Commitment." In *Rites of Ordination and Commitment in the Churches of the Nordic Countries. Theology and Terminology*, edited by Hans Raun Iversen, 553–66. Copenhagen: Museum Tusculanum Press, 2006.

Johansson, Hilding. *Bidrag till den svenska manualetraditionen*. Lund: Gleerup, 1951 [Contribution to the Swedish History of Manuals].

———. *Hemsjömanualet: En liturgi-historisk studie*. Stockholm: Svenska kyrkans diakonistyrelses förlag, 1950 [The Manual of Hemsjö. A Study in Liturgical History].

Johnson, Christopher. *Derrida: The Scene of Writing*. London, 2000 (1997).

Johnson, Elizabeth. *She Who Is: The Mystery of God in Feminist Theological Discourse*. New York: Crossroads, 1992.

Jungmann, Josef A. *The Mass of the Roman Rite: Its Origins and Development (Missarium Sollemnia)*. Vols. 1 and 2. Dublin: Four Courts, 1986.

Kärkkäinen, Veli-Matti. *An Introduction to Ecclesiology: Ecumenical, Historical & Global Perspectives*. Downers Grove, IL: InterVarsity, 2002.

Kasper, Walter. *Harvesting the Fruits: Basic Aspects of Christian Faith in Ecumenical Dialogue*. New York: Continuum, 2009.

Kavanagh, Aidan. *On Liturgical Theology: The Hale Memorial Lectures of Seabury-Western Theological Seminary*. Collegeville, MN: Liturgical, 1992, 1981.

Kitching, Gavin. *Karl Marx and the Philosophy of Praxis*. London: Routledge, 1987.

Komonchak, Joseph. *Foundations in Ecclesiology*. Supplementary Issue of the Lonergan Workshop Journal 11, edited by Fred Lawrence. Boston: Boston College, 1995.

Kompridis, Nikolas. *Critique and Disclosure. Critical Theory between Past and Future*. Cambridge, MA: MIT Press, 2006.

Kress, Robert. *The Church: Communion, Sacrament, Communication*. Mahwah, NJ: Paulist, 1985.

Kyrkovetenskap som forskningsdisciplin. Ämneskonferens i Vitterhetsakademien, 12–13 november 1998, edited by Sven-Åke Selander, 95–104. Stockholm: Kungliga Vitterhets historie- och antikvitetsakademin, 2001 [Ecclesiology/Practical Theology as a Branch of Research].

Lathrop, Gordon W. "Foreword." In *The Meaning of Christian Liturgy: Recent Developments in the Church of Sweden*, edited by Oloph Bexell, vii–x.. Grand Rapids: Eerdmans, 2012.

———. *The Four Gospels on Sunday: The New Testament and the Reform of Christian Worship*. Minneapolis: Fortress, 2011.

———. *Holy People: A Liturgical Ecclesiology*. Minneapolis: Fortress, 1999.

Latour, Bruno. *Science in Action: How to Follow Scientists and Engineers Through Society*. Cambridge: Open University Press, 1987.

———. "'Thou Shall Not Freeze-Frame'—or How not to Misunderstand the Science and Religion Debate." In *Science Religion and the Human Experience*, edited by James D. Proctor, 27–48. Oxford: Oxford University Press, 2005.

Lefebvre, Henri. *The Production of Space*. Malden: Blackwell, 1991.

Lejdhamre, Agneta. *Psalm, kön, kyrka: Könsförståelse och kyrkosyn i Den svenska psalmboken och i Svenska kyrkans kyrkomöte*. Skellefteå: Artos, 2011 [Hymn, Gender, Church: Understanding of Gender and Ecclesiology in The Swedish Hymnal and in the Swedish Church's General Synod].

———. "Genusperspektiv i förslaget till ny kyrkohandbok." *Svensk kyrkotidning* 1 (2014) 11–14 [Gender Perspectives in the Proposal for a New Worship Manual].

Lennan, Richard. *The Ecclesiology of Karl Rahner*. Oxford: Clarendon, 1997.

———. "Roman Catholic Ecclesiology." In *The Routledge Companion to the Christian Church*, edited by Gerard Mannion and Lewis S. Mudge, 234–50. New York: Routledge, 2008.

Lewis, C. S. *The Screwtape Letters*. New York: Macmillan, 1982.

Lorber, Judith. *Breaking the Bowls: Degendering and Feminist Change*. New York: Norton, 2005.

Lourde, Audre. *Essays and Speeches by Audre Lourde*. Freedom: Crossing, 1984.

Luhmann, Niklas. *Essays on Self-Reference*. New York: Colombia University Press, 1990.

Lyotard, J.-F. *The Postmodern Condition: A Report on Knowledge*. Manchester, 1984.

MacIntyre, Alasdair. *After Virtue: A Study in Moral Theory*. 2nd ed. Notre Dame: Notre Dame University Press, 1984.

Madar, Martin. "Roger Haight's Contribution to Method in Ecclesiology and Its Implications for Ecumenical Dialogue." *Journal of Ecumenical Studies* 47:2 (Spring) 207–26.

Mannion, Gerard and Lewis S. Mudge, editors. *The Routledge Companion to the Christian Church*. New York: Routledge, 2008.

Marais, B. J. "Die Christelike broderskapsleer: sy agtergrond en toepassing in die vroeë kerk." Doctoral thesis, Stellenbosch, 1946 [The Christian Doctrine of Brotherhood: its Background and Application in the Early Church].

———. *Places of Redemption: Theology for a Worldly Church*. New York: Oxford University.

Marks, Richard. *Image and Devotion in Late Medieval England*. Stroud: Sutton, 2004.

Marty, Martin E. and R. Scott Appleby, editors. *The Fundamentalism Project*. 5 vols. Chicago: University of Chicago Press, 1992–1995.

McClintock Fulkerson, Mary. *Places of Redemption. Theology for a Wordly Church*. Oxford: Oxford University Press, 2007.

———. "Theological Reflection and Theories of Practice: Rethinking Normative Memory as if Bodies Mattered." In *Pastoral Bearings: Lived Religion and Pastoral Theology*, edited by Jane F. Maynard et al., 23–42. Lanham: Lexington, 2010.

McFague, Sallie. *Models of God: Theology for an Ecological, Nuclear Age*. Philadelphia: Fortress, 1987.

McIntosh, Mark. *Divine Teaching: An Introduction to Christian Theology*. Oxford: Blackwell 2008.

———. *Mystical Theology: The Integrity of Spirituality and Theology*. Oxford: Blackwell, 1998.

Menighetsutvikling i folkekirken: Erfaringer og muligheter. Edited by Erling Birkedal et al. Oslo: Iko-forlaget, 2012 [Parish Development in the Folk Church: Experiences and Possibilities].

Middlemiss, Martha. "Divided by a Common Language: The Benefits and Problems Created by Linguistic Diversity in a Comparative European Project." In *Churches in Europe as Agents of Welfare—Sweden, Norway and Finland*, edited by Anne

Birgitta Yeung, 11–19. Uppsala: Uppsala Institute for Diaconal and Social Studies, 2006.

Milbank, John. *Theology and Social Theory: Beyond Secular Reason.* Cambridge: Blackwell, 1994 (1990).

———. *Beyond Secular Order: The Representation of Being and the Representation of the People.* Oxford: Wiley Blackwell, 2013.

Milbank, John et al., editors. *Radical Orthodoxy.* New York: Routledge, 2006 (1999).

Minear, Paul S. *Images of the Church in the New Testament.* Philadelphia: Westminister John Knox, 1960.

Mogren, Mikael. *Den romantiska kyrkan. Föreställningar om den ideala kyrkan på jorden inom nya skolan intill 1817.* Skellefteå: Artos, 2003 [The Romantic Church. Conceptions of the Ideal Church on Earth by the New School up to 1817].

Moodie, T. Dunbar. *The Rise of Afrikanerdom: Power, Apartheid, and the Afrikaner Civil Religion.* Los Angeles: University of California Press, 1975.

Murray, Paul D., editor. *Reason, Truth and Theology in Pragmatist Perspective.* Leuven: Peeters, 2004.

Myrdal, Gunnar. *An American Dilemma: The Negro Problem and Modern Democracy.* New York: Harper and Row, 1944.

———. *Asian Drama: An Inquiry into the Poverty of Nations.* Vols. I–III. New York: Harper and Row, 1968.

———. *Value in Social Theory, a Selection of Essays on Methodology.* Edited by Paul Streeten. London: Industrial Library of Sociology and Social Reconstruction, 1958.

Nadar, Sarojini. "On Being the Pentecostal Church: Pentecostal Women's Voices and Visions." *The Ecumenical Review* 56:3 (July 2004) 354–67.

Nadar, Sarojini, and Isabel Apawo Phiri, editors. *On Being Church: African Women's Voices and Visions.* Geneva: World Council of Churches, 2005.

Nordgren, Joseph et al., editors. *Quality and Renewal 2007: An Overall Evaluation of Research at Uppsala University 2006/2007.* Uppsala: Uppsala universitet, 2007.

Nordgren, Joseph et al., editors. *Quality and Renewal 2011: An Overall Evaluation of Research at Uppsala University 2010/2011.* Uppsala: Uppsala universitet, 2011.

Nordlund, Fredrik. "Isomorfismer i kyrklig organisation. En ecklesiologisk undersökning av Svenska kyrkans regionala nivå," Master's thesis, Uppsala University, 2014 [Isomorphisms in an Ecclesial Organization: An Ecclesiological Study of the Church of Sweden's Regional Level].

Nygren, Anders, editor. *En bok om kyrkan av svenska teologer.* Stockholm: Diakonistyrelsen, 1942. [*This is the Church: Basic Studies on the Nature of the Church.* Philadelphia: Muhlenberg, 1952; *Ein Buch von der Kirche.* Berlin: Evangelische Verlagsanstalt Berlin, 1950].

Oljelund, Karin. *Kristi kropp och Guds folk: En undersökning av ecklesiologin i Svenska kyrkans huvudgudstjänster 1942-2000.* Skellefteå: Artos, 2009 [The Body of Christ and the People of God. An Investigation into the Ecclesiology of the Church of Sweden Sunday Services 1942–2000].

———. "Method in Liturgical Ecclesiology: An Attempt to Understand the Formation of Primary Ecclesiology." In *The Meaning of Christian Liturgy: Recent Developments in the Church of Sweden,* edited by Oloph Bexell, 91–113. Grand Rapids: Eerdmans, 2012.

One Baptism: Towards Mutual Recognition. Faith and Order Paper 210. Geneva: WCC, 2011.

Ormerod, Neil. "A Dialectic Engagement with the Social Sciences in an Ecclesiological Context." *Theological Studies* 66 (2005) 815–40.

———. "Ecclesiology and the Social Sciences." *The Routledge Companion to the Christian Church*, edited by Gerard Mannion and L. S. Mudge, 639–54. London: Routledge, 2008.

———. "The Structure of a Systematic Ecclesiology." *Theological Studies* 63 (2002) 3–30.

Pädam, Tiit. "The Diaconate after the Signing of the Porvoo Declaration: An overview of Methods and Hermeneutics." *International Journal for the Study of the Christian Church* 13 (2013) 300–11.

———. *Ordination of Deacons in the Churches of the Porvoo Communion: A Comparative Investigation in Ecclesiology*. Uppsala: Kirjastus TP, 2011.

———. "Toward a Common Understanding of Diaconal Ministry? Recent Developments in the Diaconat among the Porvoo Churches." *Ecclesiology* 8 (2012) 326–29.

Pahn, Peter C., editor. *The Gift of the Church: A Textbook on Ecclesiology in Honour of Patrick Granfield*, O.S.B. Collegeville, MN: Liturgical, 2000.

Pannenberg, Wolfhart. *Systematic Theology*. Vol. 3. Edinburgh: T. & T. Clark, 1998.

Patelos, Constantin G. *The Orthodox Church in the Ecumenical Movement: Documents and Statements 1902–1975*. Geneva: WCC Press, 1978.

Percy, Martin. *Shaping the Church. The Promise of Implicit Theology*. Farnham: Ashgate, 2010.

Pethrus, Lewi. *Gud med oss: Predikosamling*. Stockholm: Filadelfia, 1931 [God with Us: A Sermon Collection].

Phillips, Elizabeth. "Charting the 'Ethnographic Turn': Theologians and the Study of Christian Congregations." In *Perspectives on Ecclesiology and Ethnography*, edited by Pete Ward, 95–106. Grand Rapids: Eerdmans, 2012.

Piltz, Anders. "Communicantes: Aspekter på kyrkan som solidarisk gemenskap i svensk högmedeltid." In *Svensk spiritualitet: Tio studier av förhållandet tro—kyrka—praxis*, edited by Alf Härdelin, 15–55. Uppsala: Svenska kyrkans forskningsråd, 1994 [Communicantes: Aspects of the Church as Solidary Communion in Late Medieval Sweden].

Pityana, Barney N., and Charles Villa Vicencio, editors. *Being Church in South Africa Today*. Johannesburg: South African Council of Churches, 1995.

"The Porvoo Common Statement" (PCS). In *Together in Mission and Ministry: The Porvoo Common Statement with Essays on Church and Ministry in Northern Europe*, 1–33. London: Church House, 1993.

Pospielovsky, Dimitry. "Impressions of the Contemporary Russian Orthodox Church: Its Problems and Its Theological Education." *Religion, State & Society* 23:3 (1995) 249–62.

Potgieter, F. J. M. *Die Verhouding tussen die teologie and filosofie by Calvyn*. Amsterdam: Press 2007 (1939) [The Relationship between Theology and Philosophy in Calvin's Theology].

Procter-Smith, Marjorie. *In Her Own Rite: Constructing Feminist Liturgical Tradition*. Nashville: Abingdon, 1990.

Prusak, Bernard P. *The Church Unfinished: Ecclesiology through the Centuries.* New York: Paulist, 2004.
Ramshaw, Gail. *God beyond Gender: Feminist Christian God-Language.* Minneapolis: Fortress, 1995.
Rappe, Axel. "Det liturgiska rummet." In *Kyrkans liturgi,* edited by Hugo Blennow, 174–88. Kallinge: Eginostiftelsens förlag, 1952 [The Liturgical Room].
Rasmusson, Arne. "A Century of Swedish Theology." *Lutheran Quarterly* 21 (2007) 125–63.
Reason, Peter, and Hilary Bradbury, editors. *The Sage Handbook of Action Research, Participative Inquiry and Practice.* London: Sage, 2008.
Rikhof, Henry. *The Concept of Church: A Methodological Inquiry into the Use of Metaphors in Ecclesiology.* Sheperdstown: Patmos, 1981.
Rowell, Geoffrey. "Editorial Preface." *International Journal for the Study of the Christian Church* 13 (2013) 255–57.
Ruether, Rosemary Radford. *Women-Church: Theology and Practice of Feminist Liturgical Communities.* San Francisco: Harper & Row, 1996.
Russell, Letty M. *Church in the Round: Feminist Interpretation of the Church.* Louisville: Westminster John Knox, 1993.
Ryman, Björn. *Brobyggarkyrka: Svenska kyrkans engagemang i utrikesfrågor.* Skellefteå: Artos, 2010 [Bridge Builder: Church of Sweden's engagement in foreign affairs].
———. "Church of Sweden, 1940–2000." In *Nordic Folkchurches. A Contemporary Church History,* edited by Björn Ryman et al., 49–61. Grand Rapids: Eerdmans, 2005.
Saarinen, Risto. "Lutheran Ecclesiology." In *The Routledge Companion to the Christian Church,* edited by Gerard Mannion and Lewis S. Mudge, 170–86. New York: Routledge, 2008.
Scarisbrick, John Joseph. *The Reformation and the English People.* Oxford: Blackwell, 1984.
Scharen, Christian B., editor. *Explorations in Ecclesiology and Ethnography.* Grand Rapids: Eerdmans, 2012.
Scharen, Christian, and Aana Marie Vigen. "What is Ethnography?" In *Ethnography as Christian Theology and Ethics,* edited by Christian Scharen and Aana Marie Vigen, 3–27. New York: Continuum, 2011.
Schlink, Edmund et al., editors. *Ökumenische Dogmatik. Grundsüge.* Göttingen: Vandenhoeck and Ruprecht, 1985 [An Ecumenical Dogmatics. Fundamental Features].
Schmemann, Alexander. *Introduction to Liturgical Theology.* Portland: American Orthodox Press, 1996.
———. *Liturgy and Tradition: Theological Reflections of Alexander Schmemann,* edited by Thomas Fisch. New York: Crestwood, 1990.
Schultz, Majken. *On Studying Organizational Cultures: Diagnosis and Understanding.* Berlin: Walter de Gruyter, 1995.
Schreiter, Robert, editor. *Edward Schillebeeckx: The Schillebeeckx Reader.* New York: T. & T. Clark, 1984.
Schüssler Fiorenza, Elisabeth. *But She Said: Feminist Practices of Biblical Interpretation.* Boston: Beacon, 1992.

Schwartz, Regina M. "Religion." In *Critical Terms for the Study of Gender*, edited by Catherine R. Stimson and Gilbert Herdt, 428–48. Chicago: University of Chicago Press, 2014.

Scott, Joan. *Only Paradoxes to Offer: French Feminists and the Rights of Man*. Cambridge: Harvard University Press, 1996.

———. "Deconstructing Equality—Versus—Difference: Or, the Uses of Poststructuralist Theory for Feminism." In *Conflicts in Feminism*, edited by Marianne Hirsch and Evelyn Fox Keller, 134–48. New York: Routledge, 1990. Originally in *Feminist Studies* 14:1 (Spring 1988) 33–50.

Seidl, David. "Organizational Identity in Luhmann's Theory of Social Systems." In *Autopoietic Organization Theory: Drawing on Niklas Luhmann's Social System Perspective*, edited by Tore Bakke and Tor Hernes. Oslo: Abstrakt forlag, 2003.

Selander, Sven-Åke, editor. *Kyrkovetenskap som forskningsdisciplin. Ämneskonferens i Vitterhetsakademien, 12–13 november 1998*. Stockholm: Kungliga Vitterhets historie- och antikvitetsakademin, 2001 [Ecclesiology/Practical Theology as a Branch of Research].

Senn, Frank C. "The Ecclesiological Basis of the Office of Deacon: The Contribution of Sven-Erik Brodd." *Pro Ecclesia* 3 (1994) 197–205.

———. "Protestantism och katolicitet: Aspekter på förhållandet mellan ecklesiologi och kyrkobyggnad." In *Ett mångtydigt rum*, edited by Carl-Göran Bergman and Sven-Erik Brodd, 160–84. Skellefteå: Artos 2001 [Protestantism and Catholicity: Aspects on the Relation between Ecclesiology and the Church building].

Sigurdson, Ola. "The Return of the Body: Re-imagining the Ecclesiology of Church of Sweden." In *For the Sake of the World. Swedish Ecclesiology in Dialogue with William T.Cavanaugh*, edited by Jonas Ideström, 125–45. Eugene: Pickwick, 2010.

Skjevesland, Olav. *Invitasjon til praktisk teologi: En faginnføring i samarbeid med Per-Otto Gullaksen*. Oslo: Luther forlag, 1999 [Invitation to Practical Theology: An Introduction to the Discipline in Cooperation with Per-Otto Gullaksen].

Stanton, John, and Harriet Mowat. *Practical Theology and Qualitative Research*. London: SCM, 2006.

Sterkens, Carl. "Challenges for the Modern Church in Empirical Ecclesiology." In *Hermeneutics and Empirical Research in Practical Theology*, edited by C. A. M. Hermans and M. E. Moore, 395–431. Leiden: Brill, 2004.

Stier, Jonas. *Dimensions and Experiences of Human Identity: An Analytic Toolkit and Empirical Illustration*. Göteborg: Department of Sociology, Göteborg University, 1998.

Stimson, Catherine R., and Gilbert Herdt, editors. *Critical Terms for the Study of Gender*. Chicago: University of Chicago Press, 2014.

Stringer, Martin. "Text, Context and Performance: Hermeneutics and the Study of Worship." *Scottish Journal of Theology* 53 (2000) 365–79.

Stone, Bryan P. *Reader in Ecclesiology: Ashgate Contemporary Ecclesiology*. Farnham: Ashgate, 2012.

Stuart, Elizabeth. "Exploding Mystery: Feminist Theology and the Sacramental." *Feminist Theology* 12 (2004) 228–36.

Sullivan, Maureen. *The Road to Vatican II: Key Changes in Theology*. Mahwah, NJ: Paulist, 2007.

Swinton, John, and Harriet Mowat. *Practical Theology and Qualitative Research*. London: SCM, 2006.

Taft, Robert F. *Beyond East and West: Problems in Liturgical Understanding*. Second revised and enlarged edition. Rome: Pastoral, 1997.
Tamez, Elsa. "An Ecclesial Community: Women's Visions and Voices." *The Ecumenical Review* 53:1 (January 2001) 57–63.
Tanner, Kathryn. *Theories of Culture: A New Agenda for Theology*, Minneapolis, Minnesota: Fortress, 1997.
Tavard, George H. "The Church as Eucharistic Communion in Medieval Theology." In *Continuity and Discontinuity in Church History: Essays Presented to George Huntston Williams on the Occasion of his 65th Birthday*, edited by E. F. Church and T. George, 92–103. Leiden: Brill, 1979.
Teologisk forskning, Fakultetsprogram. Reviderad utgåva Uppsala och Lund 1989. Uppsala: Uppsala universitet, 1989 [Theological Research: Faculty Program, revised edition].
Teologiska grundprinciper för arbetet i 2006 års kyrkohandboksgrupp 2009 [Basic Theological Principles for the work in the 2006 Committee on the Worship Manual]. http://www.svenskakyrkan.se/default.aspx?id=710964.
Thomson, John Bromilow. *The Ecclesiology of Stanley Hauerwas: A Christian Theology of Liberation*. Burlington: Ashgate, 2003.
Ting Jin, Yong. "On Being Church. Asian Women's Voices and Visions." *The Ecumenical Review* 53:1 (2001) 109–13.
Tjørhom, Ola. "Ecumenical Research on Ministry and Ordination: Some Remarks and Observations." In *Rites of Ordination and Commitment in the Churches of the Nordic Countries: Theology and Terminology*, edited by Hans Raun Iversen, 477–88. Copenhagen: Museum Tusculanum Press, 2006.
Troeltsch, Ernst. *The Social Teaching of the Christian Churches*. Vols. I–II. New York: Macmillan, 1956 (1931). [Die Soziallehren der Christlichen Kirchen und Gruppen," in Gesammelte Schriften, vol. I. Tübingen: Mohr, 1923 (1912)].
Tuulse, Armin. "Västra Ryds kyrka." In *Konsthistoriskt Inventarium*, 89–102. Stockholm: Generalstabens litografiska anstalt, 1956 [The Church of Västra Ryd].
van der Ven, Johannes A. *Practical Theology: An Empirical Approach*. Leuven: Peeters, 1998.
Västra Vingåkers kyrka. Sörmländska kyrkor nr 3. edited by Mats Bergman. Nyköping: Sörmlands museum, 1981 [The Churches of the Swedish Landscape Södermanland].
Vogel Dwight W, editor. *Primary Sources of Liturgical Theology: A Reader*. Collegeville, MN: Liturgical, 2000.
Volf, Miroslav. "Theology for a Way of Life." In *Practicing Theology: Beliefs and Practices in Christian Life*, edited by Miroslav Volf and Dorothy C. Bass, 245–63. Grand Rapids: Eerdmans, 2001.
Volf, Miroslav, and Dorothy C. Bass, editors. *Practicing Theology: Beliefs and Practices in Christian Life*. Grand Rapids: Eerdmans, 2001.
Walker Bynum, Caroline. *Christian Materiality: An Essay on Religion in Late Medieval Europe*. New York: Zone, 2011.
"Das wandernde Gottesvolk." In *Lund Dritte Weltkonferenz der Kirchen für Glauben und Kirchenverfassung—Kirche Gottesdienst Abendmahlsgemeinschaft—Bericht einer Weltkirchenkonferenz*, 201–10. Witten/Ruhr: Luther Verlag, 1954 [The Wandering People of God].

Ward, Frances. "The Messiness of Studying Congregations Using Ethnographic Methods." In *Congregational Studies in the UK*, edited by Mathew Guest et al., 125–38. Farnham: Ashgate, 2004.

Ward, Graham. "Bodies: The Displaced Body of Jesus Christ." In *Radical Othodoxy: A New Theology*, edited by John Milbank et al., 163–81. London: Routledge, 1998.

Ward, Pete, editor. *Perspectives on Ecclesiology and Ethnography*. Grand Rapids: Eerdmans, 2012.

Watkins, Clare. "Living Marriage, Learning Discipleship, Teaching Church: The Practices of Married Life as Embodied Theology for Today's Mission." *INTAMS Review* (2015) 236–48.

———. "Organizing the People of God: Social Science Theories of Organization in Ecclesiology." *Theological Studies* 52 (1991) 689–711.

———. "Practising Ecclesiology: From Product to Process. Developing Ecclesiology as a Non-Correlative Process and Practice through the Theological Action Research Framework of Theology in Four Voices." *Ecclesial Practices* 2 (2015) 25–39.

Watkins, Clare, and Bridget Shepherd. "The Challenge of 'Fresh Expression' to Ecclesiology: Reflections from the Practice of Messy Church." *Ecclesial Practices* 1 (2013) 92–110.

Watkins, Clare, and Helen Cameron. "Epiphanic Sacramentality: an example of practical ecclesiology revisioning theological understanding." In *Explorations in Ecclesiology and Ethnography*, edited by Christian B. Scharen, 71–92. Grand Rapids: Eerdmans, 2012.

Watkins, Clare, et al. "Practical Ecclesiology: What Counts as Theology in Studying the Church?" In *Perspectives on Ecclesiology and Ethnography*, edited by Pete Ward, 167–81. Grand Rapids: Eerdmans, 2012.

Watson, Natalie K. *Introducing Feminist Ecclesiology*. London: Sheffield Academic, 2002.

Weber, Max. *Aufsätze zur Wissenschaftslehre*. Tübingen, 1922 [Essays in Philosophy of Science].

———. *The Protestant Ethic and the Spirit of Capitalism*. London, 1976 (1930). First published as a two-part article in *Archiv für Sozialwissenschaft und Sozialpolitik*, 1904–1905.

Weman, Gunnar. "The Interplay between the Church Building and the Worship." In *The Meaning of Christian Liturgy: Recent Developments in the Church of Sweden*, edited by Oloph Bexell, 140–74. Grand Rapids: Eerdmans, 2012.

———. *Nutida gudstjänst och medeltida kyrkorum: Förhållandet mellan det sena 1900-talets liturgireform och det medeltida gudstjänstrummet i Svenska kyrkan*. Skellefteå: Artos, 2006 [Contemporary Worship and Medieval Churches: The Relationship between late twentieth century Liturgical Reforms and the Medieval Worship Space in the Church of Sweden].

Weman, Gunnar (text), and Tord Harlin (photo). *Jerk Alton: Nutida kyrkorumsarkitekt*. Skellefteå: Artos, 2009 [Jerk Alton: A Present-Day Church Architect].

Wharton, Amy S. *The Sociology of Gender: An Introduction to Theory and Research*. Oxford: Blackwell, 2005.

Williams, Rowan. "The Unity of Christian Truth." In *On Christian Theology*. Oxford: Blackwell, 2000.

Wingren, Gustaf. "Deutscher Einfluss auf Kirche und Theologie in Schweden 1870–1933." In *Nicht nur Strindberg: Kulturelle und literarische Beziehungen zwischen*

Schweden und Deutschland 1870–1933, 150–59. Stockholm: Acta Universitatis Stockholmiensis, 1979 [German Impact on Church Life and Theology in Sweden 1870–1933].

Winter, Miriam Therese, et al. *Defecting in Place: Women Claiming Responsibility for their own Spiritual Lives*. New York: Crossroad, 1994.

Wrede, Gösta. *Kyrkosynen i Einar Billings teologi*. Stockholm: Uppsala Universitet 1969 [Ecclesiology in Einar Billing's Theology].

Yates, Nigel. *Liturgical Space. Christian Worship and Church Buildings in Western Europe 1500-2000*. Hampshire: Ashgate, 2008.

Yoder, John Howard. *Body Politics: Five Practices of the Christian Community Before the Watching World*. Scottdale: Herald, 2001.

———. *The Politics of Jesus*. Grand Rapids: Eerdmans, 1972 (1994).

Zeuch, Manfred. "A comunhão na confissão é comunhão eclesiástica?" Aspectos críticos da eclesiologia da Federação Luterna Mundial, *Igreja Luterana* 55 (1996) 149–72 [Is the Confessional Communion an Ecclesial Communion? Critical Aspects on the Lutheran World Federation's Ecclesiology].

www.ingramcontent.com/pod-product-compliance
Lightning Source LLC
Chambersburg PA
CBHW071017240426
43661CB00073B/2448